CONTESTING IMAGES

CONTESTING IMAGES

Photography and the World's Columbian Exposition

Julie K. Brown

The University of Arizona Press
Tucson & London

The University of Arizona Press
Copyright © 1994
The Arizona Board of Regents
All rights reserved

Manufactured in the United States of America

99 98 97 96 95 94   6 5 4 3 2 1

Library of Congress Cataloging-in-Publication Data

Brown, Julie K.
    Contesting images : photography and the World's Columbian
Exposition / Julie K. Brown.
        p. cm.
    Includes bibliographical references and index.
    ISBN 0-8165-1382-1
    ISBN 0-8165-1410-0 (pbk.)
    1. Photography—Social aspects—United States—History—
19th century. 2. World's Columbian Exposition (1893 : Chicago,
Ill.). I. Title.
TR183.B76 1994   93-19891
779'.09'0340747731—dc20   CIP

British Cataloguing-in-Publication Data
A catalogue record for this book is available from the British
Library.

To my parents,
Robert Frederick McGraw and
Margaret Hahn McGraw,

and to my children,
Margaret Ellen Brown and Paul Francis Brown

CONTENTS

FIGURES

PREFACE

There is a particular fascination in the subject of exhibitions, expositions, and displays. As events in the public sphere, they demand our attention and challenge both our judgment and our role as spectators. They stimulate our need to know how and why they were constructed, what is being represented, and their impact—or lack of impact—on the larger picture of our culture and life. While this book does not answer all these questions in relation to the World's Columbian Exposition, held at Chicago in 1893, I hope it will be part of our continuing dialogue with the past. It may also offer some useful insights into the meaning and rationale of such events in the present.

Recent projects, such as Andrew Eskind's data base for the GEH Interactive Catalogue and the new Exhibition History File with which I have been involved at the George Eastman House, International Museum of Photography and Film, are indications of a growing recognition of the value of exhibitions and the necessity of more completely preserving the documentation of these public events.

I would like to acknowledge the help of a number of individuals in the completion of this work. Desley Deacon of the American Studies Department of the University of Texas at Austin and Grace Seiberling of the Department of Art and Art History at the University of Rochester were both crucial to sustaining my energy and my belief in the project, especially during the early years of this work. George Gurney of the National Museum of American Art generously shared materials from his own research project and stimulated me to take a broader view of the Columbian Exposition. From her own rich career in research and writing, Janet Buerger offered a special kind of encouragement and inspiration during the long period of writing and waiting. While it is not possible to cite all those from whom I have received valuable advice during this period, I would like to acknowledge the following with grateful appreciation: Howard Merritt, Charles Penney, Pete Daniel, Paula Fleming, Roy Flukinger, Elizabeth Broun, Lois Fink, Bill Johnston, Bill Deiss, Bill Cox, Michael Holley, Carl Chiarenza, and Bill Stott.

As an independent scholar, I received institutional support for this work during my tenure as Fanny Knapp Allen Post Doctoral Fellow at the University of Rochester and as a participant in the Smithsonian Institution's Visiting Scholar Program at the National Museum of American Art. In addition to the collections and archives listed in the bibliography, I am also indebted to the following libraries for their fine resources and excellent staff: the Elizabeth Maddux Library of Trinity University, San Antonio; the Rush Rhees Library and Special Collections of the University of Rochester; the Perry-Castañeda Library and the Harry Ransom Humanities Research Center of the University of Texas at Austin; and the Menchel Library of the George Eastman House, International Museum of Photography and Film. The assistance of Fotinie Efstratiador-Wisner,

Jim Enyeart, Andrea Inselmann, and Robert Tofolo is also acknowledged. I would like to thank my family and friends, who sustained my energy and good humor during the past five years. Finally, my deepest thanks to my editors, Christine Szuter and Alan Schroder, whose belief and guidance enabled the making of this book.

Julie K. Brown
San Antonio, Texas, 1993

INTRODUCTION

"It's out of sight," exclaimed Columbus, the fictional character in an 1893 poem describing part of an imaginary visit by the explorer to the World's Columbian Exposition.[1] Ephemeral the Exposition was, like other events of its kind, a juxtaposition of objects and artifacts. These artifacts were essentially fragments, detached from their original social, economic, and political context, and gathered and assembled for the duration of the Exposition.[2] The Exposition was also a carefully controlled event that mirrored a contest of struggling self-interest, a veritable microcosm of the 1890s. The fact that it fell between the financial panic of 1893 and the Pullman Strike of 1894 indicates the unsettled character of the period.[3] The Exposition was, according to Reid Badger, "a facade, a magnificent stage prop set in a landscape of fantasy in which the economic, political, racial and sexual conflicts of the times had no place."[4] This artificial vision of unity was, he notes, also a positive response to a real condition, a felt need to counterbalance a growing sense of materialism, a confusion of traditional values and symbols as well as a lack of culture and political leadership. In examining the structure, production, and meaning of international expositions, Burton Benedict has argued that they were "mammoth rituals in which all sorts of power relations" were expressed.[5]

A new window on the dynamics that drove the Exposition is opened when we look at the role of photography. As a case study it offers an insider's view of how the event worked for both exhibitors and spectators. Photography was essential to the staging of the event, providing both the necessary images for display and a means for making images of the experience of the event itself. Nothing, however, was transparent or unmediated about the presence of photography. A contest existed in which photography had to create strategies and negotiate terms for its functioning and practice. This book is not, therefore, a pictorial reconstruction of the World's Columbian Exposition; rather, it is the story of a series of contests that were integral to exhibiting and making photographs at the event. Any exhibit presents a contested terrain, as Ivan Karp and Steven Lavine have pointed out, and the Exposition was no exception.[6] Photography at the World's Columbian Exposition was much more than pictures on walls. It was a new form of popular culture for an increasing number of amateurs; it was an industry at the beginning of a meteoric rise; and it was a tool for communicating with a mass audience. In effect, photography was used to inform, persuade, record, and illustrate ideas on a scale not equaled in previous exhibitions.[7] Photography was, and still is, a cultural practice, a distinctive way of constructing, producing, and using images. Even in the 1890s, inconsistency and confusion existed concerning photography as a hybrid of art and technology, but these obstacles did not prevent its use as a tool for science, an agent of social change, and a replica of things not present.

The visionary proposal for the Exposition put forward by museum educator George Brown Goode, assistant secretary of the Smithsonian Institution, was for an

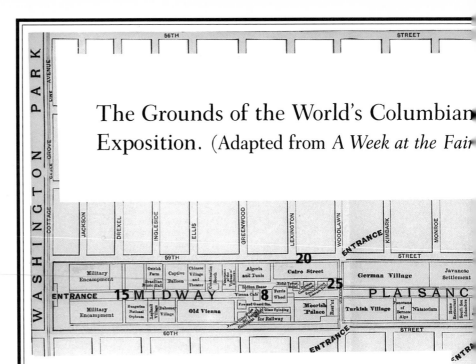

The Grounds of the World's Columbian Exposition. (Adapted from *A Week at the Fair*)

MAP LEGEND

Administration Building	1	Midway Plaisance	15
Agriculture Building	2	Mines Building	16
Anthropological Building	3	North Canal	17
California Building	4	Photography Building	18
Cliffdwellers Exhibit	5	South Canal	19
Convent of La Rabida	6	Streets of Cairo	20
Electricity Building	7	Transportation Building	21
Ferris Wheel	8	United States Government	
Fisheries Building	9	Building	22
French State Building	10	Woman's Building	23
Horticulture Building	11	Wooded Island	24
Illinois Building	12	Zoopraxographical Hall/	
Machinery Building	13	Pompeii Theater	25
Manufactures and Liberal			
Arts Building	14		

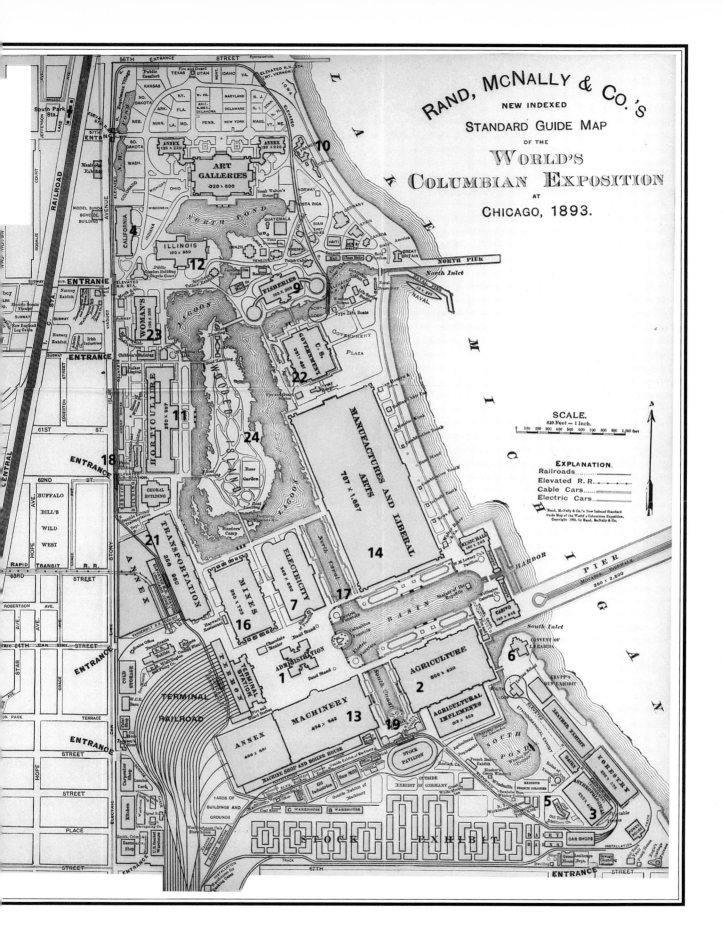

RAND, McNALLY & CO.'S

NEW INDEXED

STANDARD GUIDE MAP

OF THE

WORLD'S

COLUMBIAN EXPOSITION

AT

CHICAGO, 1893.

SCALE.
610 Feet = 1 Inch.
100 200 300 400 500 600 700 800 900 1,000 feet

EXPLANATION.
Railroads
Elevated R. R.
Cable Cars
Electric Cars

Rand, McNally & Co.'s New Indexed Standard
Guide Map of the World's Columbian Exposition.
Copyright, 1893, by Rand, McNally & Co.

illustrated encyclopedia of civilization, a book written in artifacts.[8] Goode's proposal represented part of a fundamental cognitive shift to the visual, as Robert Rydell has pointed out.[9] Not surprisingly, the plan did not prevail, as it failed to cater sufficiently to the interests of industry, the major political force behind the event. It could be argued that the Exposition was indeed an illustrated encyclopedia, but it was photography rather than Goode's specimens and artifacts that made this possible. The Exposition was, in the words of one observer, "almost a photographic exhibition," and photography was everywhere.[10]

Photography had a specialized section for its own display at the Exposition, and prior exhibitions had already formed the expectations of both spectators and exhibitors at Chicago. Competition from two other photographic exhibitions held in 1893 directly affected what appeared on the walls of the Exposition's American photographic section. The contest of representation was a product of the nature and operation of the photographic community as whole. Restrictions on space, competing self-interest, and the internal politics of photographic practices all contributed to this struggle. Every object on a wall, as Donna Haraway has observed, carries with it a "profusion of objects and social interactions," and this was particularly true for the photographic section of the Exposition.[11]

As John Tagg has reminded us, photography has no identity, its history no unity. Its practice and function must be pursued across the flickering field of its institutional spaces.[12] Various institutions exhibiting at the Exposition appropriated photographs for use in their displays. These functions overlapped and were woven together with artifacts that served specific but often complex agendas. The pervasiveness of photography in such displays demonstrated how thoroughly the culture was served by the medium and its images. The interaction between photography and the Exposition's institutional organization also revealed another more overt form of contest and control. In a period that Alan Trachtenberg has characterized as dominated by a system of incorporation in business and culture, official Exposition administrators, mostly businessmen themselves, enacted a policy for restricting and regulating photographic practices.[13] Such policies of incorporation produced a corresponding resistance that significantly affected the practice and production of photography at the Exposition.

Finally, no image of the Exposition failed to reflect the process of mediation and negotiation. This contest of representation was evident even in the work of amateurs. Subject as it was to pictorial conventions and even technical restrictions, the amateurs' work also was able to expand into new formats and explore a range of new subjects. The result was a rich pool of images of the Exposition that provide an immediacy and connection to the event not evident in their commercial and official counterparts.

Photography had just witnessed its first fifty-year retrospective in 1889, and in 1893 the assessment and acknowledgment of its achievements was still in progress. Understandably for the Exposition, photography was lavished with a rhetoric that grew out of the celebratory nature of the event itself. Photography was even referred to as a new world for exploration. Even the eighteenth-century scientist Johann Schulze was reconstituted as the "Columbus of Photography" for his discovery in 1727 of the light sensitivity of silver salts.[14] Adopting the Columbian symbol of the New World, Léon Vidal characterized the present and future possibilities of photography in a paper presented at the Exposition's congress on photography.[15] This "new era" image for photography was sustained by Vidal and others in the belief that the progress of photography was analogous to that of the science of evolution, with the present building organically on the past.[16] Vidal pointed to recent advances made possible by technologies such as electricity, which allowed stop-action photography to go beyond the human eye and see moving objects "as if they were stationary." Advances in rendering the "reality of detail and of color" based on the sensitivity of new film emulsions and "direct prototypes from nature," Vidal declared, were further evidence of the advances made by photography. Science, he continued, would further profit from the applied forms of photography, and progress would not be complete until the new portable camera reached every home. This type of inventory approach and linear history of the "progress of photography" provided a useful paradigm for photography's specialists and its popular audience alike, looking for an understandable explanation of the rapidly expanding phenomenon. Such a perception of photography presumed a unity and cohesion in the practice, production, and function of photography that simply did not exist. Photography was as elusive, tentative, and amorphous as the experience and event of the Exposition itself.

PART I
Photographs on Display

1

PHOTOGRAPHY FOR THE PUBLIC
Precedents, Competing Exhibitions, and a Forum for Ideas

No exhibition exists in isolation. It is built on the foundation of the traditions from which it was created and in the context of competing events. In the case of the World's Columbian Exposition, a whole series of exhibitions earlier in the nineteenth century provided the precedents and background for what took place in Chicago, especially in relation to photography. Both national industrial fairs and international exhibitions provided for the public display of photography. The Philadelphia Centennial Exhibition in 1876, the first United States event on an international scale, has generally been considered the precedent for the 1893 Exposition, but other national exhibits also molded the expectations of both exhibitors and spectators at the Chicago event.

The presence of photography at the 1893 Exposition was also affected by two important competing photographic exhibitions in 1893, one in Philadelphia and the other also in Chicago. The former was a spectacular exhibition of the joint amateur photographic societies in May, which attracted foreign as well as a large regional participation, and the latter was the exhibition at the annual Photographers' Association Convention in July, which was attended by both photographic manufacturers and professionals. Inevitably, the success of the photographic section of the 1893 Exposition and the Auxiliary Congress of Photographers (held in conjunction with the Exposition to provide a much-needed forum for the presentation of ideas about and uses of photography) was measured in relation to these two events.

The Philadelphia Centennial Exhibition as a Precedent

The popularity of industrial fairs in the United States was well established by the second quarter of the nineteenth century, even before the famous Great Exhibition in London in 1851.[1] Beginning in the 1850s, photographs and apparatus were regularly included in the annual industrial exhibits of the American Institute of the City of New York and the Franklin Institute in Philadelphia, as well as in various regional events.[2] The context these exhibits provided for photography reinforced its connection with industry and commerce, as well as applied science and technology, though photography necessarily competed for space and attention with a diversity of products, from engines to agricultural tools. The awards system, which was intended to stimulate participation and reward excellence, was a significant part of the industrial fairs. For photography, such competition raised essential questions about the relative importance of the technical, artistic, and scientific aspects of production, and there was little agreement on the criteria to be used in judging the exhibits. Such fairs were therefore limited in their ability to represent a broad spectrum of either local commercial photographers or photographers in the applied fields of the arts, industry, and science.

The outbreak of the Civil War brought an abrupt suspension of most annual industrial fairs in the wake of the war's massive displacement of the social, cultural, and economic fabric of the country. In response, a new hybrid exhibition was created to support the work of the United States Sanitary Commission, a civilian auxiliary organization that agitated and provided resources for improving health conditions in military facilities. To insure its independence, the commission raised its own funds from a network of support groups throughout the country and used them to purchase medical supplies, food, clothing, and bandages, and to provide for nursing care in army camps and hospitals. The idea of holding fund-raising fairs came from Mary Ashton Livermore, and the first—held in Chicago in November 1863—raised $80,000 for the cause.[3] The Sanitary Fairs were unique in combining the opportunity to display and sell goods with the opportunity to participate in a national effort. Photography was well represented at such events, and amateur photographers participated with professionals for the first time in a commercial setting. Indeed, the fairs attracted a larger and more diverse group of photographers than had any of the previous industrial fairs. The fairs numbered more than a dozen and included events in the leading eastern cities, the Great Western Fair in Cincinnati, the Mississippi Valley Sanitary Fair in St. Louis, and two fairs in Chicago. The production of souvenir photographs in the form of stereographs, books, and albums provided a lucrative commercial business for several entrepreneurs. Jeremiah Gurney and M. Stadfeld's original albumen prints were included in a publication commemorating the New York Metropolitan Fair, while R. Newall's work appeared in another on the Philadelphia event. The E. & H. T. Anthony Co. and Bierstadt Brothers published stereographs for commercial sale.[4]

In the 1870s there was a resurgence of interest in industrial fairs. The Franklin Institute resumed its annual events, and the new Cincinnati Industrial Exposition was reconstituted from an earlier society. In New York City an active photography group began meeting regularly at the American Institute.[5] Although the opportunities for the exhibitors of photography were thus expanding, participation was limited because, for photographers, a new development had eclipsed the industrial fair: the annual professional convention and exhibition of the National Photographers' Association, discussed later in this chapter. In the 1850s and 1860s, however, popular industrial fairs had provided an important connection between industry, commerce, art, and science from which photography benefited.

The most important international event in the United States prior to the Columbian Exposition was the Philadelphia Centennial Exhibition. Like the 1893 event, the Centennial Exhibition masked the serious social, economic, and political upheavals afflicting the country in 1876. The financial crisis of 1873, with its numerous bank failures and spreading unemployment, was still affecting the economic health of the country.[6] The impending presidential election of 1876 and the political crisis that ensued following the close election of Rutherford B. Hayes marked a winter of political confusion and constitutional uncertainty. As a respite from these events, the Centennial celebration offered a moment for the country to focus its identity and experiences.

The Centennial's Photographic Hall—where "everything belonging to photography" would be displayed, including pictures, chemicals, and apparatus—was the first such specialized building for photography at an international exposition.[7] The unwieldy design of the 1873 Vienna exposition had drawn severe criticism from Edward Wilson, editor of the *Philadelphia Photographer* and secretary of the National Photographers' Association. He had been overwhelmed by the "horrible arrangement" for photographs and suggested that "one grand exhibition" should be the ideal for the forthcoming Centennial.[8] For the first time at an international event, photography at the Centennial received a fine arts classification and initially was to be included in the Art Gallery of Memorial Hall.[9] But the lack of space for photography within the Art Building required the construction of a separate building, a course Wilson had been advocating for months.[10] The responsibility for raising the $10,000 needed to cover the building costs was placed on members of the photographic profession.[11] Wilson rallied his readers and members of the "fraternity" for contributions. The National Photographers' Association was suffering at this point from a lack of funds, and internal discord had even caused its 1875 convention to be canceled. The Centennial Exhibition's Photographic Hall showed a striking similarity to the traditional annual exhibits of the association, undercutting its claim to independence and uniqueness. By attempting to isolate photography in a separate building, away from both the art and industry sections of the exhibition, an artificial context was created. The Photographic Hall could not, in fact, contain everything pertaining to photography. The space was too small for the numerous national collections, and more important, photography was too integral to the arts and industries and their displays for this kind of separation to prevail.

Appropriating the space in the Photographic Hall followed a pattern similar to that found in the association's annual exhibits. The photographic trade dealers took full advantage of the first come, first served system of registration for the 19,080 square feet of hanging space. The Scoville Manufacturing Company requested 1,625 square feet, and Wilson & Hood 600, for example. The National Photographers' Association itself requested 1,800 square feet.[12] With the growing complexity of the arrangements for the new hall, as well as the impending arrival of more than three hundred exhibits, by the early months of 1876 it had become clear that a supervisor was urgently required. John Carbutt—who was an experienced photographer, the owner of the American Photo Relief Company, and a close friend of Wilson's—was appointed to this position.[13] Carbutt was the right person for the difficult job of balancing the interests of photographers and dealers. Considerable tact was needed to manage the system of display to achieve an equitable representation.

Of the 322 exhibitors in the Photographic Hall, 144 represented the United States. The space was overcrowded even though twenty-eight hanging screens and freestanding cases were added at the corners and in alcoves along the walls (see Fig. 1.1).[14] The majority of the work by foreign photographers was in the Centennial's main building rather than in the Photographic Hall. Had this material been brought together, Dr. Hermann Vogel pointed out, the foreign displays would have surpassed the American.[15] Vogel, the well-known German photo chemist, had been a judge of the photographic sections of numerous international expositions, including those in Paris in 1867 and Vienna in 1873, as well as the 1876 Centennial and later the 1893 Chicago Exposition. Following the exhibition's theme of national competition in his reviews of the event, Vogel identified individual features by nationality. He characterized the Americans by their "life-size" formats and successful technical processes, including coloring by crayon.[16]

Edward Wilson followed Vogel's lead with his own celebratory nationalistic rhetoric, which extolled the unusual large-scale portrait groups by John Kent of Rochester, New York, and the "mammoth" portraits by the well-known New York photographer William Kurtz, whose innovative photoreproduction work was later featured in the 1893 Exposition.[17] Wilson also singled out individual photographs for their content, such as the enlarged genre scenes like *Newsboy,* which James Ryder

finished in crayon and which he prominently featured in his display.[18] Wilson declared James Landy's series illustrating Shakespeare's "Seven Ages of Man" to be "one of the grandest works ever produced by photography," though this did not prevent him from noting that the aged seer had legs that were "too plump" to be authentic. Landy accommodated this criticism by making a second version of the scene with a bandage wrapped around the leg of the actor (Fig. 1.2).[19] He gave the label of "masterpiece" to a photograph by L. G. Biegelow showing a scene with two ladies viewing a painted portrait of a child, which he commended to all photographers as "the work of a young American artist."

It was this generation of photographers who had experienced the growth of photography, as one writer said in 1876, "from almost nothing, to its present colossal proportions."[20] Unlike the historically conscious European expositions, there was little on display that celebrated or even reflected the extent of the progress in photography in the United States. One exception was the exhibit by Marcus Aurelius Root, an early chronicler of photographic practices. His single-frame collection (visible in the left foreground above the number 8 in the upper view in Figure 1.1) was entitled "The Progress of the New Art Form, August 1839–May 1876." It was composed of a collection of early daguerreotypes, ambrotypes, and argentotypes, including a historic self-portrait by Robert Cornelius.[21] By the 1870s in the United States, progress in photography was identified by its commercial product rather than by its science, technology, or art, as it had been in the 1850s and to some extent in the 1860s. The feature that pervaded the exhibition in Photographic Hall was the commerce in photography.

Photographic Hall was not the sole repository of photography at the Centennial Exhibition. One reviewer noted this anomaly clearly when he said: "Anyone who will go through the whole extent of the great Exhibition, and notice the photographs in almost every department, of all kinds of wares, as well as of people and scenery, will be convinced of the multifarious applications and usefulness of our art."[22] This was a confirmation of the degree to which photography had been woven into the nation's social fabric and guaranteed its presence in the diverse displays and departments at the Centennial. This pattern would be repeated in the 1893 Exposition. An examination of several departmental displays at the Centennial similar to those in 1893 indicates the nature of this representation some twenty years earlier.

The extensive display on American educational sys-

tems used photographs as a source of information along with statistics, plans, and samples of student work. Among the fifteen state school systems represented, photographs were widespread and were presented in a range of formats, including, for example, stereographs of historic public buildings in Massachusetts.[23] The New Jersey display used a set of photographs showing school exteriors and interiors over the period 1866 to 1876 to demonstrate the progress that had been achieved. Photographs of students and buildings from the Hampton Institute in Virginia, as well as albums from various collegiate institutions, including Brown and Harvard universities, were as promotional as they were informative.

Indeed, national displays at international expositions were primarily promotional in intent. Photographs, together with selected artifacts representing cultural features, natural resources, and opportunities for development, were crucial to the nations' display strategies. The Australian colonies of Great Britain, for example, used photographs to attract investment and settlement to the growing regional urban centers in Victoria and South Australia, as well as to the rich pastoral lands being opened in its northern colony of Queensland. Acting independently, as it was also to do for the 1893 Exposition, New South Wales sent a series of well-publicized photographs that included panoramas of Sydney harbor and views of the famous Hill End goldfields. B. O. Holtermann, the entrepreneur who had made a fortune in the goldfields, provided these photographs as part of his own effort to illustrate the benefits of emigration to the colony.[24] As early as 1873 he had begun plans for his own international traveling exposition featuring photographs, specimens, and models. Holtermann hired the photographer Beaufoy Merlin to undertake the work, which was later completed by Charles Bayliss, Merlin's assistant. The ninety-foot tower on

FIGURE I.I Two views of the photographic displays in the Centennial Exhibition's Photographic Hall. Unlike the Columbian Exposition, the Centennial provided a separate building for photography for the U.S. exhibitors and some from other countries as well. (Above: Albumen print, 11.5 cm × 18.4 cm, by the Centennial Photographic Company; from the *Philadelphia Photographer* (September 1876): front., courtesy of the George Eastman House, International Museum of Photography and Film, Library Collection; below: reproduced from Norton, *Frank Leslie's Historic Register. . . 1876*, 225; courtesy of the Fine Arts Library, University of Rochester)

FIGURE I.2 James Landy's photograph of the aged seer, the last scene in his series depicting the "Ages of Man" soliloquy from *As You Like It*: "Last scene of all that ends this strange eventful history, is second childishness, and mere oblivion; sans teeth, sans eyes, sans taste, sans everything." (Albumen print, 44 cm × 28 cm; courtesy of Cincinnati Historical Society; Photographic Collection)

Blue's Point, Holtermann's grand residence in Sydney, served as a tripod for making the 18-by-22-inch negatives for the giant thirty-foot panorama print on display at the Centennial. Holtermann came to Philadelphia on his international tour, carrying one of his two original 3'2″ × 5'3″ sixty-pound negatives, which was shown in the Philadelphia studio of Frederick Gutekunst. Holtermann's role as an entrepreneur and successful businessman fit perfectly into the colonial government's carefully constructed strategy for encouraging settlement and development, and photography played a key part in the process.

The largest concentration of photographs outside Photographic Hall was in the United States Government Building. The engineering section of the army exhibit included photographs along with models, apparatus, specimens, maps, and drawings showing the nature and location of its various construction projects.[25] Similar photographs were found in the national displays of France, Brazil, Russia, and Austria. The army's surveying expedition led by George M. Wheeler was also prominently featured. In an effort to establish the preeminence of military over civilian surveys, Wheeler's work was directed less toward pure science than promotion, as William Goetzmann has pointed out.[26] The Wheeler survey material was a central feature, with photographic panoramas of the country west of the Mississippi by such well-known photographers as Timothy O'Sullivan and William Bell.[27] There was also a demonstration of the "field photography" used in the survey.

The Department of the Interior presented work from the important surveys by Ferdinand V. Hayden and John Wesley Powell, Wheeler's competitors. These were civilian rather than army-directed surveys, and they were carried out to establish information on the character of the land and its physical resources for potential exploitation and development. A less-advertised purpose was to evaluate Indian populations in preparation for implementing the government's pacification policies. Competition for government support caused these civilian surveys to be alert to ways of publicizing their work, and an international exhibition served as a useful tool in this effort. According to William Goetzmann, Hayden cultivated his role as the "businessman explorer" and creator of "the Tourist's West" through his publications and his effort to promote the photographic work of William Henry Jackson.[28] The Interior Department's display was "one of the most remarkable" exhibits, according to a contemporary observer, with "models, maps, photographs, publications, sketches, pictures in watercolor and chromos."[29] Its most innovative feature, however, was Hayden's use of a wall of brilliantly lit glass transparencies from original 20-by-24-inch plates (Fig. 1.3). These included a range of Jackson's photographs of the Rocky Mountains, the Yellowstone geyser and hot springs, and ruins in southwestern Colorado, Arizona, and Utah. To accompany his photographs of the ancient cave ruins of Mancos Canyon (recently discovered in the Mesa Verde region) Jackson and the survey artist, William Henry Holmes, had constructed a series of scale models based on photographs. Jackson later remarked that these models "attracted more attention than the many photographs and all the rocks and relics of Dr. Hayden's career."[30] Two large volumes depicting western scenery and Indians were also available for visitors to leaf through at their leisure. Hayden clearly understood

the effectiveness of visual devices that used photographs to attract an audience for the work of the survey.

The Powell Survey featured photographs by its own official photographer, Jack Hillers, whose work was also prominent at the Columbian Exposition.[31] While Hillers was in Salt Lake City in 1871, Powell had hired him as a boatman for the second survey expedition down the Colorado. At that time, E. O. Beaman was the official photographer, and Hillers learned photography from him, eventually replacing Beaman in 1872. A series of framed photographs from the Colorado expeditions included views of the Kaibab Paiute Indians, who were among the last Indian groups to come into contact with Euro-Americans.[32] One of the photographs on view, *The Arrow Maker and His Daughter,* which had been made for ethnographic purposes in the fall of 1872, was placed adjacent to a view of a similar Indian group made the following year for the stereographic trade. The second photograph showed a Paiute mother and children dressed in clothing from the Smithsonian's collection that Powell had brought along for the occasion.[33] The Columbian Exposition provided a means of continuing this type of photographic work by Hillers under the direction of Powell, who by this time was in charge of the U.S. Geological Survey as well as the Smithsonian Institution's Bureau of Ethnology. In the 1870s both Powell and Hayden emphasized ethnographic subjects in their respective displays, reflecting the overlapping nature of the work undertaken by the different surveys prior to their later amalgamation into a single agency, the USGS, within the Interior Department. The ethnographic focus of Powell's work was in direct conflict with that of the Office of Indian Affairs, whose purpose was to speed up the acculturation process. As H. Craig Miner has pointed out, the contrived picturesqueness of the display mannequins at the centennial was less than flattering and only thinly masked the difficult transitions Native Americans were then undergoing.[34] The mannequin of Red Cloud, chief of the Oglala Sioux (Fig. 1.4), obscures the fact that he was a fine-looking man, according to Miner, who had been on friendly terms with the government for years.

In addition to using photographs as display objects, international exhibitions always offered an important market for the sale of photographs. The concession for the sale of commercially produced photographs of the Centennial Exhibition was opened to bids, and in November 1875 it was granted to the Centennial Photographic Company. Not surprisingly, the company was headed by

FIGURE 1.3   Part of the Interior Department's Centennial display, a wall of transparencies, included Western views by William Henry Jackson, which he had taken while working on the Hayden Survey. (Cyanotype, 23 cm x 18 cm, photographer unknown; RU 95, box 64, no. 72-6191, Smithsonian Institution Archives)

Edward Wilson as superintendent and William Notman as president, with W. Irving Adams as vice-president and J. A. Fraser as art superintendent. The conditions of operation required the payment of a basic sum plus 10 percent of gross receipts over $30,000.[35]

The company's one-story, 130-by-30-foot structure with its attractive wide verandahs was designed to fit the style of other buildings by the exhibition's architect, H. J. Swarzmann. Three rooms were devoted to photographic manufacturing, and a southern-exposure studio constructed especially for the large-volume production of photographic prints had a slanted, glazed roof to hold a quantity of the necessary printing frames (Fig. 1.5). To minimize the effect of direct sunlight when producing the firm's albumen prints, tissue paper was placed between the negative and the print paper. Although this process was slow, it produced superior results.[36] The company employed several Philadelphia photographers, including the highly capable and experienced John L.

Gihon and the young William Rau, later represented at the 1893 Exposition. This ensured a high standard for the production of quality photographs.

The Centennial Photographic Company also made the identification photographs for the Centennial pass books that were issued free to visitors, exhibitors, and employees. This was, in fact, a large part of the company's business, in peak times amounting to more than 700 photographs a day. The company's premises offered a "picturesque sight," according to one writer. It was like a "true Babel" with Tunisians, Algerians, Turks, Chinese, and Japanese "all jabbering in their native tongues, scrambling for their turns in their national way, showing their international measure of push and enterprise in getting ahead."[37] A collection of portrait photographs by the Centennial Company entitled "Our Foreign Visitors" was displayed in Photographic Hall, reflecting the widespread interest in this type of portraiture, an interest that persisted into the 1893 event.

Souvenir photographs were also available from the company in a wide range of formats, including lantern slides, stereographs, and prints. The popular stereograph sold for twenty-five cents, and the larger sizes (6" x 7", 8" x 10", 13" x 16", and 17" x 21") ranged from fifty cents to five dollars.[38] The 52-page catalogue listed more than 3,050 different views, which included a thorough inventory of the exhibition, views of important buildings from multiple angles, interior views of various international displays, images of works of art from the Art Gallery display, and views of the exhibits of individual manufacturers and businesses.

The Centennial Photographic Company held a veritable monopoly on photographic work at the exhibition. Amateur photography was still on a very small scale and was not considered competitive with commercial work, but there was at least one exception to the company's monopoly—a commercial print produced by the well-known Philadelphia photographer Frederick Gutekunst, who, to make his exposure, erected a special scaffold near the Belmont reservoir that was reminiscent of the tower Holtermann erected in Sydney. To prepare a print, he had to print seven negatives individually on a single piece of silvered paper measuring 18 inches by 10 feet, with the final gold toning done before fixing and washing. Gutekunst continued to produce these prints for years after the event.[39] The print was a fitting symbol for the entrepreneurial and technical skill that characterized professional photography at the Centennial Exhibition.

FIGURE 1.4 Detail of a commercial stereograph of the Centennial's mannequin of Red Cloud, chief of the Oglala Sioux, which was on view at the Centennial. (Albumen print, stereograph 2613, 10 cm x 7.8 cm, by Centennial Photographic Company; Historical Society of Pennsylvania; Centennial Exhibition, Stereograph Collection)

Competing Exhibitions

While there were precedents for the public display of photographs and while the Centennial had created a certain set of expectations for the 1893 Exposition, two other contemporary exhibits, one in Chicago and one in Philadelphia, significantly influenced the Exposition's photographic section. In July 1893 Chicago was the venue for the 13th Annual Convention of the Photographers' Association of America. The association had been founded as the National Photographic Union in 1868, and a year later it had become the National Photographic Association. Its stated purpose was to relieve the "present state of isolation among photographers," as well as their vulnerability to what was seen as "the process monger, the patent-seeker" and "cheap and incompetent" practitioners.[40] In this period the association was an uneasy alliance that grew out of a sense of

cooperative self-interest and protectionism that arose among photographers in response to economic competition and rapidly developing technology. At a time when photographers needed a national rather than just a regional identity, the association provided a regular, centralized forum. It offered a venue for the display and discussion of photographic work—its practice and progress—and its meetings attracted participants from a wider region than had the previous industrial fairs. It held annual exhibitions in connection with each of its conventions from 1869 to 1874 and beginning in 1880, when the group reformed as the Photographers' Association of America.[41]

These early exhibitions provided an opportunity for photographers to present their own work, compare it with the work of others, observe demonstrations of new techniques, and examine the apparatus of various photography dealers. At a time when professional photography relied solely on the apprentice system, the educational function of these events was important. Maintaining this focus was problem, however. Critics of the association's exhibition in 1873 cited the "family gathering," self-congratulatory approach of such displays and asserted that they were becoming more like "picture shows" than opportunities for instruction.[42] The exhibitions had always addressed two audiences—the specialized photographic membership and the general public, who were encouraged to attend—and the public success of the exhibitions gradually came to overshadow their educational role as a venue for advancing professional practice. Further, powerful photographic dealers fostered this change to serve their own interest in marketing their goods. Eventually the precarious balance between the photographers and the dealers shifted toward the promotion of goods over practices. The Centennial temporarily drew the association together in the cooperative effort of preparing its Photographic Hall exhibition, but the tensions soon resurfaced, and the association dissolved in the late 1870s. The association was reformed in 1880 under the new name of the Photographers' Association of America and with James F. Ryder as president. The new group passed a resolution stating "that our association [should] be oriented more towards the needs of photographers than those of trade, which had previously dominated."[43]

The association's 1893 exhibit had no formal connection with the Columbian Exposition. Efforts by a committee of the association set up in 1891 to lobby for a proper representation of photography at the Exposition proved ineffectual. Attendance at the association's 1893 convention was deemed "slight," with just over two hundred members present.[44] Yet its exhibition, according to *Wilson's Photographic Magazine,* "appeared to more advantage than did the regular display at the World's Fair."[45] Considering that the Wilson in the magazine's title was the same Edward Wilson who had been such a pervasive advocate for photography at the Centennial Exhibition, such an observation justifies a closer look at the event.

The association's exhibition, held in the large, rambling Chicago Second Regiment Armory just outside the Exposition's grounds, offered participants the opportunity to compete for cash prizes—a regular feature of such events but an even greater inducement in the hard times of the 1890s. Frank Place, the association's president, emphasized the awards in his opening remarks to the convention. "I believe in investing a large amount of our income in prizes," he said, because it creates competition among photographers and sends each one "home with new life and vigor, to start anew and improve his or her observation."[46] The 1893 competition included prints illustrating the narrative poem "Lucile" by Owen Meredith, genre photographs (which depicted scenes of everyday life and work), portrait collections, landscape collections, and a set of enlargements. There were also separate prizes for operators and retouchers, and for technical improvements and foreign entries. Several of the prizewinners, such as J. C. Strauss, George Steckel, James Inglis, and Adam Heimberger, were also represented in the Columbian Exposition's photographic section. In addition to the association's own cash prizes, manufacturers offered substantial prizes at the annual conventions. In 1893 the Photo Materials Company provided a number of lucrative prizes for work on its new "Kloro" gelatin chloride paper. This enticement made it "practically an 'aristo exhibition,'" according to one reviewer, who noted that more than 80 percent of the prints were on aristotype paper.[47] The writer was probably referring to both gelatin and collodion chloride printing papers, which offered both a faster and a simpler process, as well as sharper print quality, than the traditional albumen paper. Professional photographers were being offered a number of American brands from which to choose.[48] Firms that produced aristotype papers were always evolving new ways to attract the attention of customers from both the amateur and professional communities, and the convention was an ideal site for this purpose. The association's 1893 convention was, then, a

FIGURE 1.5   An exterior view of the Centennial Photographic Company's working studio, showing the slanting glazed roof of the printing studio, where large quantities of photographic prints and stereographs were made. (Albumen print, detail of commercial stereograph no. 2854, 10 cm × 7.8 cm, by the Centennial Photographic Company; courtesy of the Historical Society of Pennsylvania; Centennial Exhibition, Stereograph Collection)

lucrative exhibition as well as a readily accessible venue for professional photographers to show their work. Both of these features were absent from the Exposition's photographic section.

There was at least one other reason for the relatively greater success of the convention's exhibition. The policy of offering cash awards for photographs was under critical scrutiny by amateur societies but was supported, maintained, and stimulated by the growing number of manufacturers eager to gain a market for their new products, particularly in light of the fact that the country was in the midst of a depression at the time. The association's active promotion of the prize system to encourage participation had the support of a large part of the photographic business community, but this had the effect of isolating professional photographers from the wider social and cultural context.

In sharp contrast to the Photographers' Association Chicago event was the Sixth Joint Annual Exhibition, held in April just a month before the official opening of the Exposition. The combined exhibition was deemed by one observer to be "an exhibition of photographic progress . . . second to none ever held in this country, the great Centennial Exhibition in 1876 not excepted."[49] Held jointly by the amateur groups of New York, Boston, and Philadelphia, it was staged in the spacious rooms of the Pennsylvania Academy of Fine Arts in Philadelphia.[50] Amateur photographers had always had their own alternative exhibition sites, but the move toward cooperation in these events contributed to expanding their representation. Revisions in the exhibition practices, such as the removal of rigid classification types like genre, landscape, and architecture subjects, also contributed to their renewed importance. On view at the exhibition were 1,200 framed pictures and 62 sets of lantern slides by 187 individual photographers, nearly three times the number of photographic exhibitors at the Exposition itself.[51]

A feature of these exhibits was the number of overseas participants they attracted. A number of British exhibitors, as well as several of the foreign award winners from this exhibition, also had work on display in Chicago. Among them was George Davison, whose large pinhole photographs executed on rough platinum paper included *The Onion Field*. Cited by Janet Buerger as the beginning of the "aesthetic movement" in photography, this photograph departed significantly from the previously dominant naturalistic mode.[52] Alfred Stieglitz, during his period of study in Germany, had written a number of articles on photography and had exhibited work in various European exhibits.[53] In 1891, after his return to the United Stated, Stieglitz joined the Society of Amateur Photographers in New York City and wrote for the *American Amateur Photographer,* assuming the editorship on the departure of Catharine Barnes in July 1893. In his extensive review of the Philadelphia event, Stieglitz called Davison's work "the most remarkable of the exhibition."[54] Stieglitz had been developing a terminology or critical language, later adopted by other writers, to distinguish the technical "photograph" from the artistic "picture." He exhorted photographers to emulate the British model by returning to simplicity and originality in their work, especially through the use of tone in printing. Stieglitz's critiques were often characterized by a thinly veiled abrasive arrogance. In referring to William Rau's photograph *On the Blue Juniata,* which was reproduced in the catalogue, Stieglitz concluded

that it "might be called a picture" in a tone of condescension hardly appropriate to a photographer of Rau's professional reputation.[55]

Throughout the exhibition there was a noticeable presence of "artistic" photographs, especially platinum prints. The delicate tonal qualities of these prints gave a distinctive look to the exhibit, one that was significantly different from the high-pitched, purplish brilliance of the aristotypes of the Photographers' Association exhibit. Despite the efforts of the organizers of the Philadelphia event to stress the function of photography as "the handmaid of science" as well as an artistic medium, there were few exhibits in the applied fields to support this view. There was, however—in one corner of the exhibition and far from "the finest and most pretentious specimens of modern photography"—a set of five plain oak frames. These frames held facsimile photographs of the earliest daguerreotypes by Joseph Paxton and Dr. Paul Beck Goddard, as well as Robert Cornelius's "first portrait of the human face," which had also been present at the Centennial.[56] The interest in presenting this display on the history and progress of photography was due to the efforts of Julius Sachse, editor of the *American Journal of Photography,* who had copied original daguerreotypes, collected reminiscences and accounts of the earliest practitioners, and published several articles on the subject.[57] A rival version of this history was presented in an Exposition display by the University of the City of New York, discussed in chapter 3.

The Philadelphia exhibit included prominent American amateur photographers such as John Dumont, W. B. Post, Robert Redfield, and Emma Farnsworth. Farnsworth (one of whose photographs is shown in Fig. 1.6) was the only woman to have received an award at the Philadelphia exhibition, and Stieglitz described her work as "unaffected and full of individuality."[58] This failure by the Exposition to elicit participation from most of the leading Philadelphia exhibitors was due in part to the perceived need to separate "artistic" and "aesthetic" photography from contact with the Exposition's industrial and commercial aspects. This was the basis for the idea of creating a separate exhibit format for "aesthetic" photography, an idea that was promoted by Stieglitz and that was dramatized in the next decade in the struggle among different camps of amateurs. In 1893 there was still, however, a somewhat fluid relationship among the amateur groups, and a number of proposals were made for accommodating amateur work in general at the Exposition. One suggestion was to set up separate exhibits of amateur photography in the various state buildings through the auspices of the American Photographic League.[59] The various exchange societies, which circulated work by amateurs and others, were urged to come forward with proposals for coordinated displays on themes related to individual states. Amateur practitioners had little recent history of working cooperatively with professionals and manufacturers, however. They failed to exert the necessary pressure on the already resistant Exposition administration and the suggestion was rejected.

The Exposition's photographic section thus lacked both the wide range of professional work on view at the Photographers' Association convention in Chicago and the lavish demonstration of what was claimed to be "modern" in art photography by the amateurs at Philadelphia. Instead, the contest enacted at the Exposition reflected both the growing distinction between amateur and professional commercial photographers, which led to the increasing isolation of both groups. The spectators at the Exposition therefore did not see either the full range or depth of photographic work being done in the United States in this period.

The World's Columbian Exposition's Auxiliary Congress of Photographers

An important counterpoint to the static displays of artifacts at the Exposition itself were the activities of the World's Columbian Exposition's Auxiliary Congress of Photographers with its motto, "Not things but men." The congress sought to draw together the international leaders of various disciplines for lectures and exchanges, and it was here that some of the more interesting and dynamic ideas circulating within the photographic world were given space for presentation. Among the proposals heard were those on the unification of practices, an international photographic survey project, and a proposed training institute on photography. The audience for the sessions averaged only fifty people. In fact, just over half of the fifty scheduled papers for the congress were delivered, and those in the last two sessions were presented in a greatly abbreviated form. Most of the papers were later published, however, and thus reached a much larger public.[60] The importance of the event lay in the fact that it provided a forum for ideas relating to photography not addressed by the Exposition itself, with its focus on commerce and industry.

The Auxiliary Congress of Photographers, held from July 31 to August 5, was put together by a committee of several leading Chicago photographers, with Judge

FIGURE 1.6 Emma Farnsworth's photograph *To a Greek Girl,* shown as a glass transparency in the Joint Exhibition in Philadelphia, was characteristic of the quality of the work that earned her a medal at this event. (Green-toned silver print, 18.7 cm x 13.2 cm; cat. no. 77.92.21, neg. no. 81-12790, Division of Photographic History, National Museum of American History, Smithsonian Institution)

James Bradwell as chairman and Gayton Douglass as vice-chairman. Judge James Bradwell's versatility was well known. It was said that he could earn his living at seventeen different trades, including several elected positions. He was an early supporter of voting rights for women, and while he was the manager of the judiciary review *Legal News,* edited by his wife, he invented a halftone process for illustrating the journal with photographic portraits.[61] Gayton Douglass was an amateur astronomer, chemist, skilled photographer, and vice-president of a Chicago photographic supply business. Also on the committee were Charles Gentile, editor of the Chicago-based journal *The Photo Eye;* M. J. Steffens, a well-known Chicago portrait photographer; Alexander Hesler, whose reputation had been made with daguerreotypes in the 1860s; and Mrs. D. M. Stevenson, a leading Chicago amateur who served as vice-chairman of the Women's Committee of the Auxiliary Congress. Critics, however, were not wholly satisfied with the larger "advisory council" of national representatives from professional and amateur interests and manufacturing. They complained about the slowness of the congress's planning and the fact that the advisory members came from only twenty-three states and selected photographic publications.[62] While the council included three editors from the *Photo-Times* and one each from *Anthony's Bulletin* and the *American Amateur Photographer,* there were none from the *St. Louis Photographer, Wilson's Photographic Magazine,* the *American Journal of Photography,* or the Chicago-based journal *The Photo Beacon.* Given the important role of the photographic media, this kind of selectivity reflected the factionalism that was present in the world of photography.

In his opening remarks, Judge Bradwell characteristically noted the contributions of five women. Their participation on the program may also have been due to the presence of Mary Bartlett, who served as the chairman of the Women's Committee of the Auxiliary Congress. Their papers included presentations on amateur photography by Catharine Barnes, who had recently married H. Snowden Ward, with whom she helped create a link between the photographic communities of Great Britain and the United States.[63] There were also papers by Elizabeth Flint Wade of Buffalo on the camera as a source of income, and photography in the Alps by Elizabeth Main.[64] Main's work was as technical as it was artistic, dealing as it did with the ways to use light to capture the unusual and sometimes elusive qualities of snow subjects.

Not surprisingly, the subject of color in photography led off the congress, as it was of great interest at the time, especially with the prominence given the French display on color photography at the Exposition, discussed in chapter 2. Even so, not all the scheduled papers were delivered, some because they arrived too late. Frederick Ives did not even alert the organizers to the fact that he would be absent despite the considerable international attention then being focused on his Kromskop camera and viewer, a system based on an additive color process.[65] This instrument, provided with three color-separation filters, allowed for the creation of a single negative because it employed a system of mirrors that divided the light rays and focused them separately on a single sensitive plate. The resulting positive lantern slide, when viewed in the same device in reverse through the three color filters, appeared in natural color. It is surprising that his device was not on view at the Exposition, but it was shown at the Photographers' Association convention in St. Louis in 1894. The process of manufacturing orthochromatic plates, which enabled the correct tonal rendering of colors on black-and-white plates, was presented by the two leading plate producers, Gustav Cramer and John Carbutt, whose papers were published in the September issue of the *Photo-American.* Both men had large displays in the Exposition's photographic section and are discussed in detail in chapter 2. Considerable discussion took place among the participants about the use of these plates and the reluctance of professional photographers to adapt them for use.

Four papers on the medical applications of photography were presented, although this important field was seriously underrepresented in the displays of the Exposition itself. Otis G. Mason argued that photography was the best "illustrated record of the facts," and that "no human hand can rival" it in degree of detail for the study of disease. Mason had been the photographer at Bellvue Hospital in New York for twenty-five years, and his view was that photography gave the "correct location, form and size, with an amount of detail otherwise unattainable." His paper described the setup for photography on the seventh floor of the hospital, and the photographic apparatus and developing and printing techniques used.[66]

Similar arguments for the use of photography in anthropology were scheduled to be made by Frederick Starr, a popular lecturer from the University of Chicago. His paper was among those not presented, but he discussed his photographs of fingerprints of Cherokee Indians in a published article, and they were included in a display in the Anthropological Building noted in chapter 3.[67] While there were single papers on the application of photography to religion and to education, none dealt with photographic practice itself, especially the use of hand-held cameras by either professionals or amateurs. These were obvious omissions and reflected the growing separation of the groups representing professional and amateur photographers from those in the developing fields of applied photography.

A plan to overcome this isolation and unify all photographic activities at the level of the conventions was the subject of a key paper by H. Snowden Ward, editor of the English journal *The Practical Photographer.*[68] Ward outlined a sweeping proposal for national representation in the European International Congress of Photography. This would be, he said, a "combined conference on all subjects that are of interest to amateurs and professionals alike."[69] As a journalist, Ward had a broad view of photographic practice, and he drew attention to the absence in the United States of an active mutual benefit association for photographers, the previous attempt having ended badly through mismanagement.

The idea of an international congress on photography was not new. A European congress had been formed in conjunction with the 1889 Paris Exposition, and a second followed in Brussels in 1891.[70] This European effort focused on the scientific and technical aspects of photography—especially with regard to standardizing lenses, plate sensitivity, and the measurements to be used for formulas—rather than on current practices of professionals or amateurs. The treatment of professionals and amateurs at the annual photographic association conventions held in England and the United States was significantly different. While the English convention drew both amateurs and professionals, few amateurs in the United States participated in the annual exhibits of the Photographers' Association of America. Similarly, manufacturers and dealers had a controlling presence in the American conventions but were not well represented in the British and European events. What prevented the achievement of unity among such groups in the respective associations, according to Ward, was that in "the great things they are powerless, and the multitude of little things they can do they despise."[71] Ward's proposal for an international union of photography was impressive for its inclusiveness. It would encompass amateurs, professionals, and manufacturers, and also employees of both industrial and professional firms. The breadth of Ward's concept was visionary, to say the least. What is interesting is that even during this period, when the pressure for specialization was increasing, Ward's call for a unified photographic community on an international scale that would exchange work, ideas, and practices struck a strong positive response from the audience at the Auxiliary Congress.

Another proposal on an international scale was presented in a paper by Jerome Harrison, who called for the establishment of a bureau to record the physical features of each country by photographic survey. Harrison's idea of making a "true pictorial history of the present day" by enlisting the participation of local photographic societies across the country had already begun in the form of the Warwickshire Record Survey in England. But Har-

rison's background in natural science and geology allowed him to bring a systematic approach to the concept of record photographs that had never before been applied to amateur work. The use of survey maps, keyed panoramic views, standard plates, and platinum prints (which were more permanent prints available in this period) were some of the features of his program. He suggested the Smithsonian Institution as the repository for the record negatives, as the British Museum had been in the United Kingdom.[72] As indicators of official interest in Harrison's proposal, Judge Bradwell commented on it in his opening remarks, and Harrison's paper was moved up in the program to avoid its being missed in the later sessions, several of which were canceled.

Harrison's proposal met an enthusiastic response, and a committee was formed to examine its feasibility.[73] The attractiveness of a cooperative ideal, also expressed in Ward's proposal for union, was deeply felt by photographers in the United States who were searching for an alternative to the growing fragmentation of their community. Lacking in the United States, however, was the strong, well-organized regional network of amateurs that was present in Great Britain. Harrison's success came later, and then only indirectly, with the British Photographic Record project.[74] Léon Vidal, a fellow participant in the Auxiliary Congress, was so impressed by Harrison's proposal that he founded the Association du Musée des Photographies Documentaires the following year.[75]

The most interesting proposal from the United States at the Auxiliary Congress was for the creation of a teaching and research institution for photographic practice. It was put forward by Dr. John Nicol, editor of the *Photo Beacon*. In his paper, Nicol argued that even though there was a "suspicion on proposals for centralization . . . there are matters in which the nation and not the state should take hold, and the recognition of photography is one of these."[76] This call for a photographic institution was not new, having been put forward in the 1860s and 1870s in a proposal for government support that met with no success. The European model of technical training in photography remained Dr. Hermann Vogel's Technische Hochschule outside Berlin.[77] Training in photography in the United States was available at the Chicago College of Photography, some local technical institutions, and the Chautauqua School of Photography, under the direction of Charles Ehrmann, which catered to 150 correspondence students. Classes were also available at the University of Michigan under the direction of Professor A. B. Stevens. In his presidential address at the Photographers' Association convention in 1890, J. M. Appleton called for the creation of a permanent home for the association linked to the establishment of a school and collection.[78]

Nicol envisioned a wide context for such training, which struck a responsive note in a period when professional technical training was generally gaining credibility. The period of the "self-made and self-instructed men" who had been the country's "famous photographers," he said, was coming to a close. By the end of the century, in response to the pressure of growing competition within the trade, regulations with respect to photographic businesses, and a move to more complex technical practices in specialized work, professional photography was being transformed. Nicol did not touch on the complexity of these issues, although he clearly saw that responsibility and control rightly lay outside the professional associations.[79] Few listeners or readers would have considered Nicol's proposal for a teaching and research institution to be attainable, given the severe economic conditions of the times. Such proposals were, however, a recurring theme throughout the second half of the nineteenth century in the United States and an essential part of the process of defining the occupation of photography.

Precedents for the Columbian Exposition had been established by the industrial fairs, the annual photographic conventions, and the Centennial Exhibition. Through these events, both a popular and a specialized audience for photography had come into existence by 1893, and both audiences looked to the coming exposition's photographic section as a place that would resemble what they had come to expect in public photographic exhibits. While professional photographers and dealers-turned-manufacturers enjoyed a history of cooperation in the Photographers' Association annual conventions, there was no direct link between these groups and the photographic section of the Exposition.

In its Photographic Hall, the Centennial had produced a highly innovative solution to the question of its international exhibitors. Still, this turned out to be a synthetic construct for the representation of photographic practice and production. It failed because it did not acknowledge photography's broader social and cultural function. The Columbian Exposition saw a similar, though enlarged, pattern of representation. It was, in the words of Charles Gould, "almost a photographic exhibition."[80]

Missing from the photographic section of the Columbian Exposition, however, was a selection of the most "modern" or "aesthetic" photography by amateurs who had exhibited in April 1893 in Philadelphia. Clearly, the developments separating amateur from professional photography contributed to a substantial number of amateurs deciding not to participate in the Exposition. The absence of this important constituency reflected the extent of the struggle between the artistic, scientific, and industrial aspects of photographic practice.

While the applied forms of photography appeared throughout the Exposition's displays, it was only in the Auxiliary Congress of Photographers, with its forum for discussion, that these applications were presented and discussed. The congress provided a wide spectrum of papers on subjects ranging from applied photography to its technological development. It brought an exchange of ideas into the somewhat arid, frenzied, and fragmented atmosphere of the Exposition.

2

EXHIBITING PHOTOGRAPHY
Photographic Sections in the Manufactures and Liberal Arts Building

In no small part, the failure of a world's fair to present a true picture of the art and industry of the several nations is in the nature of the case . . . [of] the man who sought to sell his house by exhibiting "a specimen brick." To show by sample the products of some countries is to omit what is really characteristic concerning their industry, notable perhaps not for the perfection of growth or manufacture, but for the scale of production.

FRANCIS A. WALKER, *Professor, Sheffield Scientific School, Yale University*[1]

This appraisal of the "true picture" of international exhibitions as places of only a limited representation of a nation's art and industry provides a useful focus for examining the Columbian Exposition. Particularly for the photographic section, there were specimen bricks rather than a true picture of the art and industry of contemporary photography. The photographs presented in the section reflected the dynamic social processes at work both within the organizational framework of the Exposition itself and in the photographic world generally.

To begin with, photography was defined and classified according to a system imposed by the Exposition. In contrast to the policy followed by the Centennial Exhibition, photography was not given a separate building or a fine-arts classification for the 1893 Exposition. Nor was it placed in the liberal arts along with educational apparatus and processes, as it had been at the 1889 Paris Exposition. Nor did the organizers for the 1893 Exposition follow the classification system that George Brown Goode had proposed, which would have placed photography with the "Decorative, Plastic and Pictorial Arts," a category that included architecture, sculpture, and painting.[2] By 1893 the climate for photography at such events had changed significantly. It was no longer possible for individuals like Edward Wilson to lobby successfully, as they had in 1876. Now, the carefully managed corporate structure of the Exposition proved impervious to pressure, even that coming from groups of professional associations and amateurs who attempted to see that photography was properly represented. Ultimately it was lumped with precision instruments as Group 151, which one observer concluded was "a sad come down."[3]

The structure of the Exposition simply reflected the developing polarization between industry and art, and in this division the interests of the photographic manufacturers carried by far the greatest weight. In the contest for representation in the very limited space available for the photographic section, there was no question who the winners would be. Because administrators, exhibitors, and the various special interests within photography were pitted against each other, it is not surprising that the photographic section seemed more like a specimen brick than a true picture of the medium. The precarious balancing of interests between manufactures and practitioners, professionals and amateurs, all of whom were further fragmented into specialized interest groups, created the dynamics of the process. Photography in its dual role as science and art had created "a house divided against itself," according to Catharine Barnes, describing current photographic practice in 1892.[4] In addition, photography was a thriving new industry with a number of forces jockeying for position on the international stage.

The United States in the Photographic Section of Group 151

The photographic section for exhibitors from the United States within Group 151 began with several handicaps, especially a lack of space. Well before the event, efforts were made to replicate conditions at the Centennial. During the 1891 Photographers' Association convention, Charles Gentile, editor of the *Photo-Eye,* exhorted his colleagues to "make a demand on the authorities to give us a building specially adapted for an exhibit of photography."[5] Efforts in the summer of 1892 for the creation of a "magnificent photographic exhibit collected from the whole world" had resulted in the appointment of a committee to confer with the Exposition officials.[6] These attempts to provide an adequate representation of photography were deflected by the larger and more focused effort to limit the restrictions placed on photographic practices at the Exposition (discussed in chapters 4 and 5). The lack of organized pressure on the part of professionals, amateurs, and manufacturers made it impossible for them to affect the Exposition's decision-making process. Like other display sections, photography was simply provided with a specific physical space, a

FIGURE 2.1   Part of the Exposition's Austrian exhibit in the huge Manufactures and Liberal Arts Building, showing the kinds of display booths found there and the scale of the building's interior. (Albumen print, detail of stereograph no. 8040, 7.5 cm × 8 cm, by B. W. Kilburn; courtesy of the American Antiquarian Society)

method of admission for exhibitors, and a system of awards.

The vast Manufactures and Liberal Arts Building, where the photographic section was located, celebrated "progress, and invention, and art," the alliance of art and industry. On display was the "comfortable and luxurious life." Here was the visual delight of what one writer called a "vast ingathering of objects" (see Fig. 2.1).[7] For photographers, spectators and exhibitors with memories of the 1876 event, the building's massive space was daunting. Indeed, the fatigue that spectators regularly experienced was generally remarked upon by writers, noting "how tired and cross were some people" after hours at the Exposition.[8] The photography displays necessarily competed for their attention with very elaborate presentations of porcelain, furniture, glass cabinets, and other objects.

Another disadvantage was the fact that the photographs were split up among the various national displays rather than presented in a unified section, as had been done at the 1889 Paris Exposition. The U.S. display suffered from being placed in the north gallery on the second floor of the building, a less-than-prime location. Further, the space allotted to it was some 14,000 square feet, which was 5,000 square feet less than had been allotted to it in the Photographic Hall at the Centennial. Organized along a central aisle with seventy screens that were ten feet high and from sixteen to twenty-five feet long, and that were placed at ten-foot intervals, the section had to accommodate fifty photographic exhibitors, including manufacturers, dealers, professionals, and amateurs. While the better light may have been a feature in selecting its second-floor location, the unprotected glazed roof made the summer heat a severe trial for visitors. Even in the early summer, panes of glass began to fall from the roof as the structure expanded in response to the heat, leading many exhibitors to place awnings or canopies over their booths to protect their displays.

Applications for exhibit space were again processed on a first come, first served basis, and the lack of adequate space meant that few were accepted. Technically, amateur and professional practitioners and manufacturers were all included in Group 151, but their representation was by no means equal. Announcements of the registration procedures began to appear in the photographic journals in February 1893, but by then, according to Selim Peabody, chief of the Department of Liberal Arts, space had already been fully allocated.[9] Among those entries that arrived too late was certainly that of Frances

FIGURE 2.2 The front and back of the bronze medal inscribed for the photographer and manufacturer John Carbutt, a medal of the type the Exposition presented to award winners. (9 cm in diameter; courtesy of William Brey)

Benjamin Johnston, who made her inquiries in February.[10]

Well before the Exposition opened, the outlook for the United States photographic section was not good. Only the "occasional master" had submitted photographs, one writer noted, and "it will end with there being not a single exhibit by an American amateur photographer, where they should outnumber those of the professional."[11] The initial requirement that entrants submit a design for their display was waived, and the responsibility for selecting the photographs was left with the exhibitor. There was no restriction on photographic processes, which included photogravure and halftone work, but pictures involving crayon or pastel work were excluded. This was an obvious response to the controversy over current commercial practices, but it was also a statement against the popular taste for certain hybrid

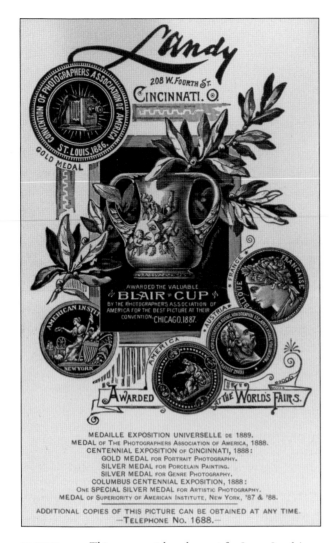

FIGURE 2.3 This commercial card mount for James Landy's Gallery of Photographic Art in Cincinnati demonstrates the advertising value of the various medals and awards exhibitors earned at international exhibitions like the World's Columbian Exposition. (Commercial card mount, 16.8 cm × 11 cm; courtesy of the Cincinnati Historical Society; Photographic Collection)

photographic forms involving hand artwork applied to the photographic image available from commercial studios.

The Exposition had a uniform system of awards, with no differentiation among the grand prize, silver and bronze awards, and honorable mention. The Committee of Awards decided to "have medals enough to go around" in order to avoid the exhibitors' appeals and dissatisfaction that had characterized previous international juried exhibitions.[12] Nevertheless, various protests were submitted at the close of the Exposition. One noted that a German judge, possibly Vogel himself, declined to exam-

ine the American and British work, and seven medals were awarded to German microscope makers.[13] The award winners received a diploma—an elaborate steel engraving that measured eighteen by twenty-four inches—and a three-inch bronze medal with an image of Columbus on one side and the *Santa María* on the reverse (Fig. 2.2). The incentive for professional photographers and manufacturers was in their subsequent use of awards in advertising and promotions, as seen in the display card of Landy's Gallery of Photographic Art shown in Figure 2.3.[14] Similarly, an 1892 *Photographic Mosaics* advertisement for the Eastman Company's bromide paper used a reproduction of a gold medal the company had been awarded in Paris in 1889 and cited other international expositions and exhibitions at which the company had won thirteen first-prize medals. In addition, the international events served as an opportunity for many businesses to advertise their specialties with brochures or pamphlets. Circulated advertisements, such as that by the Russian photolithographic business of Franz Kroiss (Fig. 2.4), were a feature of the materials distributed at the Exposition.

Appointed to represent the United States as judges for the photographic section were Charles T. Stuart, who was the vice-president of the Photographers' Association, and Catharine Weed Barnes, the sole woman and the only spokesperson for the amateurs. The international judges were Professor Max Jaffé of Vienna and a Professor Burger-Hofer of the Zurich Politechnicium, Georg Scamoni, director of photo-engraving at the Imperial Russian Institute, and of course Dr. Hermann Vogel, who had been prominent at the Centennial.[15] Compared to the 187 exhibitors at the 1893 Philadelphia event and the 136 at the Centennial, the 50 individual displays at the Exposition (including photographers and manufacturers in the Exposition's Group 151) were hardly representative of current photography in the United States. Among the 50 exhibitors, 32 were individual photographers, and all but 4 of them were professionals (see Appendix). Well before the opening there was general dissatisfaction with the photographic section among both professionals and amateurs.

The photographic section was, however, only one of several sections in which photographers' work appeared. Chapter 3 illustrates the limitations of dealing only with individual photographers and only with the photographic sections of the international expositions. The presence of William Henry Jackson is a case in point. At the Centennial, because he was a government photographer, Jackson's work was concentrated within the Hayden Survey display in the Government Building and did not appear at all in the Photographic Hall. Jackson's career had taken many turns by the time of the Columbian Exposition, however, and his photographs were dispersed among several venues. In the Group 151 photographic section, there were several of his large prints, including *Washington, D.C., Squari Cañon Rio,* and *Las Animas.* The last two had been made in 1882 in connection with his promotional work for the Denver and Rio Grande Railway. Jackson had worked with the painter Thomas Moran, whom he had been with on the Hayden Survey in 1871 and who had influenced his work both then and in the present project.[16] Jackson's photographs in this context were not considered advertisements but "pictures in every sense of the word, and pictures that are once seen and not forgotten," according to John Nicol, writing in the *Photo Beacon.*[17] In the Transporta-

FIGURE 2.4 This pamphlet advertising Kroiss's "photo-zincography" firm in St. Petersburg is characteristic of the promotional materials various commercial firms handed out at the Exposition. (14.8 cm × 10 cm; Miscellaneous Pamphlets, Engineering folder, World's Columbian Exposition; courtesy of the Chicago Historical Society; Library Collection)

tion Building, in contrast, Jackson's photographs subordinated the artistic function to that of promotion. Here, his commissioned work for the Baltimore & Ohio Railway included panoramic views such as the 17″ × 40″ print from the Buckhorn, Pennsylvania, series. Jackson completed the works for the B & O commission in the late summer of 1892, and Jackson was accompanied by "Major" Joseph Pangborn, the former journalist and current publicist for the railway. He was paid ten dollars each for the large 18″ × 22″ prints and more than a hundred of his photographs—including the panorama captioned "On Picturesque B. & O. Railway, 30 Buckhorn Wall, 2,500 feet above sea level"—which appeared in the Transportation Building exhibit.[18] Jackson noted the value of using Cramer's isochromatic plates in the "smoky Pittsburgh" area. The plates compensated for the area's hazy conditions by increasing the tonal contrast. Similarly, in the Wyoming Building another special commission Jackson completed in 1892 included a collection of photographs of the Yellowstone valley, where he had worked in 1871 and 1882. These were again made with his companion Thomas Moran, who like Jackson was part of the "booster forces of the railways," whose work reflected an accommodation to promotional tourism, as Hales has noted.[19]

Another enterprising professional who took advantage of the Exposition's range of commercial opportunities was William Rau, who also provided 250 photographs for the Pennsylvania Railway's display. Rau had been commissioned by the Pennsylvania Railway in 1891 to produce exhibition-size photographs, including panoramas of sites on its main line between New York and Pittsburgh. The railroad even rigged a special photographic car for the equipment Rau needed for this work.[20] Such photographs served a wide range of functions when placed on display outside the confines of the photographic section of the Manufactures and Liberal Arts Building.

In surveying the national and international photographic sections in this chapter, I have selected particular aspects of the production, practice, and function of photography in order to highlight characteristic features of the displays. A list of all the exhibitors from the United States is given in the Appendix. Surprisingly, not all the photographers were concerned with showing new work; some chose to repeat the display of well-known pieces. Some photographers had become exhibition "regulars" through their participation on the circuit of international expositions and were obviously familiar with the system. Younger professionals were not totally absent, however, and there was even a place for women within this heavily male enclave, though as amateurs they made only a token appearance. As they did with other display strategies, photographers used techniques of exaggeration such as "giantism" and miniaturization to draw attention to individual pieces and impress their rivals in the competitive environment of the photographic section.[21] Further, although progress was the theme of the Exposition's rhetoric, the photographic section, especially the U.S. display, held a curiously mixed representation.

Amateur and Professional Photographers in the Photographic Section of Group 151

There was nothing new about James Landy's *Seven Ages of Man,* first shown in 1876 and now one of his key displays at the Exposition. The series had even been awarded a bronze medal at the recent 1889 Paris Exposition, indicating a popularity that was not merely a phenomenon in the United States, at least among the Exposition's judges. James Landy was a regular on the exhibition circuit, and a key aspect in the continued attraction of his work, especially his staged pieces, was certainly its familiarity to a wide public audience. These Shakespearean tableaux depicting the famous soliloquy from *As You Like It* used various actors prominent in 1876. Included were Russell Soggs as "the justice" and Freddy Hall as "the whining schoolboy," both of whom were from Wood's Theater, and Ezekiel Walker in the role of the aged seer (Fig. 1.2). According to an account by Landy's wife, Walker was a proud, well-educated man, originally a lawyer but then living in impoverished conditions on an income of eighty-eight dollars a year.[22] Landy had been regarded as "persevering and progressive" in the early 1870s, and the popularity of his staged pieces of the 1880s, including *Hiawatha* and *Moses,* had diminished little, it seems, for a popular audience in 1893. Of course, this was the same audience that was offered a free advertising Exposition souvenir by the New Home Sewing Machine Company entitled *Shakespeare Boiled Down,* a condensed narrative version of all the Shakespearean plays.[23] The illustration of literary themes was a prominent feature of the Photographers' Association annual competitions, and this strain of "artistic" commercial photography was popular, lucrative, and pervasive. The 1891 Tennyson competition drew twelve submissions and was won by J. E. & J. A. Roesch of St. Louis, but according to one reviewer in the photographic trade, not "one photographer in ten had heard

of" the poem "Lancelot and Elaine" in Tennyson's *The Idylls of the King.*[24] Considered a complex poem, it was seen as requiring five rather than three illustrations to do it justice.

The most recognized works in the photographic section, according to contemporary accounts, were the photographs that exemplified the professional "artistic" formula. The strength of this tradition was shown in the reception given to *The Old Sculptor,* the 1879 portrait of sculptor Thomas D. Jones by James Madison Elliot. This was seen as "a gem," "a picture once seen never to be forgotten" in its pose, expression, and textural rendition (Fig. 2.5).[25] An updated version of this formula, considered the best in the section, was the work by Hezekiah McMichael. The Canadian-born McMichael had a photographic business in Hamilton before coming to Buffalo in 1870 and had received a degree of international recognition with his acceptance for the prestigious Vienna art exhibit in 1891. At the Exposition he exhibited a series of ten large platinum prints—religious illustrations focusing on the figure of Christ. Their large format, Charles Gould noted, gave an effect of "grandeur," and

FIGURE 2.5 James Madison Elliot's highly praised portrait photograph of William D. Jones entitled *The Old Sculptor,* which was on view in the Exposition's Group 151 photographic section. (Albumen print, 63 cm × 45.2 cm; courtesy of the Ohio Historical Society)

in their concentration on a single figure, they were without the distraction of accessories.[26] An engraved text on the frames linked the biblical references directly with the image for a combined visual/textual effect. McMichael had produced similar tableaux with literary themes in the 1891 "Elaine" competition series, which concentrated more on feeling and dramatic effect in the placement and positioning of figures than did Landy's work.[27] McMichael was working from a tradition of the staged tableau, which had been raised to a individual, expressive art form beginning in the 1870s with the work of the well-known English photographer Julia Margaret Cameron. This kind of work attempted to balance the literature of fiction with the reality of the photographic image. McMichael's move into religious themes was therefore natural and skillfully done, according to contemporary assessments. McMichael's reputation within the professional field made him a leading exponent of this type of "artistic" photography, which had a popular commercial following, in contrast to the newer "aesthetic" version coming from the amateur community, which was as yet devoid of commercial or popular overtones.

Photographs, like other artifacts on display at the Exposition, employed exaggeration to attract the viewer with examples of the largest print, the largest negative, the largest piece of paper. The St. Louis photographer Julius Caesar Strauss produced what was for some photographers "the greatest achievement of the World's Fair exhibit."[28] This was a photograph devised from nineteen different negatives and printed on a single piece of paper fifteen feet long and two feet wide, provided by the American Aristo Company. The photograph entitled "The Largest Photo in the World" was formed from the letters spelling out the title, with a figure decoratively positioned for each letter. The individual negatives, made on 18″ × 22″ Cramer plates, were placed on a giant frame to make a single negative with all the backgrounds evenly opaqued, leaving only the figures and the printing on aristotype paper. Understandably, the print's toning, fixing, and mounting required special equipment. Strauss was reported to have said that it cost $390 to produce the first print. The tonal features of the photograph were noted by Dr. Hermann Vogel as being representative of a "fashionable" style indigenous to the United States which used a light tone with an architectural or botanical background, blended out at the corners of the picture.[29] The question of style seemed secondary to the intriguing adaptation to photography of a popular advertising design. A hybrid production of photography and manufacturing, it was evidence of the fluid relationship between industrial and entrepreneurial practices in the modern business of professional photography during this period. The size and scale of such "pieces" caused one reviewer to note with pragmatic sarcasm: "Once they have served this little day at Jackson Park what is to become of them? Who has space to accommodate such leviathans? I suppose the lumber room will be the fate of most of them, and in after years we can fancy their authors mournfully surveying them and agitating over their fallen greatness."[30] Forgotten and untraceable they have become, but they were, in any case, an aberrant form of the traditional panoramas, which, because of their exaggerated size, had always gained a certain audience at the expositions. Gutekunst, for example, had commercially exploited this format in connection with the Centennial, and the Australians were to repeat their 1876 strategy in 1893.

A few members of the younger generation of photographers were also present in the American photographic section, although most preferred the alternative exhibition site of the Photographers' Association convention, discussed in chapter 1. George Steckel of San Francisco, winner of several awards at the convention, exhibited his photograph *Grecian Maidens* (Fig. 2.6). The *Photo Beacon*'s reviewer considered it "a beautiful production, almost faultless, both from the artistic and technical point of view."[31] The prominence of classical themes was part of the style of the new "aesthetic" photography, a style that was interestingly adapted in the commercial work of photographers like Steckel. Also on view in this section was the photograph *Ariadne and Bacchus,* by James Lawrence Breeze.[32] Breeze was one of the photographers—along with Hezekiah McMichael, Alfred Stieglitz, Mrs. Grey Bartlett, and Miss M. Martin—whose works had been accepted for the prestigious 1891 Vienna "art photography" exhibit, which showed only 600 of the 4,000 photographs submitted. The Exposition also provided Breeze with material for a later photograph of a model as the "Statue of the Republic," which was reproduced with a series of his portraits in the December 1894 issue of *The Cosmopolitan.*

For the "most important and interesting photographic object on exhibition," according to Hermann Vogel, one had to look to the photographic reproductions "in natural colors" by William Kurtz.[33] This was not exactly a disinterested judgment, since Kurtz's work was an application of Vogel's own successful research. The German-born Kurtz, after being drafted into the army during the Crimean War, moved to London, where he worked in lithography and taught drawing. After a series of sea voy-

FIGURE 2.6   George Steckel's *Grecian Maidens,* showing the prevalence of classical themes in the artistic work of commercial photographers. A print of this work was part of the Exposition's Group 151 photographic section. (Photoengraving, 17.8 cm x 9.8 cm; from the *Photo Beacon* 6 [September 1893]: front.; courtesy of the George Eastman House, International Museum of Photography and Film; Library Collection)

ages and shipwrecks, Kurtz came to the United States, served in the Civil War, and in 1866 became the proprietor of a photography studio. His reputation had been established with the introduction of the Rembrandt effect of lighting in portraiture, for which he won medals at the 1867 Paris and 1873 Vienna expositions. By the 1890s, Kurtz's highly successful photographic business had become secondary to his original interest in printing, seen especially in his early use of the halftone process in 1883 and later his work on an experimental

color halftone process in 1892. In 1892 Kurtz hired Dr. Ernest H. Vogel, Hermann's son, at an exorbitant fee—reportedly $40,000 for six months—to work with him on the process.[34] The process developed by Kurtz was unpatented and not yet commercially viable, and his expenses were estimated to have been as high as $200,000. He achieved satisfactory results in 1893 with the publication in March and May of his three color halftone prints of a still life with fruit (later shown at the Exposition) and a still life with vegetables.[35] Kurtz's efforts, which marked the beginning of modern commercial color printing and the fulfillment of a half century of effort to produce permanent color printed photographs, went unnoticed by the general public. The feat was said to have cost Kurtz both his career and his health, a high price even for the Exposition award he received.

Few amateur photographers were present in the United States Group 151 photographic section, and Selim Peabody pointed out that not many had even applied for space.[36] Still, considering the size of the amateur population, the presence of only four photographers is surprising. Of more interest is the fact that each of these "amateurs" had been participants in the highly successful Philadelphia exhibit in May, and they were all women. The criteria used to differentiate between amateur and professional practice was never spelled out for potential exhibitors and probably went unnoticed by the general public. This was, however, a highly contentious issue in this period and was part of a significant debate on the nature of photographic practice in general, as discussed in chapter 5. The fact that the amateur work was by women makes their presence even more noticeable, because, strictly speaking, their work should have been in the Woman's Building with the seventeen other female amateur and professional photographers listed in the Appendix. Marie H. Kendall, a professional photographer from Connecticut whose work *was* shown in the Woman's Building, was the only woman to receive a diploma among the forty-two awards in photography at the Exposition.[37]

Emma Farnsworth had work in both the photographic section in the Manufactures and Liberal Arts Building and in the Woman's Building. None of her photographs on display at the Exposition was cited by title, but the 1893 photograph *To a Greek Girl* (Fig. 1.6), a transparency of which was shown in Philadelphia,[38] can be taken as representative of the work she displayed in the photographic section. The signature aspect of her work was the use of semiclassical themes employing her friends as models in landscape settings. The apparent ease and fluid style of the photographs mask the difficulty of their execution. Photographing the subjects meant "having to go miles sometimes for the proper backgrounds, wind, time of day and sun," according to Farnsworth, who found the work hard and "a tremendous nervous strain."[39]

The other amateurs who displayed their work in the photographic section of the Manufactures and Liberal Arts Building were Louise Deshong Woodbridge and Mrs. J. G. Long, both of Chester, Pennsylvania, just southwest of Philadelphia, and Elizabeth Almy Slade of New York City, whose work was also shown in the Woman's Building. All three women, like Farnsworth, had been represented in the Philadelphia exhibition, but unlike their East Coast colleagues, they had not found it necessary to boycott the Exposition, with its industrial and commercial overtones. Conditions for women amateurs were still problematic, as illustrated by the fact that Slade, Farnsworth, and Catharine Barnes were all required to join photographic societies in New York City because their local society in Albany did not admit women.[40] Woodbridge's print *Marcus Hook Looking Northeast* appeared in both the Philadelphia and Chicago venues and represented her straightforward, naturalistic style, which was based on a deep interest in botany and the sciences generally. Woodbridge, a prominent social figure and supporter of the arts, had taken up photography in 1884 and was closely associated with the Philadelphia circle of amateur photographers. As Mary Panzer has shown in her study of the period, an appreciation for scientific and natural subjects was not a feature favored in the growing "aesthetic" climate of photography in Philadelphia during the 1890s.[41] The presence of these women photographers in the photographic section of Group 151 speaks to the independence of their individual positions within the much larger context of photographic practice. It also represents an important statement on the absence of their male colleagues.

Manufacturers' Booths in the Photographic Section of Group 151

The winners in the United States photographic section in terms of representation were manufacturers and dealers, with some eighteen different companies present. This is not especially surprising, considering the industrial nature of the Exposition itself, but it represented a shift from previous expositions. One possible explanation was the apparent skill and experience man-

ufacturers and dealers had in displaying their products, an expertise gained at the exhibits at the Photographers' Association annual conventions dating back to the 1870s. The Exposition booths and displays in 1893 were simply more elaborate versions of those at the conventions, where the manufacturers and dealers competed with one another for the attention of potential customers.

One display strategy several companies used was to feature work by leading photographers as product endorsements. Although this was not new in 1893, the increased competition in paper, plate, and camera production meant that it was definitely a practice used more often in this period. Thus it is not surprising to find not only the work of a photographer like William Henry Jackson in the booth of the Gustav Cramer Company but also a published recommendation by him promoting Cramer's orthochromatic plates. The booth presented a display of colored drawings and photographs demonstrating the dramatic effects gained with the use of such plates. Jackson had used Cramer orthochromatic plates for his 1892 landscape work in order to correct for any conditions "from the excessive clearness of the high Rockies to the October haze of Indian summer along the Atlantic seaboard."[42] One reviewer noted that of the twenty-nine individual photographers' displays at the Exposition, all but four were using Cramer plates.

Following the 1893 Philadelphia exhibition, Alfred Stieglitz posed a challenge to photographic manufacturers: "Why will manufacturers insist upon always exhibiting mediocre work? . . . Why not collect an interesting set of negatives and make prints from them for exhibition purposes? That would attract attention, in other words advertise the manufacture."[43] Stieglitz's remarks were directed to John Carbutt's display at that venue, and they certainly provided the stimulus for the company's comprehensive display at the Columbian Exposition. There, at the twenty-foot-long booth of Carbutt's Keystone Dry Plate and Filmworks, 8″ x 10″ transparencies of work by noted photographers from all over the world were set into the entrance.[44] Carbutt's son, John Carbutt, Jr., had designed the display, and he had obviously heeded Stieglitz's advice. The company also marketed a new product for the Exposition: the "Columbian" plate, a special coated plate that prevented halation, a light-bursting effect produced under conditions of strong contrasting light. Several interior prints showing the successful use of these plates were on display. The young Carbutt also made 800 lantern views of the Exposition sites, a selection of 432 of which were avail-

FIGURE 2.7   The elaborate Eastman Kodak Company exhibit in the photographic section included a wide range of manufactured goods and a selection of the prizewinning photographs from a special competition held for the Exposition. (Halftone reproduced from the *St. Louis and Canadian Photographer* 12 [February 1894]: 90; courtesy of the George Eastman House, International Museum of Photography and Film; Library Collection)

able for purchase or order, presumably from this Exposition display even though this was officially prohibited. Just inside the doorway of the booth was a frame on an easel of early 1860s stereo views the elder Carbutt made during the time he practiced as a professional photographer in Chicago before moving to Philadelphia in 1870.

The booth of the Eastman Company (Fig. 2.7) illustrated the degree of sophistication and design that was possible for commercial displays. The open architectural design—with columns surmounted by cherubs holding cameras and low display cases for easy viewing of the apparatus—was both visually inviting and practical. The company's previous success at the 1889 Paris exposition, where it was awarded one of only four gold medals given to Americans, was a factor in the elaborate character of the display booth.[45] Rather than soliciting recommendations from photographers for its display, the Eastman Company followed what was, again, a regular practice at the Photographers' Association exhibitions. To provide photographs for its booth, the company held a special prize competition for photographs on their new Solio

paper. The judges for the Eastman competition were two veteran professional photographers, J. F. Ryder and W. F. Van Loo, and Charles T. Stuart, the official United State judge for the Exposition. Such strategies were not always completely successful. The *Photo Beacon* noted in its review of the display that the prints "prove the excellent qualities of the paper, [but] artistically most of them are very ordinary productions."[46] Realizing the importance of the international context of the Exposition and the need to maintain the reputation of their awards, the Eastman Company also included a photograph by J. Lafayette, the well-known photographer of British royalty, to show what could be done if Solio paper were put into "good hands." Lafayette's work gave an international tone to the display, as he was also represented in the British section with excellent platinum and carbon work. Vogel called them the "grandest" photographs, especially the "suspended angel, almost life-size and taken from life."[47] The bromide print enlargements, which were a feature of the Eastman display, highlighted the technical abilities of the company. Elsewhere in the Exposition—

in the Bureau of the American Republics in the United States Government Building—there was a large display of Eastman's commercial enlargement work, discussed in chapter 3. The company also used the tactic of product endorsement, in this case displaying a Kodak camera of the type that Lieutenant Robert Peary had used during his 1200-mile, thirteen-month expedition through northern Greenland by sledge in 1891–92. Peary benefitted from the publicity as well, because he was seeking to create and maintain a public image to gain the necessary support for his work. During the expedition he had taken some 2,300 photographs, including ethnographic studies of many isolated Eskimo tribes—single views, group shots, and nudes, which were considered "invaluable in the scientific study of new peoples."[48] The Exposition included a selection of these photographs in the Anthropological Building because Peary had been paid by F. W. Putnam, who was in charge of the Exposition's anthropology section, to make photographs and collect artifacts. The Eastman advertising slogan "Peary Pushed the Button" was an acknowledgment of popular interest in the Arctic and was perhaps the best in a series of innovative endorsements the Eastman Company obtained in this period.

Other manufacturers used their displays to promote some of their commercial products associated with the Exposition, subverting the official restrictions that attempted to control the marketing of photography and protect the sales of official photographs. In addition to displaying the most up-to-date projection apparatus, for example, the T. H. McAllister Company, a prominent New York lantern-slide manufacturer, offered for sale a large stock of commercial slides, including an "excellent series of the World's Fair."[49] These had been made by the company's photographer, and the wide range of popular subjects and catchy titles for the lantern views showed that the firm's thinking was similar to that of the official maker of stereographs, B. W. Kilburn, who is discussed in chapter 4. McAllister's views included *An Idea of a Crowd* and *Visitors Eating Their Lunches, Scene North of Government Building,* and views of building interiors. A selection of these slides was also intended to accompany a lecture text.[50] Written by R.E.A. Dorr, the assistant chief of the Department of Publicity and Promotion for the Exposition, this combination of spoken and visual presentation was a very popular form of parlor entertainment that enabled people to re-create a walking tour of the Exposition (see Figure 4.4).

Photographic Displays in the International Exhibits

When visitors had examined the self-contained unit of the U.S. photographic section to their satisfaction, finding those for the various foreign countries required a lengthy and sometimes unrewarding search among the exhibits in the "City Under One Roof," which is the way the Exposition described the Manufactures and Liberal Arts Building. The layout of the building reflected the political status of the national exhibitors, with the key positions going to Germany, France, and Great Britain on the ground floor and other nations on the periphery.

Entries in the *Official Catalogue of Exhibits* for the liberal arts give the names of individual exhibitors and a description of the material they were displaying. The catalogue, however, was long delayed and was not necessarily complete, and other sources—such as the *Index to Awards*—provide some names that are absent from it.[51] In a number of cases the index gives the names of the photographs on display, although none of the French section is included, since the French had declined to participate in the awards. Neither source includes last-minute or late participants, like Nadar, the pseudonym for Gaspard Félix Tournachon, who had not planned to participate in the Exposition but who was asked to do so. The discussion that follows is not intended as an inventory of all the photographs in the international displays but only those that speak to a characteristic feature that is of interest in comparing the displays of photography at the Exposition.

Immediately to the left of the south entrance of the Manufactures and Liberal Arts Building was the space given to Italy. Among the eleven photographic exhibitors who displayed there were several Italian firms, regulars at such international venues. It was the combined efforts of these firms that had created, sustained, and provided the photographs for marketing the Italian artistic heritage and scenic travel industry in the last quarter of the nineteenth century. The firms of Fratelli Alinari in Florence and Domenico Anderson in Rome, for example, had been established in the 1850s and had become production companies by the 1890s.[52] With large staffs of assistants, they operated on a factory-like production scale and also distributed the work of other photographers. Firms like that of the Venetian Carlo Naya functioned effectively through several generations, well past the death of their founders.[53] Naya had died in 1882, having made his reputation at various international expositions, including the 1876 Centennial. International expositions provided the means of maintaining their reputations with displays that catered to an audience that was favorably disposed toward a specific type of commercial imagery: the largely formulaic "view." The sole exception to this pattern in the Italian photographic section was the work of Count Luigi Primioli, a member of the growing movement of international "aesthetic" photographers. Primioli and Carle de Mazibourg, the French amateur photographer, were the only exhibitors from their respective countries who were identified with this important group.[54] Both had contributed substantial displays to the large October 1893 Hamburg exhibition for international "aesthetic" amateur photography.

Just behind the Italian section in an area where lighting conditions were less than adequate was the Mexican section, which included forty-two photographic displays, more than half of which received diploma awards. Technically, these photographs were intended for the photographic section, but their importance lay more in their subject matter, which served to illustrate, inform, and persuade viewers about the resources of the country. The work of professional photographers was interspersed with extensive collections of promotional photographs from the municipal governments of the states of Oaxaca, Yucatán, Zacatecas, Puebla, Durango, and Querétaro. In addition, several Mexican government branches, including the War Department and the Commission for Geological Exploration and Railways, were represented in displayed photographs and view albums. Many countries, including the United States, subsumed photographs under the broad classification of photography even though the photographs were intended to fulfill a range of purposes.

Moving to the center of the building on the opposite aisle, the French section had one of its large rooms handsomely decorated and furnished for its display of photographs and photogrammetric apparatus, both old and new, as well as the current techniques from the pioneer of camera surveying, Aimé Laussedat. In fact, the French section overall, according to one reviewer, presented photographs not as works of art but as material products.[55] This reflected the dualistic attitude about the industry and art of photography, a dilemma underlying the Exposition itself. Featured were photographs by Albert Londé that were used for medical research in neurology and psychology. Londé was the director of the Photographic Service Laboratory, which was connected with the clinic for the study of nervous diseases at the Salpêtrière Hospital in Paris. His reputa-

tion in the study of sequential photography was comparable to that of the eminent Etienne Marey in France and Eadweard Muybridge in the United States. Londé's work was given additional prominence with the presentation of his paper "Photography as an Aid to Medicine" at the Auxiliary Congress of Photographers. Further, his book *La photographie médicale: Application aux sciences médicales et physiologiques* had just been published, and it included details of his hospital laboratory studio, the methods he used for recording aspects of various diseases, the applications of such photographs for medical research, and the care and reproduction of photographic data (see Fig. 2.8).[56] As Nicholas Graver has shown, Londé early recognized the importance of the hand-held camera in less-formal studio settings for recording some types of medical symptoms.

Another example of the use of photography for measurement was the work of Alphonse Bertillon, although it was located outside the photographic section in the French state building. At a time when there was no systematic method of criminal identification, Bertillon, who had been trained in anthropology, devised a method of identifying repeat offenders.[57] By applying anthropological methods, he devised a system in the early 1880s based on eleven body measurements, observations of defining features, three standardized record photographs, and a data-retrieval cabinet filing system. Bertillon insisted on specific procedures for "judicial photography," with standard-focal-length lenses, consistent lighting, and his new method of frontal and profile portraits, including features of the ear. His display at the Exposition included the apparatus used to photograph dead crime victims and to make police photographs for identification (Fig. 2.9). Bertillon's system was also presented in a paper at the Auxiliary Congress for the section on charitable and correctional institutions rather than photography. Interest in his work among United States judiciary officials, especially in Chicago, was enhanced by the publication of his work in English in 1893, with illustrations of his methods. The 1896 English translation of Bertillon's "signeletics" was a complete handbook on the use of the Bertillon system prepared under the supervision of the former general superintendent of the Chicago police, R. W. McClaughry, and its use was recommended for anthropologists, social and political reformers, insurance companies, and lawyers.[58] While Alan Sekula has argued that Bertillon's "police archive" was a "complex biographical machine" for the purposes of social engineering, Bertillon's use of photographs was similar to techniques employed in other emerging scien-

FIGURE 2.8 Albert Londé's work at the Salpêtrière Hospital in Paris included photographs recording the nervous disorder suffered by this female patient. Londé's photographs appeared in the photographic section of the French display on the first floor of the Manufactures and Liberal Arts Building. (*Transfert de* *contracture chez une hystérique*, from Londé's *La Photographie Médicale*, detail from pl. 9; courtesy of the George Eastman House, International Museum of Photography and Film; Library Collection)

tific disciplines, such as anthropology, psychology, and social work, as discussed in chapter 3.[59] Photography in its applied forms was used extensively for data accumulation, which is not a pernicious activity except when it becomes a tool of social or cultural management.

A prominent feature of the French photographic section was the work of Gabriel Lippmann, a professor of physics at the Sorbonne who was the first to achieve successful chemically based color photography. Based on the well-known phenomenon of light interference, such as occurs in soap bubbles or mother-of-pearl surfaces, Lippmann made a camera exposure of one to two hours on a plate backed with a coating of mercury, which reflected the light waves and created an interference pattern that was recorded on an emulsion. As with daguerreotypes, the resulting positive plates had to be viewed at a certain angle.[60] While some specimens of Lippmann's work had already been exhibited in 1891 at the National Conference of Amateur Photographers in

New York, the display at the Exposition was an opportunity for a much wider audience of photographers and members of the general public to see examples of the process for the first time.[61] The response to the specimens was, however, mixed; many people were not persuaded that this was the answer to color photography. Abraham Bogardus described the images as having a halo of unregistered colors and was irritated at having to wait two hours for a French official to arrive and unlock the cabinet so that he could handle the specimen.[62]

More successful were the recent improvements in Lippmann's process made by the Lumière brothers, Auguste and Louis. Their images, which were also on display at the Exposition, were presented in projected form by the official in charge of the French scientific exhibits to the Chicago Camera Club's August 1893 meeting.[63] For the purposes of projection, the lens, removed from the lantern, was placed six inches from the specimen. The limelight lantern, placed at right angles

Vue d'ensemble de l'exposition de la section photographique.

FIGURE 2.9   The display of the photographic apparatus and methods developed by Alphonse Bertillon for documenting criminals and their crimes. This display was shown in the French state building rather than with the other photographic displays in the Manufactures and Liberal Arts Building. (Albumen print, 16.6 cm x 23.5 cm, album entitled "Service d'identification de la Préfecture de police pour l'Exposition universelle de Chicago"; courtesy of the National Gallery of Canada, Ottawa; PSC80:286:9)

to the arrangement, projected an image about two feet in diameter onto a viewing screen. Charles Gentile, editor of the *Photo Eye,* stated that what he saw "looked very natural," although this was not confirmed by all reports. Among the seven images shown were those of a bouquet of flowers, a landscape, a cottage surrounded with shrubs, colored placecards, and a Japanese screen. Unlike Lippmann's work, according to the American color researcher Frederick Ives, they "showed many delicate shades of color which impressed the spectators."[64] The subtleties and difficulties of the technology were appreciated by a few specialists, like Ives, but not by the general public, whose expectations for color photography had been unrealistically raised by inflated publicity.

Across the main central aisle from the French section, along the west wall of the Manufactures and Liberal Arts Building, was the German section. Actually, only part of the German photographic display was here. An-

other substantial section was assigned to an exhibit some distance away in the Machinery Building because the devices used in photomechanical reproduction—like collotype, photogravure, and photolithography—were classified as mechanical instruments in Group 76. Hermann Vogel reacted sharply to this situation. "I have been at all the larger exhibitions since 1867," he said, "but a similar arrangement I have never met with before."[65] Germany had the strongest tradition and the strongest representation in photomechanical reproduction processes, and the German representatives as a whole considered this fragmentation of its display offensive, especially since it was one of the few countries shown separately in the Machinery Building.

Another point about international expositions illustrated by the German photomechanical display is that they functioned like vast markets, especially for museums and other institutions. The huge variety of objects assembled from all parts of the world always gave them the opportunity to enhance their collections by donation or purchase at the Exposition. With the presence of the excellent specimens of German and Russian photomechanical printing processes, the Smithsonian's curator of graphic arts, S. R. Koehler, moved to take advantage of the opportunity. Writing to George Brown Goode from the Exposition in September, Koehler suggested that the institution should consider purchasing German and Russian specimens for the collection. Contacts Koehler made during the Exposition led to a substantial donation to the Smithsonian's collection by Wilhelm Roese of the Government Printing Office in Berlin.[66]

Several of the German displays were by prominent technical innovators of the earlier generation, including Josef Albert, Franz Hanfstängl, and Johan Obernetter of Munich, all of whom were deceased by this period but whose work was still being carried out by firms under their names. The newer halftone reproduction process, pioneered in the early 1880s and suitable for illustrated publications with large pressruns, was represented by one of the major innovators in this work, Georg Meisenbach.[67] Not surprisingly, the German firms received a number of awards for their work on photomechanical processes.

Hamburg, poised to become the site of the first annual exhibit of amateur photography in October 1893, was one of the primary centers of the new international "aesthetic" photography movement, as Janet Buerger has shown.[68] Through the skillful management of Ernst Juhl, founder of the Society for the Promotion of Amateur Photography in Hamburg, together with Alfred Lichtwark, director of the Hamburg Kunsthalle, more than 450 individual exhibitors from Italy, France, Great Britain, Russia, Hungary, Australia, and the United States were drawn to this event, which opened just as the Chicago Exposition was closing. Given the importance of this upcoming international photographic event, it is surprising that the work of only one member associated with the aesthetic photography movement, Michael Dietrich, was present in the German photographic section. Even though there was only token representation from the Italian and French members of the movement, their combined presence was larger than that from the United States. Only the British photographers made the optimum use of the Exposition as an opportunity to show a comprehensive collection of work by photographers of the emerging aesthetic movement.

Great Britain was prominently placed in the central west section of the Manufactures and Liberal Arts Building and clearly understood the value of imperial display both culturally and politically. Beginning with the 1886 Indian and Colonial Exhibition, there was, according to Paul Greenhalgh, a noted change from a complacent pride in empire to a more propagandistic defense.[69] The politicization of the process was evident in the recent establishment of the Imperial Institute as the "Empire Under One Roof," complete with exhibition hall, library, and meeting rooms, which opened in May 1893. The striking photographic enlargement called the *British Lion,* by Gambier Bolton, at the entrance to the British section was a fitting symbol for this carefully constructed display.

Canada, because of its dominion status, had a large space separate from Great Britain's. It had a photographic section that included work from the studio of William Notman, who had been prominently associated with the Centennial Photographic Company in 1876. By the time of Notman's death in 1891 a number of Notman studios had been established outside of Montreal, including one in Halifax, two in Boston, and one in New York City. William McFarlane Notman, son of the original owner, had undertaken several commissions for the Canadian Pacific Railway in the early 1880s, similar to those by William Rau and William Jackson.[70] Photographs he made as a result of these commissions, showing land-related and Indian subjects, were probably among the works on display, and they would have offered a sharp contrast to his father's tableaux and composite genre scenes, which were so celebrated in the 1870s.

The less-than-uniform presence of the Australian colonies was due to agitation by New South Wales for a display separate from that of Great Britain. Rather than being subsumed into its traditional colonial status, New South Wales regarded this as "the first step" in the transition between colonial and federation status, which was not effected until 1901.[71] While it proceeded with its own government building, as it had at the Centennial, this seemed a premature effort to several of the colonies, including Queensland. Like Victoria, it opted to accept the status quo and remained in the main British section. Among the photographs of the colony in the New South Wales photography section was the striking twenty-four-foot-long enlarged panorama of Sydney harbor. This photograph had been produced by the New South Wales Government Printing Office and was an obvious reference to Holtermann's extravaganza of 1876.[72] The Government Printing Office of New South Wales, like those in other colonies, such as Queensland, used photography in connection with extensive lithographic work for government survey as well as in publications that promoted immigration.

According to the English amateur photographer the Reverend F. C. Lambert, photographers who regularly exhibited their work in public displays recognized that exhibition prints required a "stronger and more pronounced scheme" than those for home use because of the "stronger light, crowded company and larger surroundings."[73] Framing for exhibitions, too, was different, the key being to keep the mount and frame subordinate to and in coordination with the tones, lines, and content of the print. The booth belonging to the British photographer Henry Van der Weyde drew considerable attention because of its unusually careful attention to these elements of display strategy. Van der Weyde used a green-toned color scheme throughout for framing and mounting the prints, thus integrating the photographs with the physical exhibit space. This practice would later be a feature of the London "Salon" exhibits of art photography by the Linked Ring.[74] Van der Weyde did his portrait work, for which he received an award, with an invention he called the "photo corrector," which adjusted for the distortion of hands and bodies. In his display he included original and corrected versions of the same portrait to demonstrate the efficacy of his invention. His device once again raised the controversy over optical versus visual truth in photography. This issue—between the "correctness" of the machine image and that perceived by the eye—was of current interest, and Van der Weyde asserted that it was the visual image of the eye that was preferable because it was subtler and depended on the appreciation of the individual viewer.[75]

The collection of photography on special loan in the British section earned the most acclaim from photographers. It was, one critic said, "a collection which may well be taken as representing the highest achievements of the art to this day."[76] A committee had been appointed by the secretary of the British commission for the Exposition, Sir Henry Trueman Wood, an avid amateur photographer. Wood had been prominent at the administrative level for several international expositions, most recently the 1889 Paris event where, in the absence of government support, he raised private funds to finance the British display. He was closely associated with the Society of Arts, serving as its secretary, and was president of the Royal Photographic Society from 1894 to 1896.[77] It is not surprising that the committee—composed of George Davison, Colonel Joseph Gale, and

H. P. Robinson—were the leading photographers of the "old" and "new" art photography.[78] They invited a select group of "the best" photographers to send prints for this collection. Several photographers were members of the newly organized Linked Ring, a breakaway association of English photographers. The Linked Ring was formed following an incident in which the Photographic Society refused to hang George Davison's prints at its annual exhibit in September 1891. After the resulting council dispute, Robinson, Davison and twelve other members left the society and with twenty-eight photographers, including Van der Weyde and Lydell Sawyer, formed the Linked Ring in May 1892.[79] The group conspicuously avoided conventional terminology, preferring to describe themselves as "links" and their meetings as "unions." They held no elections and had no officers or subscription lists. The Linked Ring sponsored the first international "Salon" of art photography in November 1893, a month after the closing of the Chicago Exposition. The portrait by William Crooke on display at the Exposition (Fig. 2.10) was representative of this kind of "aesthetic"

FIGURE 2.10 This portrait of John Stuart Blackie, the noted Scottish classicist, is by William Crooke, whose work was included in the British Loan Collection. (Photogravure, 33 cm × 25 cm; from Exposition d'Art Photographique, *Première Exposition d'Art Photographique*, pl. 13; courtesy of the George Eastman House, International Museum of Photography and Film; Library Collection)

FIGURE 2.11 Frank Sutcliffe's photograph *Water Rats*, showing a group of boys from Whitby, was already prominent by the time it was shown in Chicago as part of the British Loan Collection. (Photogravure, 12.5 cm x 17.8 cm; from *Sun Artists*, no. 8 [July 1891]; courtesy of the George Eastman House, International Museum of Photography and Film; Library Collection)

style, which was featured at the salons sponsored by the Ring as well as at the other international exhibits held in France and Germany during the 1890s.

Lydell Sawyer was among the founding members of the Linked Ring, the brotherhood of English photographers devoted to aesthetic photography. His photograph *Smokey Tyne* was among a number of river scenes that attempted to "individualize" such views "by varying phases of atmosphere, motion, and form."[80] This he regarded as a more difficult enterprise than his more popular figure pieces. The photograph *Sleepy Hollow*, done in 1889 by Colonel Joseph Gale, was considered by one reviewer from the United States as "abundant evidence that photography is entitled to rank as a 'fine art.' "[81]

The Water Rats, by Frank Sutcliffe (Fig. 2.11), was one of the most popular and well-known photographs from the English art photography movement, and was also included in the British loan collection on view at the

Exposition. The photograph, originally made in 1886, had begun with the casual placement of a few truant boys, with others added to the group as they appeared to take a swim. The result, a carefully balanced image that combined artfulness with naturalism, was a highly successful example of this version of English aesthetic photography. Sutcliffe concluded that the "old" and "new" schools in photography were different means to the same end; that is, that the photograph presents the "naked truth which has to be clothed by the imagination."[82] The scene of nude young swimmers was common in the harbor at Whitby and asserted its claim to status as a picture.

The proximity of the Philadelphia exhibit meant that several of the English prints were shown at both venues. Adam Diston's *A Rehearsal*, George West's yacht-racing picture *Mohawk*, and the unusual series of prints entitled *Initiation of a Parsee Priest*, by N. Sharpoor Bhedwar (which was also shown at the Photographers' Association convention), were among the photographs brought from Philadelphia. George Davison, the undeclared leader of the "new English school," also had work present at both venues. He had initially espoused the "naturalistic photography" preached by Dr. Peter H. Emerson in 1888 but was often associated with the "fuzzy" school, a contemptuous reference to the pictorial effects that characterized work by photographers moving away from the clarity of sharply focused images and that John Nicol and other American photographers were recognizing as preeminent.[83] By the 1890s, however, Davison had moved well beyond Emerson's art-through-science approach, both in his writings and in his distinctive use of a lensless or pinhole camera to produce images. Davison's *Farm in the Marsh,* on view at the Exposition, was close to, if not identical with, the platinum print *The Homestead in the Marsh,* shown in the May 1893 Philadelphia exhibit. It represented the essence of his naturalistic belief that photography should be "used to express our impressions of natural scenes," a position with deep historical links to English artistic traditions.[84]

The presence at the Exposition of such a striking collection of photographic "pictures" by British members of the new movement of aesthetic photography highlighted the absence of a comparable display from the United States. The *Photo Beacon* attempted to rationalize the situation by saying that the "American show" was "the outcome of enterprise or ambition of individual exhibitors" who "do not always possess artistic ability, nor are the truly artistic always enterprising or ambitious."[85] The belief that business and artistry were incompatible was an idea peculiar to American culture in this period. It contributed substantially to narrowing the definition of art in relation to its practice in photography. Turning away from the more popular commercial "artistic photography," the shift was to a more exclusive and elitist form of high art "aesthetic." Neither ambition nor enterprise were absent among the East Coast amateur photographers who were responsible for the highly successful Philadelphia exhibit in May. The photographic section of the Exposition was too strongly associated with industry and commerce for photographers who were seeking to establish photography as a separate art form. The basic polarization between industry and art, an underlying construct of the Exposition itself, was a theme that resonated deeply in the practice and production of photography in the United States in this period. The British, on the other hand, with their longer history of observing the symbiotic relationship between industry and culture (dating from at least the time of the Great Exhibition in 1851), were more assured in their moves. The U.S. photographic section reflected the tenuous nature of the period itself in its uncertainty and its less-than-balanced representation, its lack of cooperative effort, and the unfocused image it presented of the national culture.

3

APPROPRIATING THE IMAGE
Using Photographs for Display

It is a gratification to see to what extent photography is used by every department of industry at the Fair; scarcely a room in which there is not a photograph or some part of its machinery, contents or the uses to which its products are adapted. Boys, we've got 'em. The employment of photography will be as universal as light, air and water.
ABRAHAM BOGARDUS[1]

The exhilaration that Abraham Bogardus expressed on the pervasiveness of photography at the Exposition, as well as his optimism about its future, was shared by many others. It was proof that photography at the Exposition could not be limited merely to a special section of the Manufactures and Liberal Arts Building. Because of this we have to look at the larger context of the Exposition to get a real picture of the display of photography. The Exposition, just like the society it represented, demanded replica images, textual illustrations, and images designed to persuade and inform. Photography was there to provide them all.

Various rationales were expressed to justify the use of photographs for display. For Professor Charles Himes, photographs were more than facts; they are things, he said, that "speak for themselves, are in the main permanent, can be referred to at any time, and are comparable with subsequent results."[2] For Captain William L. Marshall of the army's Corps of Engineers, photographs were to be preferred because they "don't lie, don't deceive and can be instantly comprehended."[3] Marshall was not being naive about the transparency of the photograph; he was simply choosing to privilege their factual character and inherent attractiveness.

Photographs function on several levels, often simultaneously. Moving as they do between persuasion and illustration, information and picture, there is a contest whenever these functions are subsumed under a specific cultural authority to convey content and create meaning.[4] Once appropriated, photographs no longer perform the single function of being a picture or an advertisement but enter into a new matrix of meaning. W. H. Jackson's and William Rau's railway photographs in the Transportation Building, for example, were assimilated into an interplay of functions within the overall display of engines, timetables, steel joints, and promotional hype in a way that was quite different from their counterparts in the photographic section of the Manufactures and Liberal Arts Building.

The Exposition depended on artifacts for its existence, especially the original objects and replicas used in displays. An impressive number of such replicas was on display at the Exposition—a reconstructed mountain of the cliffdwellers (Fig. 4.16), for example, and a diorama of one of the army's Arctic expeditions of the 1880s. Photographs were integral to a middle-class culture that readily accepted reproductions in its furnishings, art, and architecture, as Miles Orvell has pointed out.[5] As substitute images, photographs were ideally suited for use in an exhibition, where there was a necessary absence of originals and where vicarious experiences were in such high demand. What follows is a selective overview of the Exposition's departments of anthropology, social welfare, and government-sponsored services, all of which drew heavily on photography to fulfill the purposes noted above. What is interesting here is the way in which the functions of the photograph as illustration, record, advertisement, source of information, and picture overlapped, as well as the ways that exhibitors used these images in their displays with artifacts and text.

The Education Department Photographs

Just south of the U.S. photography section on the second-floor gallery of the Manufactures and Liberal Arts Building was the Education Section, or Group 149. While photographs had also been present in educational displays at the Centennial, now they were pervasive. Educational displays earned numerous awards, and among these were forty-three displays that relied on photographs, indicating how central they had become for the exhibitors' purposes.[6] The exhibits employed various ingenious methods to display photographs. The free-winged frame, for example, which stood six or seven feet high, provided a compact and flexible format here as elsewhere in the Exposition. This efficiently designed stand could hold fifty double-glazed, swinging hinged frames, accommodating 100 22″ × 28″ mounts for a total capacity of 600 individual photographs (see Fig. 3.1). The Exposition's administrators circulated directions on how to prepare photographs for educational displays, along with information on the standard format required for photographs.

Another less-expensive display format was the self-contained collapsible portfolio for a wall or table presentation. The arrangement of photographs and other materials was controlled directly by the exhibitor, which ensured a more individual and distinct image for the group or institution being represented. Such a portfolio was used by the Van Norman Institute, a private school for "ladies and children" in New York City. It opened like a screen with four cord-hinged 24″ × 19″ panels and included photographs of the students (see Fig. 3.2) as well as pamphlets, curricula, and views of its building and faculty.[7]

The strategy of these educational exhibits was to present "the school itself." Moves to set up a live model school like that of the Bureau of Indian Affairs, the ultimate replica, were deemed inappropriate by William T. Harris, the U.S. Commissioner of Education, because the "atmosphere of the Exposition was one of intense excitement and distraction of mind."[8] Deliberations on how best to represent the nature of education at the Exposition had begun in 1892, and photographs were clearly to play a part in the strategy.[9] As one organizer said, "Pictures alone, however beautiful, or essential to the imparting of knowledge, are not in themselves enough—the intellect as well as the eye must be entertained."[10] Educational exhibits were therefore designed to integrate photographs of students, buildings, and activities with statistics, publications, and samples of student work.

"Nothing gives a better idea of an institution than good photographs."[11] This was the rationale for the New York State Education Department's exhibit, which included some 3,500 photographs. What the department meant by "good photographs" were those that went beyond the stereotypical view of the school building or static group portrait. They conveyed something individual about the institution, the school's activities, and the students in a classroom situation. Such a display was created by the Workingman's School of the Ethical Culture Society in New York City. The society, founded by Dr. Felix Adler in 1876 as a nonsectarian institution, had as one of its aims the moral education of children. It combined manual training with ethical instruction in its "Learning by Doing" academic curriculum, and it was

FIGURE 3.1   One of the winged frames that proved so useful at the Exposition for displaying large numbers of photographs in a relatively small area. (Halftone reproduction, 15.5 cm × 11.2 cm; New York Board of General Managers, *Report,* opp. p. 204; courtesy of the Rush Rhees Library, University of Rochester)

one of the earliest schools to offer free education to tenement residents. The display, "among the most admired exhibits at the fair," was arranged by Dr. Max Groszman, the superintendent of the school.[12] The photographs, by the firm of Pach & Brothers, a leading New York photographic company, showed students engaged in school activities, including assemblies, gymnastics, kindergarten exercises, and classes (see Fig. 3.3). The educational exhibits were considered so successful that state officials sought to preserve the extensive collection of photographs covering New York's educational institutions at the state museum, and other states also moved to keep portions of their displays intact.[13] The educational displays themselves were the subject of photographs used in subsequent state reports by New York and Massachusetts. Only one educational exhibit was systematically recorded in photographs, however, and that was of the Catholic educational institutions. This unusual display included photographs of some 1,300 institutions from the United States, Canada, Spain, and France, and it covered an area of 29,000 square feet, nearly twice the space allotted to the whole photographic section. The photographs were made as a record to illustrate a comprehensive report on the exhibit that was prepared following the Exposition. Credit for developing the halftone reproductions for the report went to Mrs. W. E. Rothery, whose work was also present in the Woman's Building.[14] A selection of these photographs was also prepared in print format, and several albums of the photographs were presented to church leaders. Pope Leo XIII was given a white leather volume by the Columbus Club of Chicago, and Selim H. Peabody, director of liberal arts at the Exposition, who had been instrumental in obtaining the space for the exhibit, was also given a copy. Each view showed a display as it had been arranged specifically for photographing. The view of Alcove 17, for example (Fig. 3.4), showed the work of the Jesuit teaching institutions in California. Here the clearly defined formula used in educational displays can be seen. Photographs of students and institutions were juxtaposed with volumes of bound school work in various academic subjects and, in this case, works of art rather than statistics. As Denis B. Downey has shown, the overall exhibit was intended as an object lesson to show that it was possible to be both American and Catholic. With the Catholic church perceived as an immigrant church in a time of nativist reaction, the exhibit attempted to demonstrate the moral and intellectual achievements of Catholic education.[15] Photographs

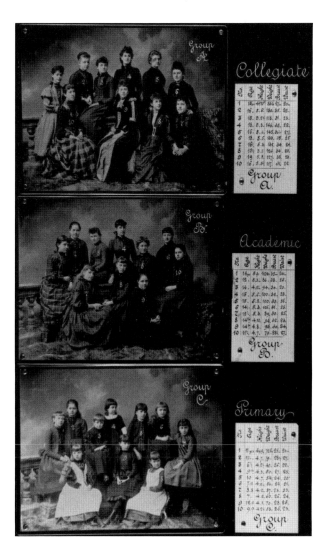

FIGURE 3.2 One of the panels from a self-contained collapsible portfolio, which gave exhibitors more flexibility in the use of text and photographs than did the winged frames, and at much less cost. The Van Norman Institute of New York City used this portfolio to show the work of the institution and its students in its primary, academic, and collegiate levels. (Albumen prints, photographer unknown, Series A0300, D80; Dept. of Public Instruction, Exhibit of Public School Students Work, vol. 2, New York State Archives, Albany)

were a way of providing facts and information to an American society divided both in its attitude toward its developing institutions and in its understanding of the social implications of the rapidly expanding population.

For many universities and colleges, the Exposition offered a forum for promoting their own image in a competitive setting. While Harvard University was accorded the largest amount of space for its displays, Amherst

FIGURE 3.3   The Ethical Culture Society used photographs like this view of a kindergarten group at its Workingman's School in its large display in the Education Section. (Albumen print, 20.4 cm × 25.4 cm, by Pach & Bros.; courtesy of the Ethical Culture Fieldston Schools)

College was judged by the Massachusetts Board of Managers for the Exposition to be more effective in its presentation because it limited itself solely to pictorial and photographic work.[16] Amherst displayed several enlarged 30″ × 40″ views of its buildings, of course, but it also presented photographs of the transit of Venus in 1882 taken at the Lick Observatory. Other institutions also pointed to the work of their distinguished faculty members as part of their promotional work.

The careers of Dr. John Draper and his son, Dr. Henry Draper, two prominent contributors to the history of photography, were the focus of a display by the University of the City of New York (now New York University). This was, in fact, the only display of strictly historical photographic artifacts in the whole Exposition. John Draper accepted an appointment at the university in 1839 to teach chemistry and help set up the medical school.[17] Continuing his early research on the chemical effects of light, he came into contact with Samuel F. B. Morse, Professor of Fine Arts, who had met with Daguerre in the spring of 1839 in Paris. Draper quickly began working with the daguerreotype

process, experimenting with ways to reduce the exposure time required for portrait work by using a short-focal-length lens and substituting chloride for iodine in sensitizing plates. Included in the central cabinet of the display were John Draper's early photographic apparatus and microscopes. His mercury box for developing daguerreotypes, on the bottom shelf, was identical in shape to that held in the Photographic History Collection of the Smithsonian Institution. Henry Draper followed his father's early interest in lunar photography and built his own observatory at Hastings-on-Hudson in about 1860, a photograph of which may have been included in the display. A bust of Henry Draper was placed just in front of a five-foot photograph (visible on the wall of the display) showing the last quarter of the moon that had been enlarged from a 2½″ negative and printed on four sheets of paper (Fig. 3.5). Draper had taken the photograph on August 24, 1872.[18] Three smaller stellar views were also on view.

The other major group of photographs in the university's display was placed together under the large caption "Oldest Sun Picture of the Human Face" (seen just to the right of the large lunar photographs of the moon in Fig. 3.5). This series of photographs included the original daguerreotype made by John Draper of his sister Dorothy Catherine on the roof of the university in 1840 (Fig. 3.6), alongside a more recent portrait.[19] Through the personal efforts of the university chancellor, Henry MacCracken, the university had made contact with Sir William J. Herschel, son of the original owner of the daguerreotype, and arranged for its use in the Exposition. Herschel noted that the daguerreotype had never been opened and gave permission to have it copied "by any process which does not involve contact of any substance with the surface."[20] The copy of the daguerreotype in artotype was made by the New York City firm of Edward Bierstadt at this time, and if the seals on the

daguerreotype were removed, this may have initiated the deterioration process that later damaged the image so severely.

The claim that the Herschel daguerreotype was the first portrait ever taken did not go unchallenged. Julius Sachse, editor of the *American Journal of Photography*, was severely critical of the claim because he had been collecting evidence on two Philadelphians, the late Robert Cornelius and Dr. Paul Goddard, indicating that this honor belonged to them.[21] In fact, facsimiles of their work had been included in a special display at the Joint Exhibition in Philadelphia in May 1893. Even within New York circles there was no consensus that the plate in question was Draper's "first" daguerreotype portrait. After examining the original, Henry J. Newton and Otis

FIGURE 3.4 In some displays, photographs were used along with books, artifacts, and tables of statistics. Alcove 17 in the huge Catholic education exhibit depicted the work of the Jesuit Fathers at their colleges in San Francisco, San Jose, and Santa Clara. (Albumen print, 19 cm x 24.2 cm, no. 55 in album "Photographic Views of the Catholic Education Exhibit, World's Columbian Exposition, Chicago," Lot 6847; Prints and Photographs Division, Library of Congress)

FIGURE 3.5 The University of the City of New York's exhibit honoring the photographic work of John Draper and his son Henry. On the far left is the bust of Henry Draper, and on the wall were displayed his 1872 photograph of the moon, examples of his photographs of the spectrum, and his work in astronomy. (Bromide print, 20 cm x 24.8 cm, by Charles L. Bristol; New York University Archives)

G. Mason, early colleagues of Draper, concurred that the Herschel daguerreotype was a different portrait from the one Draper himself had shown them as being his earliest.[22] In this way the original purpose of the display—to promote the university and honor its distinguished faculty—was obscured in the jockeying by various participants and regional centers for a place in the history of photography.

The Anthropology Department Photographs

The location of the Anthropology Department, near the lake southeast of the central axis of the Exposition, was an accommodation to its two featured outdoor attractions. These were the living-people displays of American Indians from Maine, Wisconsin, Minnesota, and the Northwest Coast, and the large facsimile models of the ruins of Uxmal and Labná in Yucatán. The Anthropology Department, with its sections on archaeology, ethnology, and physical anthropology, was under the direction of Frederick Ward Putnam, a professor of anthropology and ethnology at Harvard. Putnam had been the curator of the Peabody Museum since 1874 and had struggled to establish scientific archaeological collection focusing on North America at a time when funding was inadequate, interest was focused on European classical subjects, and trained staff members were nonexistent. The chair in anthropology was created in 1887, and institutional support for the Central American work followed in 1891, supplemented by funds for the Exposition.[23] Putnam was well aware of the role of photography both in conducting research and in creating a visual context for archaeological artifacts. He also understood from his own experience how it could be used in convincing the public of the potential value of such work.[24] Before the opening of the Exposition, Putnam had even suggested that souvenir photographs would be a lucrative sales item, but restrictions on the photography concessions probably prevented this plan from being carried out. Putnam did employ John Grabill in an official capacity to photograph the Exposition's Kwakiutl Indians and exhibits about them for the department, but this was with the provision that no commercial use be made of them.[25] In making photography serve the dual role of providing information and promoting his department, Putnam was repeating a strategy used by the various federal government surveys since the 1870s for recording and developing the West.

Putnam organized a number of archaeological research projects supported by Exposition funds, including excavations at the spectacular archaeological ruins of important Mesoamerican sites like those at Labná and Uxmal in the Yucatán by Edward H. Thompson, the United States consul at Mérida. John G. Owens, Putnam's first graduate student, undertook the work on the Copán site in Honduras, and Marshall Saville, another assistant of Putnam's, took the photographs for the Honduran and Labná expeditions. Saville arrived in Honduras with Owens in December 1891 and made photographs of the general layout of the sites' large sculptural monuments, some of which he showed in the Joint Exhibition in Philadelphia in his role as a member of the Boston Camera Club. With E. E. Chick he was also in charge of the making casts for the Exposition from the molds taken in Honduras. Finally, he undertook the extensive job of arranging and labeling the photographs and casts in the archaeology section in the Anthropological Building.[26] The strength of the archaeological section, as Nancy Fagin has pointed out, was the combination of the work done by field researchers and artifacts from donors' collections, although the latter lacked uniform labeling and presentation.[27]

In the fall of 1892, Thompson had supervised the construction of the full-scale architectural reproductions of the twenty-seven-foot-high arch of the Governor's Palace at Uxmal and the Portal of Labná, which were placed just in front of the Anthropological Building (Fig. 3.7). Inside the building, 162 photographs from the same sites, like that shown in Figure 3.8, comple-

mented the replicas. These photographs made it possible for the public to view these remote and inaccessible archaeological sites during the progress of excavation work, when key artifacts were being removed. Such expeditions were impressive and confirmed the usefulness of photography in bringing archaeology before the public. A comparison of the on-site photographs with earlier illustrations revealed the extent of the monuments' deterioration. Zelia Nuttal, a juror for the anthropology department, projected that in thirty years they would be "a shapeless mass of ruins."[28] The visual impact of the Central American material was from its unified presentation, made possible by the combination of photographs and site replicas.

Adjacent to this display was a selection of the famous Charnay casts from Palenque and Chichén-Itzá made by Désiré Charnay, a pioneer explorer and photographer of the region. Désiré Charnay attended the Exposition in Chicago and presumably saw his casts installed in the display, which had been provided by the French ministry of education.[29] The casting process required only a spe-

FIGURE 3.6 John Draper's 1840 daguerreotype of his sister, Dorothy Catherine Draper, was on view in the display by the University of the City of New York. Here it was cited as the "Oldest Sun Picture of the Human Face," although this claim was being actively disputed in this period. (Artotype print of the original daguerreotype by E. Bierstadt, 8.2 cm × 6.5 cm; courtesy of the Spencer Museum of Art, the University of Kansas, loan from the Robert Taft Collection, Kansas State Historical Society)

FIGURE 3.7   A view of the replicas outside the Anthropological Building depicting the ruins at Uxmal and Labná in the Yucatán. They were constructed from molds and were authenticated by photographs of the site. (Albumen print by the Algeier Company, a Chicago architectural photography firm, 20 cm x 25 cm, from the album "The Book of World's Fair Photographs," p. 22; Prints and Photographs Division, Library of Congress)

cial molding paper, which was light and easily transportable. Expeditionary photography was, by comparison, still cumbersome even in the era of dryplates, and darkrooms were often difficult makeshift facilities. All replication work done at archaeological sites, especially photography, required months of extensive site-clearing operations. Sometimes it was necessary to construct special scaffolding to obtain a proper viewpoint, and artifacts were treated to increase their tonal contrast for photographing.[30]

In addition to photographs of these recent expeditions, there were forty large carbon photographs of work done by the celebrated British archaeologist Alfred P. Maudslay. Maudslay's methods included surveying the site, taking building measurements, photographing the best preserved buildings, and photographing and making molds of sculptural monuments. Photographs were especially important in verifying drawings of inscriptions made later from casts. From February to July 1889,

Maudslay was at Chichén Itzá, where he was assisted by Henry N. Sweet, a "careful and finished photographer" from Boston who had also worked for Thompson in 1888.[31] Sweet photographed while Maudslay conducted the survey, although both men were severely debilitated by fever. A selection of the 1889 photographs was later enlarged into carbon prints for the purpose of display, and a number of Maudslay's views of Palenque initially appeared in the Madrid exhibition of 1892 before being sent to Chicago (see Fig. 3.9). These carbon prints, made by the Autotype Company in London as part of the official British contribution, were among the large number of department materials donated to the new Field Columbian Museum in 1894. It is not surprising that the excellence of this remarkable collection of photographs depicting Mesoamerican archaeological sites impressed visitors and officials alike. Some were struck by the juxtaposition of the ancient and the modern. One reviewer acknowledged the "weird effect produced on

FIGURE 3.8 This photograph by Edward H. Thompson of the arch of the Governor's Palace at Uxmal was probably included in the large number of photographs of Central American archaeology on display inside the Anthropological Building. The replica of the arch is seen in the left background in Figure 3.7. (Albumen print, 19.2 cm × 15 cm, by E. H. Thompson; no. 112, 20-44; courtesy of the Peabody Museum of Archaeology and Ethnology, Harvard University; Photographic Archives)

FIGURE 3.9   Alfred P. Maudslay's photograph of House C of the palace complex at Palenque, made during his expedition there, was included among his archaeological photographs on display in the anthropology exhibit. (Carbon print, 58.5 cm x 74 cm; courtesy of the Field Museum of Natural History, Chicago; neg. no. A111836)

the imagination by these old monuments of the unknown past standing in stately grandeur amidst all the magnificence and beauty that landscape art and architecture of to-day could devise."[32]

While archaeological photographs were vehicles for revealing the monuments and artifacts of remote civilizations to Exposition viewers, photographs in physical anthropology showed the degree to which the medium had been appropriated by the newly emerging disciplines, with their orientation toward science. This section included displays on craniology, neurology, and psychology and was under the direction of Franz Boas. Boas had come to the United States in 1886, and he began his career as a docent, teaching anthropology in the Department of Psychology at Clark University. He was employed by Putnam in 1891 to organize exhibits

for the Exposition while also conducting fieldwork on the Northwest Coast.[33] Photography was an accepted method of archaeological research by this time, but its application to scientific research in physical anthropology was still being developed. The need to make systematic study photographs was articulated by Frederick Starr, a professor of anthropology at the University of Chicago, who complained that most collections, including those of the federal government, were unusable for scientific anthropology. He pointed out the need to include both frontal and profile portraits in 4″ x 5″ size, as well as groups engaged in specific activities. During a visit to a Seneca reservation in upper New York state in August 1893, Starr instructed a group of amateur photographers from the Chautauqua Institute, as well as Charles Erhmann, who was in charge of the institute's photography correspondence course.[34] Boas himself had studied photography with Hermann Vogel in Berlin in 1882 and 1883 and regarded the camera as a valuable data-collecting instrument for fieldwork. He had collected portraits of "physical types" and had made anthropometric measurements as part of his fieldwork on the Northwest Coast during and after 1888.[35] It is not surprising, therefore, that Boas knew and admired the work of Alphonse Bertillon on the standardization of photography and measurement techniques for criminal investigation, which was on display in the French government's building at the Exposition.[36]

In another aspect of the physical anthropology section, Dr. Dudley Sargent had used photographic data to construct two life-size "anthropometric statues" representing the typical college male and female, based on his study of average measurements from incoming students at Harvard and Radcliffe (Fig. 3.10).[37] Three nude photographs were taken of each entering member of the freshman class, and these were combined with other data to assess the need for corrective training and exercise. A selection of these photographs were on view in

Harvard's educational display in the Manufactures and Liberal Arts Building. Room 8, one of the most popular rooms in the physical anthropology section, was the physical anthropology laboratory (Fig. 3.11), where visitors were able to have themselves measured at a nominal cost using the various standard instruments and to have their measurements compared to standard types. Visible on the righthand wall are several frames of composite portrait photographs used to identify social types. There were also frames of skull photographs demonstrating the superimposition of skull images used in studies of craniology. These were similar to, if not identical with, those displayed by John Shaw Billings, curator of the United States Army Medical Museum. Billings had been making cranial measurements in collaboration with Dr. Washington Matthews since the early 1880s, and his methods and apparatus for photographing skulls had been published.[38]

Anthropology and psychology were both newly emerging methods of study in this period, and both were undergoing significant change and development, shedding their former roots in the humanities and philoso-

FIGURE 3.10   The two "anthropometric statues" and accompanying data that Dr. Dudley Sargent prepared in connection with his measurement study of incoming members of the Harvard and Radcliffe freshman class were shown in the physical anthropology section of the Anthropological Building. (Albumen print, 15.5 cm x 20.5 cm, attributed to John Grabill; no. H6320; courtesy of the Peabody Museum of Archaeology and Ethnology, Harvard University; Photographic Archives)

phy.[39] Both fields appropriated photography as the perfect tool to provide data and illustrations, as well as a means of persuading a nonspecialist audience of the authenticity and validity of the work. The psychology section at the Exposition, under the direction of Professor Joseph Jastrow of the University of Wisconsin, had a model laboratory to demonstrate various testing procedures. On the walls were photographs showing the universities that were undertaking this work. Clark University (one of the earliest institutions to offer training in psychology, including a doctoral program) displayed forty-two photographs illustrating a wide range of apparatus for testing certain physical laws or types of perception.[40] Several photographs showing the work of the psychology department at Harvard showed similar devices and models, although they were in the institu-

tion's education display in the Manufactures and Liberal Arts Building (Fig. 3.12).[41] These photographs were not made for research purposes but rather to show the nature of the new laboratory-oriented experimental and testing work in psychology to a widely diverse public unfamiliar with recent academic and scientific developments.

The Bureau of Charities and Corrections Photographs

Group 147, for the Bureau of Charities and Corrections, was placed in the same building with anthropology in order to facilitate comparative viewing of its materials by state and nationality. The Exposition's administration especially wanted a comprehensive exhibit of the chari-

FIGURE 3.11   The physical anthropological laboratory—which included apparatus, photographs of crania, and other material used in anthropometric research—was one of the most popular rooms in the Anthropological Building. (Albumen print, 16 cm x 20.2 cm, attributed to John Grabill; no. H6329, courtesy of the Peabody Museum of Archaeology and Ethnology, Harvard University; Photographic Archives)

FIGURE 3.12 Photographs showing the new experimental work of university departments were prominent in the anthropology section. This view of a set of wax specimens of the brain and related organs was part of the display of the Harvard University psychology department, though it was placed with Harvard's own educational exhibit rather than with the other psychology displays in the Anthropological Building. (Albumen print, 32.5 cm x 40.5 cm, photographer unknown, Series HUP-SF; Harvard University Archives)

table, penal, and correctional institutions in the United States and had set up a bureau to solicit displays from state boards of charities and prisons, as well as private institutions and groups. Such a scheme presumed a strong state and national organizational structure, which was not yet present in the 1890s, a period in which the new movements for social reform were just getting underway. Thus coordination of the institutional and private groups was impeded by differences about the nature of the social question itself. The older explanations for the causes of poverty and crime were being challenged by a more scientific and pragmatic examination of the underlying conditions that contributed to them.[42] Given this situation, it would have been surprising if the resulting exhibit had been as comprehensive as anticipated. Photographs were used in displays of this department just as they had been at the Centennial, although not as pervasively as in the Department of

Education. Only a few institutions and societies dealing with the care and reform of "adult delinquents" employed photographs in their displays, though nearly all the institutions for the mentally handicapped included photographic material.[43] Absent entirely from the Exposition were the dramatic "reform" photographs associated with the New York journalist Jacob Riis, which are so often associated with this period.[44] Even though Riis had been in Chicago in March 1893 to deliver lantern-slide lectures to audiences at Hull House and to society ladies, his absence from the Exposition went unnoticed in the large and varied display of photographic work in the Bureau of Charities and Corrections.

Photographs, like other materials for display in this department, were subject to strict procedures designed for their standardization. The procedures were outlined in a booklet circulated among potential exhibitors from the social agencies by Nathaniel S. Rosneau, superintendent of the Bureau of Charities and Corrections. It stipulated the use of statistical charts, architectural plans, products made by inmates, bound reports, dolls in uniform, and photographs of exteriors and typical interior rooms, showing "the arrangement of furniture" and "groups of inmates."[45] When corresponding with one exhibitor, Rosneau pointed out that statistics without illustrations were of little value, just as an "exterior view of the building tells no story whatever" without accompanying charts.[46] Photographs were limited to eight-by-ten-inch prints, though in special cases the prints could be fourteen by twenty-two inches. They were to be sent directly to the bureau unmatted, with descriptive labels for display on 22" x 28" boards in winged frames. Each double-sided frame cost the exhibitor three dollars. These requirements and the expense clearly prevented many exhibitors from using photographs in their displays. While not an issue for state institutions, whose displays were financially underwritten, it was certainly a crucial factor for independent agencies. For these smaller groups there was little precedent and little money to hire photographers to illustrate the work of their organizations.

With the initial circulation of the guidelines to potential exhibitors, it became clear, at least in New York State, that a coordinated effort was necessary to ensure that all agencies were represented. The State Board of Charities assumed responsibility for coordinating the effort.[47] Public and private groups were solicited for photographic collections in books or albums, as well as individual histories of all the state's institutions and societies, but no payment was offered for the expenses incurred by this work. The oldest private agency in New York, the Children's Aid Society of New York, founded by Charles Loring Brace in 1853, sent a collection of pamphlets for the state exhibit, but Brace noted that he did not have any "photographs of interest."[48] This is surprising, because photographs from the society's affiliates in Philadelphia, Chicago, and Boston were used in the display. Some state institutions were able to allocate substantial monies for the exhibit, such as the Elmira State Reformatory, which spent $3,000.[49] This made it possible for the board to employ a whole range of exhibit devices, including models of buildings, mannequins dressed in uniforms, a boat made by inmates, and numerous photographs of the reformatory's premises and activities displayed in the standard winged frame.

The comparative exhibit format, while useful for archaeological material and the growing scientific work in anthropology, was not successful in this section due to the paucity of representative material from institutions and societies. State governments were keen to present a forward-looking image of their region with such displays, but dispersing the material for a comparative arrangement would necessarily undermine this. The dis-

FIGURE 3.13   In this photograph from the Lincoln State School and Colony exhibit in the Illinois Building, the students are shown at work in a woodworking class. (Albumen print, 19 cm x 23.2 cm, by Brouse & Martin of Chicago; RG 253.123, Photographic File, Lincoln State School, box 1, Illinois State Archives, Springfield)

parity between the resources available for the displays of state and private agencies was another factor in the lack of adequate materials, especially photographs. For Illinois, a number of private agencies in Chicago exhibited photographs, including the Children's Aid Society, the Chicago Relief and Aid Society, and the Germans' Old People's Home. The State of Illinois, as it had with its educational exhibits, chose to show its display of state charitable and correctional institutions in its own building. In doing so, it missed an opportunity to make a comprehensive state display, but it increased its audience significantly because of the prime location of its building (see the map of the Exposition grounds).

The Illinois display of charitable and correctional programs was primarily a photographic exhibition. Comprising over 250 photographs, together with a published booklet, it covered the following state charitable institutions: the Institute for the Blind and the Institute for the Deaf in Jacksonville, the Charitable Eye and Ear Infirmary in Chicago, the Soldiers' Orphans Home in Quincy, and mental hospitals at Anna, Elgin, Jacksonville, and Kankakee.[50] In the final committee report there was a complete title listing of all the photographs, their sizes, and the institutions represented. The committee in charge of the display had been allocated an extraordinary appropriation of $20,000 for the exhibit, of which three-fifths was returned unspent at the close of the Exposition. Unlike the restrictive standardized format of the bureau's own display, here there was an array of formats and sizes. They included 140 18″ x 22″ prints, 79 24″ x 26″ oak-framed photographs, and 34 prints mounted on stretcher-type frames. Twenty-four photographs had been made by the Chicago firm of Brouse & Martin for the Lincoln State School and Colony.[51] Three of seven original Brouse & Martin photographs have been identified with titles given in the catalogue listings. The prints were enlarged from their original 8″ x 10″ format to an 18″ x 22″ size for exhibition, as shown in Figure 3.13. These were unusual photographs in their representation of classroom interiors that included students working at lace making, wood carving, and shoe making rather than just views of the buildings themselves. For an audience far removed from contact with students with specialized learning abilities, these photographs reflected the effort the state institutions had made to create an environment similar to conventional learning situations, as in Figure 3.3. Several of these photographs required heavy retouching to compensate for the movement of the figures. While several other photographers, such as J. W. Taylor, also provided work for the committee, Brouse & Martin was the primary contractor, receiving $1,750 for its work.[52] These photographs on the second floor of the Illinois Building were described in the official committee report as "tastefully suspended around the wall of the rooms," indicating that their function as social information may not have been fully recognized. It was significant that there was no acknowledgment of the unusually comprehensive photographic survey of life at the charitable institutions. No effort appears to have been made to retain this collection at the close of the Exposition, when the photographs were given to the respective institutions.

There were, however, moves to preserve and utilize some of the materials and photographs of the larger Bureau of Charities and Corrections display for the Antwerp International Fair to be held in May 1894. Proposals were put forward to several of the state boards before the close of the Exposition to preserve the display as a means of "diffusing knowledge and awakening interest in correct charitable and penal methods."[53] Recognition of the potential photography had for illustrating the work of social institutions and societies increased significantly during the 1890s. The 1900 Tenement House Exhibition, sponsored by the Charities Organization Society under Lawrence Veiller, was so successful that it was shown in the Paris exposition in the same year. The "Tenement Committee" included such leading advocates of building reform in New York City as Felix Adler, Lawrence Veiller, and Robert De Forest, president of the Charities Organization Society. The exhibition was held as part of the effort to pass legislation to supersede the negligent building codes approved by the city with state legislation.[54] Some 1,100 photographs were displayed, along with plans, maps, and models. The public response was strong, with more than 10,000 people attending the exhibition.

Francis Peabody, a Harvard professor of social ethics, was one of many present for the important Congress of Religions at the Exposition. In his paper "Christianity and the Social Question" he argued that perfectly developed individualism must be made to serve the common good. Peabody's social-ethics pedagogy drew on the tradition of moral philosophy and attempted to integrate it with the scientific study of social phenomena, which was just beginning in this period.[55] Peabody would certainly have visited the displays of the Bureau of Charities and Corrections in the Anthropological Building. A decade later, following the close of the St. Louis World's Fair, he acquired the extensive collection of photographs

and other display materials from the social welfare section, which formed the basis for his pedagogical Social Museum at Harvard University.

The United States Government Photographs

The diversity of the displays in the United States Building, located just north of the Manufactures and Liberal Arts Building, made it almost a microcosm of the larger exhibition. The exhibits were the responsibility of the Government Board of Management for the World's Columbian Exposition, appointed by the president and composed of the head of each government department. Delays in allocating funds created uncertainty about the amount of money that could be spent for displays, however, and delays in completing the building led to similar uncertainty about the amount of space that would be available.

THE SMITHSONIAN INSTITUTION'S U.S. NATIONAL MUSEUM PHOTOGRAPHS

The exhibits of the United States National Museum, which had been under the auspices of the Smithsonian Institution since 1858, were the first that visitors encountered on entering the south entrance of the Government Building. The planned expenditure for the museum's displays had been cut in half to $150,000, seriously reducing the plans and scale of many of its divisions' exhibits. George Brown Goode's original plan of June 1892 allocated $6,000 "for illustrating the history and development of photography and the graphic arts and the use of photography in the arts and sciences," but in the revised version the figure was reduced to $2,500, and eventually it was simply eliminated.[56] Goode's plan for the photography exhibit reflected his belief in technology as the basis for a new arts and industries department that would reflect a broad interpretation of anthropology. As Arthur Molella has indicated, this reorganization was to affect the whole museum, with the focus on the "needs of man" in their economic and technical manifestations rather than on the traditional areas of botany and geology.[57] Goode died in 1896 before he could implement the plan, and the photography collection lost its chief patron.

The photography collection had no curatorial position as such, but Thomas Smillie, the institution's photographer, undertook the initial collecting and preparation of photographic displays in addition to his regular duties. By 1893 Smillie had already acquired several items, including the Samuel F. B. Morse camera that had originally been in the collection of the National Photographic Association.[58] Smillie continued to solicit donations, and at the 1890 meeting of the Photographers' Association in Washington, he called on his colleagues to support the "proposed Smithsonian collection." The museum's successful display on the history of photography for the 1888 Ohio Centennial Exhibition, which Smillie organized, was a forerunner of what he thought would be possible on a larger scale for the Exposition in Chicago.

The list that Smillie prepared for the proposed photography exhibit included space estimates totaling 1,760 square feet. Included among the sixty-eight types of items to be displayed were camera apparatus; lenses and lens cases; busts of Niépce, Daguerre, and Talbot, and portraits of other inventors; a folding screen presenting a "Bibliography of Photography"; photomicrographs; portrait, genre, landscape, astronomical, and marine photographs; various silver and nonsilver printing processes; daguerreotypes; and an historical section on early apparatus and processes.[59] Clearly this was to be an exhibit dealing with the history as well as the current forms of photography. The plan for this comprehensive photography exhibit existed in some detail, but the substantial resources in time and funds necessary to implement it were lacking. Smillie, as the National Museum's photographer, was responsible to several divisions to provide materials for their respective displays, and his lack of time must have been a major factor in the project's demise. Further, the idea of a comprehensive display on the history and practice of photography was not taken up by any other group at the Exposition. The failure to implement such a project indicates a serious lack of both vision and coordination on the part of the museum administrators, who were intent on accommodating themselves to economic interests and institutional politics. To some extent this situation paralleled the lack of representation by members of the new aesthetic movement from the United States discussed in the previous chapter. In both cases there was a clear lack of national focus and direction.

The Ethnology Division, with its more powerful position in the museum, was less jeopardized by cuts because it benefitted from the combined efforts of the U.S. National Museum's ethnology department under Otis T. Mason and the Bureau of Ethnology under John Wesley Powell, and as Simon Bronner has noted, ethnological collections were a useful mediator between the arts and industry for late nineteenth century American society.[60]

J. K. Hillers had followed Powell to the bureau, where he directed the photography section, conducting fieldwork for anthropologists and continuing to photograph Indian delegations when they visited Washington.[61] The photographs of these delegations, along with those collected in the 1870s by the various government surveys, provided an important source of exhibition material for the bureau in the 1880s and 1890s. As part of the preparation for the Exposition displays, a large selection was pulled from the bureau's photography collection for reference and possible display.[62] Most of the photographs in the selection were Indian portraits by earlier photographers, such as those by A. Zeno Shindler from the 1860s and Alexander Gardner, Julius and Henry Ulke, and William Henry Jackson from the early 1870s. These photographs were in the "classical" portrait style characterized by a studio rather than a field setting. They were the kind that Frederick Starr had indicated were not useful as sources of scientific data for anthropometric purposes, but they were prime exhibition material. The bureau displayed a large selection of these photographs, for example, at the Madrid exposition of 1892.

The Columbian Exposition was the first event at which "life groups" of mannequins were used for display in the United States, and the groups were the centerpiece of the museum's exhibits.[63] These realistic models were the result of important recent advances in figure construction and animal taxidermy, and they were significantly different from the Indian mannequins used at the Centennial (see Fig. 1.4). Goode pointed out that the best work was done by "studying . . . the living model or the best attainable pictures," and that nothing could replace "the eye of an ethnologist who has been among the people."[64] Research, he went on, should continue on improving materials and the coloring of plaster of paris to make "figures still more truthful and life-like." Constructing the life groups was essentially a reproduction process that "counterfeited nature" and that was made possible by the use of sketches and photographs from life, which constituted substitute images. Two key figural groups just inside the entry to the National Museum's display consisted of freestanding, life-size Comanche figures modeled from photographs collected and made by James Mooney during his 1892 fieldwork (see Fig. 3.14). During the course of his important fieldwork on the Ghost Dance cult—work that was significantly different in its historical and ethnographic emphasis from Powell's—Mooney made his own field photographs. He also collected a photograph used as the horse's pose for the

FIGURE 3.14 A life group of a Comanche family in the U.S. National Museum's exhibit. Like the replicas of archaeological ruins, the preparers used photographs as guides in its construction. (Albumen print, 15.3 cm x 20.4 cm, by the Government Board's Committee on Photography; Government presentation album transferred from the Treasury Department, Lot 8355, no. 50, Prints and Photographs Division, Library of Congress)

model in the Comanche family group.[65] The verification of other figural groups was further enhanced by photographing models in the specific pose. Sometimes it was the curators who undertook such roles, such as Frank Hamilton Cushing who posed as the Comanche chief whose model was on the opposite side of the entrance (Fig. 3.15).[66]

The museum's ethnology displays at the Exposition, unlike those in the Anthropological Building, had a distinct and conscious educational purpose, with a careful structuring of artifacts, photographs, and related life-groups. Several model figures of Zuni women weaving and making pottery, for example, were placed just in front of a wall of photographs from the original sites. This wall included the photograph of the Zuni Pueblo's council of secular leaders shown in Figure 3.16. Hillers had made the photograph during his several years of work for the Stevenson Expedition beginning in the winter of 1879.[67] Hillers's bureau photographs continued a style of work begun in the survey years, although his fieldwork ceased after 1883. They included display "pictures" that were more palatable to the general public than the hand-camera research work then being done by field anthropologists like Mooney. Hillers's

FIGURE 3.15   One of the ways in which photographs were used for authentication was to verify original dress and natural poses. In this case, Frank Hamilton Cushing, of the Bureau of American Ethnology, is posing as an Indian of the Great Plains for one of the life groups in the U.S. National Museum's display. (Modern copy print; neg. no. NHM 8255, National Anthropological Archives, Smithsonian Institution)

photographs contributed to the popular interest in "primitive" Indians. As Robert Trennert has noted, visitors "mobbed the pageant of traditional Indian culture" at the Smithsonian displays while virtually ignoring the Office of Indian Affairs model school with its Indian students outside the Anthropological Building.[68] The Indian school exhibit featured Indian groups in an actual school building, with photographic transparencies in the windows. Absent entirely from the Exposition, with its narrowly focused view of the Native American in the ethnology section, was any reference—photographic or otherwise—to contentious issues of the time, such as the effects of acculturation on Indian life and the 1890 massacre at Wounded Knee. One of the first photographers to arrive at Wounded Knee was John Grabill, who was well known for his Indian photographs from the Deadwood area of South Dakota.[69] None of the Wounded Knee photographs, however, are known to have been among those in Grabill's display of Indian portraits and photographs of Indian life in the Anthropological Building at the Exposition.

An unusual series of paintings of Peruvian Indians provided a main attraction along the walls of the central aisle and alcoves (some of them can be seen behind the Comanche model in Fig. 3.14). These had been collected by William E. Safford, a navy lieutenant, when he was a member of a team sent by William Curtis to collect material for the Bureau of the American Republics exhibit.[70] Safford was provided with a Kodak camera with which he made numerous exposures of Peruvian and Bolivian groups during the course of his travels. In writing back to Curtis, he enthusiastically reported on how these photographs were used: "I have struck a splendid thing. There is an old artist here [in Lima], who copies photographs excellently. He has done an Indian woman for me, and is finishing a Chola fruit-woman, his coloring is remarkably good, and his pictures true to nature. I make him utilize every canvas. . . . These pictures will beat any black and white Eastman reproductions you ever saw."[71] Safford was correct in estimating the impact of these canvases and their superiority over the black-and-white enlargements then being made by the Eastman Company for the bureau. When he received them, Curtis immediately transferred this sizable and diverse collection of large-format paintings to the National Museum for use in its Ethnography exhibit at the Exposition. The striking quality of these subtly colored hybrid images—photographs translated to canvas by the gifted but unknown native artist—was unique (see Fig. 3.17). Their ability to retain the particular quality and strength of the photographic image without anything being lost through the artistic process of enlargement and coloring was clearly superior to any reproduction. These paintings, which arrived in late 1892, probably replaced the extensive group of Indian photographs from the Madrid exhibit intended for display in the Ethnological section of the Exposition.[72]

Other divisions of the U.S. National Museum in the Smithsonian section of the Government Building also contained photographs, but none of these divisions had original photographic resources or field material comparable to that of the ethnography section. In the Division of Oriental Antiquities' display, a frieze of mounted pho-

FIGURE 3.16 John K. Hillers's photograph of the council of secular leaders taken at the Zuni Pueblo in New Mexico in 1879 was part of a display that also included artifacts and life groups from the area in the U.S. National Museum's ethnology display. (Modern copy print; neg. no. 2255-C-1, Zuni, National Anthropological Archives, Smithsonian Institution)

FIGURE 3.17 *Aymara,* one of the unusually fine paintings an unknown Lima artist made from photographs of South American Indians, was on display in the exhibit of the U.S. National Museum. William E. Safford had taken the photographs while on a collecting expedition to Peru for the Bureau of the American Republics in 1892. (80.5 cm x 57.6 cm; Safford Collection, cat. no. 1985.66.164,683, National Museum of American Art, Smithsonian Institution)

FIGURE 3.18   In the U.S. National Museum's Division of Oriental Antiquities display, photographs showing the sites and ceremonies of major world religions lined the walls. (Cyanotype, 20.5 cm x 26.2 cm, by the Government Board's Committee on Photography; RU 95, box 61, neg. no. 12350, Smithsonian Institution Archives)

tographs showing divinities, biblical sites, synagogues, and mosques was placed above display cases of artifacts (Fig. 3.18). This was part of a comparative exhibit on religious ceremonies of the Jewish, Islamic, Greek, Roman, Asian, and Christian religions.[73] It would have been of direct interest to people at the widely attended World's Congress of Religions, one of the Exposition's auxiliary events—the first such international congress and the first that was open to the public. A selection of some original Exposition labels with captions and catalogue numbers, and an outline of the exhibit in the museum's report for 1893, provide verification for some of the photographs at the Exposition.[74] One was an 1866 view of Jewish rabbis by Henry Phillips, made during

the earliest photographic survey of ethnic groups for the British-based Palestine Exploration Fund. Louis Vaczek and Gail Buckland have identified the men in the photograph as Ashkenazi, and Yeshayahu Nir has noted that some of the seven men were represented in another photograph in different positions and wearing different coats, suggesting a scarcity of willing models.[75] Since neither the National Museum nor any other museum was systematically acquiring religious photographs for research purposes in this period, it was necessary to rely on foreign commercial photographic firms like the Bonfils studio in Beirut.[76] The company's successful style rested on its ability to isolate architectural subjects from distracting restoration work or encroaching urban clutter, producing a carefully constructed image that satisfied Western audiences but that often lacked accuracy in representation. As Nir has pointed out, there was a substantial overlay of Western visual and cultural conventions in such commercial imagery. This can be seen in the photographs used to illustrate the World's Congress of Religions publication.[77]

Another section with extensive photographs in the National Museum's display was the Geology Division, under the direction of George P. Merrill. This exhibit drew many of its photographs for the Exposition from the collection of the Geological Society of America housed in the offices of the United States Geological Survey, as well as from individual donors. From original labels for some of the display photographs and details in the annual report of the National Museum, we know that there were 203 photographs measuring 7″ x 8″ and 84 measuring 6″ x 8″ mounted in large frames on the left wall and that there was a central frieze of ten large-format photographic

transparencies illustrating the formation of volcanoes, glaciers, and caves (see Fig. 3.19).[78] These included views depicting characteristic volcanic phenomena, and two of the enlarged views were of Bogoslof Island and its volcano in the Bering Sea. The photographs of limestone caves included twenty-five views from the caverns at Luray, Virginia, made by C. H. James in 1882, and of Mammoth Cave in Kentucky by Frances Benjamin Johnston, which had been acquired by the department in 1891.[79] Following the close of the Exposition, the Geology Division acquired more than 400 photographs for its collection. This was another example of the value that such exhibitions had for the development of the National Museum's divisions, especially their photographic holdings.

THE CORPS OF ENGINEERS PHOTOGRAPHS

From its earliest planning in 1891, the Corps of Engineers preferred photographs to expensive sketches and

FIGURE 3.19 The National Museum's Geology Division display included hundreds of photographs along its left wall and a series of large transparencies at the rear. (Cyanotype, 20.4 cm x 25.5 cm, by the Government Board's Committee on Photography; RU 95, box 61, neg. no. 12346, Smithsonian Institution Archives)

FIGURE 3.20   The Corps of Engineers exhibit in the U.S. Government Building made extensive use of photographs, including large window transparencies, framed bromide prints, and a spectacular panorama of Chicago's lakefront and outer harbor. (Gelatin print, negative by the Government Board's Committee on Photography; RG 111-RB-3323, Still Pictures Branch, National Archives)

drawings as a means of showing the progress of its work. Photographs were "instantly comprehended," according to Captain William L. Marshall, the astute planner of the corps' Exposition display. He foresaw that "a very complete exhibit" could be made just with photographs if they were provided by the district engineering officers of works in progress.[80] Indeed, the participation of these officers was the key to success in Marshall's efforts to collect the material he needed for the exhibition, and he sought contributions chosen by them that would best represent the work of the corps in their district. Marshall decided to use photographic transparencies because this format ensured, he said, "a more comprehensive and popular exhibit of the work of the Corps than can be obtained in any other way at many times the

cost."[81] A certain amount of rivalry between government departments stimulated efforts to present a distinctive image of the work of each branch. For the Corps of Engineers this meant spotlighting its participation in major building projects, including the Washington Monument, the Capitol, the Library of Congress, and important bridges, dams, harbor facilities, fortifications, and reclamation projects throughout the country.

Nothing was wasted in the space allotted to the corps in the southeast corner of the Government Building, and photographs were integral to the efficient and effective design. The outside window sections provided a perfect space for 24″ x 30″ glass transparencies. At about twenty-five dollars each, these transparencies were expensive, and they required negatives with high-quality definition

FIGURE 3.21 To promote trade, the Bureau of the American Republics exhibit on the second floor of the Government Building used an extensive collection of photographs made by U.S. officers sent to Central and South America to collect materials for the display. (Gelatin print, 19 cm × 23.5 cm, negative by the Government Board's Committee on Photography; RG 111-RB-3384, Still Pictures Branch, National Archives)

and no retouching or added features such as clouds. The call for bids on the work in January 1892 specified that the transparencies were to be 24″ × 30″ and mounted on a ground-glass back plate. The bromide enlargements would be of the same size, including retouching of the prints, matting, and framing, and allowing a margin for a caption.[82] Bids were to be for 100 transparencies and 200 bromide prints. Considering that most of the photographs were solicited from officers in the field, this meant that high-quality original photographs were a prerequisite.

For the final display, twenty-seven large, framed bromide photographs were placed in a frieze arrangement along the high wall, which was dominated by an impressive panorama photograph of the outer harbor of Chicago

(Fig. 3.20). Another set of smaller framed photographs was placed at the base of the windows beneath the transparencies and just behind a group of models of Corps of Engineers projects. Seventeen photograph albums, some of which were duplicates, were placed on tables for individual viewing, possibly including photographs from the Rock Island (Illinois) District assembled by the photographer and draftsman Henry Bosse.[83]

The entire display was a model of the exploitation of photography for exhibition purposes. In eliciting the support of its participating officers for the process of collecting original negatives and prints, Marshall bypassed the expense of a field photographer. He was therefore able to use his funds for more elaborate photographic formats, such as the transparencies. The presentation of complicated technical models and projects along with photographs of their construction and operation made comprehensible an otherwise difficult, perhaps inaccessible, technological subject for the general public. Not surprisingly, the Corps of Engineers received an award from the Exposition for its efforts.

Following the close of the Exposition, Marshall prepared a complete report furnished with forty photographs of the display taken for the War Department's Committee on Photography. The report also included thirty-six photographs used in the display and thirty-five other tracings and engravings. Marshall was candid in his references to the general lack of leadership on the part of both the War Department and the Government Board regarding the planning for the Exposition. He also noted that, despite the paucity of funds and lack of direction, the individual officers of the corps "were so interested in the success of the exhibit, that they freely contributed models, photographs and descriptions of their works."[84] The key to the success of the display was the cooperative nature of its organization under Marshall's skillful direction.

THE BUREAU OF THE AMERICAN REPUBLICS AND THE "LA RABIDA" PHOTOGRAPHS

The display of the Bureau of the American Republics—representing independent nations of the American continents—was organized by William Eleroy Curtis, an assistant secretary of state and a former journalist with the Chicago Inter-Ocean. The bureau, begun as a recommendation at the International American Conference, held in 1890 and which Curtis had also initiated, maintained its base in Washington. Initial support from New York merchants under the auspices of the Chamber of Commerce included a plan to remove the entire Exposition collection to a new commercial museum in the city after the Exposition.[85] The bureau's display was essentially a photographic exhibition whose purpose was to advertise the resources and promote the commercial and industrial progress of its member countries. It was held under the auspices of the State Department and was housed in the Government Building. William Curtis's ability to exploit photography for display purposes and to coordinate the preparation of such an extensive number of contemporary photographs from Central and South America was without precedent. Such an undertaking, which cut across departmental lines and Exposition red tape, was a work of inspired entrepreneurship.

To ensure the participation of the Latin American members and to provide materials for exhibit, Curtis

seconded eleven officers from the navy and the army and hired three civilians as agents to work on his behalf. Before leaving the United States in early 1891, seven of these agents were equipped with compact No. 4 Kodak Junior camera outfits similar to the one Peary took to the Arctic, which was included in the Eastman Company display, and they received instruction in their use from Thomas Smillie at the National Museum.[86] In addition, the officers were instructed in taxidermy and specimen preparation. Among the twelve officers enlisted were Roger Welles and William E. Safford. Welles collected specimens and made photographs in Venezuela, the Guyana Colonies, and the West Indies. On his return he became Curtis's assistant in Chicago, undertaking much of the organization for the two Exposition projects. Safford's Peruvian acquisitions have already been discussed in relation to the museum's ethnology exhibit. He noted in his 1891 letter to Curtis on the progress of his work: "I am taking photographs on sunny days, and on cloudy ones I go to the markets and stores to glean information regarding the products of the country. . . . In the meantime I am at work on photographs illustrating the life of the people, and now gleaning information concerning the various departments I shall visit."[87]

Curtis's plan was to enlarge the 4″ × 5″ photographs made by his agents to create display prints. The Eastman Company was the main contractor for this work. Frances Benjamin Johnston had been acting as agent for the company for government work since early 1891, and she now made the necessary arrangements for Curtis.[88] The contract with the Eastman Company, for which it was to receive exhibit credit, covered some 700 photographs used in the bureau display and the large number of reproductions of Columbian artifacts displayed in the reconstruction of the Convent of La Rabida.

Almost 2,000 photographs, maps, charts, and commercial objects made up the bureau's exhibit, located in the gallery along the eastern end of the second floor (Fig. 3.21). As a promotional and instructional exhibit, it was meant to persuade United States merchants and manufacturers of the potential for development and trade with the member countries. The photographs were not the work of trained professionals and were certainly different from the ethnographic and commercial tourist photographs available in other international displays. The range of subject matter was varied and can be gauged from a selection of the captions from the 183 items in the Mexican section: "Husking coffee, Vera Cruz Mexico," "Group of Mexican newsboys at play," "Young Mexican nurse," "Package Express in Mexico,"

FIGURE 3.22   View of the Convent of La Rabida, reconstructed from plans and photographs of the original in Palos, Spain. The east side of the Agriculture Building is in the background. (Cyanotype print, 20.3 cm x 25.3 cm, by the Government Board's Committee on Photography; RU 95, box 61, neg. no. 12189, Smithsonian Institution Archives)

"National Library of Mexico," and "Kodak Views of Mexico."[89] Frederick A. Ober of Boston, a naval officer on the USS *Enterprise* and one of Curtis's agents, made a number of photographs of Santo Domingo representing typical scenes, native life, and general views of the city.[90] Surprisingly, no permanent use was made of this important photographic survey of eighteen Latin American countries following their display at the Exposition.

The 1892 Madrid exposition had provided a preliminary staging ground for several government exhibits later shown in Chicago. These included the replicas of Columbus's three ships built in Spain and sailed to Chicago. A photograph representing these ships by John E. Dumont was admired as the epitome of artistic progress in amateur photography.[91] Madrid also provided the stimulus for Curtis's other ambitious Exposition project, the reconstruction of the Convent of La Rabida. Here were to be housed the Columbus relics on loan from

important European and American collections, as well as reproductions. Curtis had made some of the photographs used in building the reproduction of the Convent of La Rabida while he was in Spain for the Madrid exposition, and he also provided the architect, Henry Ives Cobb, with plans, and maps of the original site in Palos, Spain. The task was to create a structure that would be both a historical replica and a display space for valuable artifacts, and once again photographs provided the necessary template. In early 1893 Curtis sent Cobb photographs and tracings of La Rabida that included photographs keyed to points on the plans.[92] Although they were late in arriving, Curtis was anxious that the reconstruction be accurate and was willing to go to additional expense to obtain this result. The unpretentious nature of the convent, the original of which dated back to Roman times, offered a sharp contrast to the other Exposition buildings (Fig. 3.22). Spectators were en-

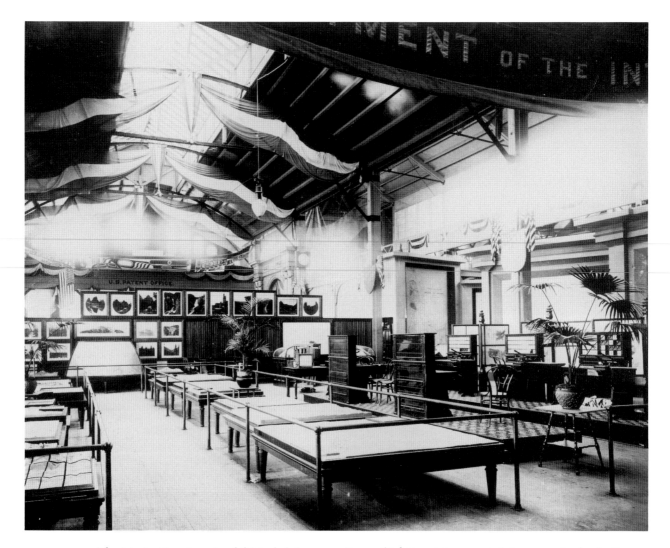

FIGURE 3.23   The Interior Department's exhibit included maps, models, and a series of large photographic transparencies by John K. Hillers, the photographer for the U.S. Geological Survey. (Gelatin print, 21 cm x 26.8 cm, negative by the Government Board's Committee on Photography; RG 111-RB-3977, Still Pictures Branch, National Archives)

couraged to experience the simplicity and quaintness of the convent, especially in contrast to the Exposition's magnificent architecture. Thomas Wilson suggested that this represented "the Alpha and Omega of American civilization."[93] The location of the convent on the spit of land behind the Agriculture Building and outside the main complex had not been chosen with photography in mind, as had the locations of the other, vista-oriented structures.

The interior rooms of the convent were filled with a mixture of photographic reproductions of portraits of Columbus, photographic facsimiles of letters and documents, and photographs of sites associated with Columbus, including the newly acquired Lorenzo Lotto

portrait of Columbus belonging to James W. Ellsworth of Chicago. Enlargements were made from photographs by Curtis's agents, and there were also copies of original paintings, prints, and maps, several of which measured 40″ x 30″ or 40″ x 60″. Charles O. Thompson, the Eastman Company's artist, described some of his two years of work on the photographic reproductions of the numerous painted portraits of Columbus, especially the care he took to reproduce the cracks and blemishes of the originals.[94] The display was a visual cacophony for the viewer, which required constant adjustment to the reproductions, the originals, and replicas on display. Yet this jarring mixture, combined with lengthy descriptive catalogue texts and poor lighting conditions, did not

FIGURE 3.24   Hillers's photograph *Reflected Tower, Rio Virgin, Utah* appeared as a transparency in the Interior Department's display. (Modern contact print from original negative by J. K. Hillers; RG 57 (PS) no. 73, Still Pictures Branch, National Archives)

FIGURE 3.25   The segment of the General Noble sequoia on display in the main rotunda of the Government Building had its own interior staircase and a display of photographs documenting the process of cutting it down. (Gelatin print, negative by the Government Board's Committee on Photography; RG 111-RB-3389, Still Pictures Branch, National Archives)

deter spectators. Indeed, the attractive inner courtyard of the convent offered a respite from the distraction and turmoil of the Exposition itself.

THE GEOLOGICAL SURVEY PHOTOGRAPHS
The United States Geological Survey display in the Department of the Interior exhibit provides an appropriate conclusion to this section on government displays. While the great independent surveys of the 1870s by Powell, Hayden, and Wheeler were all represented at

the Centennial, just three years later the surveys had been combined to form a single unit: the United States Geological Survey. During the ensuing fourteen years, J. K. Hillers played a key role in the photographic section of the survey, dividing his time and work between it and the Bureau of Ethnology, both of which were under the direction of John Wesley Powell. Hillers returned to the survey's payroll in 1881 but continued to do work for the Bureau of Ethnology in the National Museum's updated photographic laboratory, completed in the same year. In the early 1890s, with the increased fieldwork being done more by researchers themselves, Hillers spent most of his time in the laboratory processing photographs with his assistant photographer, C. C. Jones, and two or three printers. In 1892 the Division of Illustration was nearly dissolved as a result of the drastic reduction in funding, and only two of the ten employees were retained—Hillers and De Lancey Gill, the illustrator.[95] The others were transferred to other sections. The following year, all of the photographic positions except that of one of the printers were restored. Other government photographers, like Thomas Smillie, worked for several different museum departments, but Hillers worked directly for John Wesley Powell for twenty-five years.

Like Hayden and other early survey leaders, Powell continued to use photography as an important tool for informing the public as well as promoting government projects. Just as illustrated publications and commercial stereographs had widened the audience for western photographs in the 1870s, public exhibitions were an important vehicle for similar purposes during the 1880s. The U.S. Geological Survey had been given the highest award—the prestigious Grand Prix—for its display at the 1889 Paris exposition. This was the only award given for photography at the event, and it indicated the degree of recognition accorded the department's transparencies, maps, and charts.[96] It was also an acknowledgment of the degree of sophistication and expertise the survey had attained in the techniques of public display using photographs. It was Hillers who had so successfully applied the skills of making glass transparencies for exhibit purposes, and it is not surprising that he was called upon to make an unusually large 4'2" × 7' specimen for the Chicago event. The photograph was a relief map showing oil fields in the United States as part of the Standard Oil Company's display in the Mines Building and was later given to the Geology Division of the National Museum. In order to make a transparency of this size, a complete room had to be made into a camera, and processing in the silvering vat was reported to have used $250 worth of silver nitrate.[97] Washing with hoses took an hour, and finally the ⅜"-thick glass positive print was varnished. Three photographers assisted Hillers in exposing and developing the transparency. At the close of the Exposition, the transparency, which was valued at $5,000, became part of the collection of the Geological Division of the National Museum, although no trace of it has been found.

Glass transparencies in a more standard format also featured prominently in the survey's Exposition display,

with forty views by Hillers placed on the outside window spaces in the northwest section of the Government Building.[98] By now, the Geological Survey was not the only government department to recognize the potential of these photographs for exhibition purposes. Unlike the other government exhibitors, however, the appearance of the main section of the survey display—with its topographic maps, well-spaced and carefully mounted photographs, and the occasional potted palm—represented an image of assurance in the art of public display that balanced attractiveness with the transmission of information (Fig. 3.23). A number of key photographs by Hillers, some dating to 1872, were included in the ten large transparencies mounted above the separating wall as the central focus of the display.[99] *Reflected Tower* (the first on the left, in an oval format) was taken in 1873 from the Rio Virgin in present-day Zion National Park in Utah (Fig. 3.24). This photograph and others, like *Captains of the Canyon* (fifth from the right in the central frieze), were representative of a seamless style and a continuity of purpose in photographic landscape representation stretching back to the 1870s.[100] Because they were not marred by references to settlement, tourism, and the exploitation of natural resources, the federal government continued to use these Geological Survey photographs in displays in which, for cultural and political reasons, it was seeking to promote a particular view of, even a nostalgia for, the American land. Such photographs, however, were impervious to significant changes in American landscape photography in the 1880s and 1890s, as Peter Hales has pointed out.[101]

A year prior to the Columbian Exposition, Hillers made one of his last field trips, traveling to the Yosemite Valley and Kings River areas of California.[102] Yosemite was an appropriate subject for the Exposition because, after Niagara Falls, it was probably the most famous site in the United States. Through the work of such early photographers as Carleton Watkins, Eadweard Muybridge, and William Houseworth, it had become deeply embedded in the popular visual consciousness.[103] Elsewhere in the Exposition, other pictorial works also celebrated this subject—the vertical-panel paintings of the mammoth redwoods by Thomas Hill, for example, in the California state building—and just steps away from the Hillers views, in the main rotunda of the Government Building, there was the thirty-foot-high section of the original 300-foot-tall General Noble sequoia, named in honor of the Secretary of the Interior, General John Noble (Fig. 3.25). Complete with a carved interior staircase for spectators to ascend in order to view the building, the exhibit also featured a room with photographs illustrating the stages of the tree's dismantling.[104] This was perhaps the perfect Exposition artifact: authentic, imposing, and without replication, a chastening counterbalance to the mythologizing image of the western lands in the Hillers photographs hanging just a few steps away. It also represented the ambivalence and conflicting struggle between the land as a natural environment and as a potential resource for development.

The Exposition demanded photographs, and they were prominent in the displays of education, anthropology, and social welfare, and under the broad umbrella of the government departments. Photographs complemented the statistics of educational institutions and were integral to the network that linked exhibition artifacts and objects with their origins. Substantial state and federal funds provided the necessary resources for the photographs for the Bureau of the American Republics and the various social service institutions, and the lack of such resources prevented completion of the comprehensive photographic exhibit planned by the Smithsonian Institution. Remote geological and archaeological sites were made accessible by photography and by the imposing replicas of Mesoamerican ruins, the accurate ethnographic models of Indian life, and the reconstructed Spanish convent of La Rabida, and even their construction was aided by photography. Photography contributed to the development of the new scientific methods of physical anthropology, with its demand for measurable data. To serve the new educational focus of the National Museum of the Smithsonian Institution more effectively, the informational function of the photograph was subordinated to its pictorial function in order to draw a popular audience to the ethnographic displays. The Corps of Engineers, too, recognized that photographs were both popular and easily comprehended, and it quickly adopted a successful strategy of presenting carefully designed photographic formats for its displays. Finally, the Geological Survey maintained its long tradition of using the photograph as a vehicle to persuade, attract, and inform. Despite the various functions served by the photographs appearing within such diverse displays were never merely transparent images; they were a carefully constructed, multilayered edifice of meaning and use.

PART II
Photographic Practices

4

INCORPORATING PHOTOGRAPHY
The Contest of Practice and Production

The dominant cultural force of incorporation was played out in the Exposition's administrative organization through the restrictive controls Exposition officials imposed on the practice and production of photography for the event.[1] The contest set administrators and photographers in opposition, and the kinds of photographs made—the images that were available for public consumption—were a direct result of this contest.

The Exposition's administration was not a monolithic structure; it was made up of two distinct groups. The Washington-based World's Columbian Commission was composed of an unwieldy number of national representatives appointed by the president, with George R. Davis as director general.[2] The World's Columbian Exposition Board, however, which controlled the finances, was made up of forty-five prominent Chicagoans, with Harlow N. Higinbotham acting as president. Clearly there were problems with such an unbalanced and divided organization, and by August 1892 the need for a centralized administration was acknowledged with the formation of the Council of Administration, which had representatives from both groups. The Chicago board early recognized the possibility of using photography as its "visual arm," in the words of Peter Hales.[3] The decisions on photographic practice and production were implemented by the Chicago board's Committee on Ways and Means, a group it carefully removed from democratic debate and public pressure. Finally, as part of its strategy of incorporation, the board decided to set up a photographic department to engage in the commercial production of photographs.

Official Photography for the Bureau of Construction

In examining the business of official photography, we must begin with the Exposition's Bureau of Construction because this agency was the source of the later enterprise. As part of its procedures for keeping track of the progress of construction for the Exposition's administrators, designers, and architects, the bureau turned to photographs for official use. It is worthwhile to point out that this official photography began in June 1891, just when the earliest applications for the commercial photographic concessions were arriving at the Chicago board. The Bureau of Construction had hired the Canadian photographer Charles D. Arnold for this work (Fig. 4.1).[4] Arnold had early come to the attention of Daniel Burnham as an architectural photographer suitable for the Exposition work. He was a photographer who could follow a photographic "style" that satisfied the utopian visions and "urban grand" designs that the Exposition architects and planners were seeking to create in the neoclassical edifices of the White City.[5] The Exposition buildings, numbering well over two hundred, were basically iron and timber sheds faced with various architectural details, claddings, and decorative sculptures made of "staff," a mixture of plaster, jute, and cement (see

Figure 4.2). Harlow Higinbotham, in defending Arnold at a later period when a conflict was raging in the photographic press about his appointment as official photographer, said that his photographs drew "many compliments from people well qualified to judge of their artistic merit, notably the different architects who have designed and constructed the different buildings in Jackson Park."[6] Arnold's bureau photographs were distinctive in their quality and execution, unlike the later commercial material produced for the Department of Photography. The Exposition's architects, designers, and planners (whom Arnold had previously provided with photographs of European architecture) were well served by these official photographs.

To enhance the vista approach to the Exposition buildings, Arnold's architectural photographs followed a standard formula that utilized a set of viewpoints created by the architecture itself. Throughout 1892 and 1893 these photographs were regularly published in architectural journals like the *American Architect and Building News* of Boston, the *Inland Architect and News Record,* and James B. Campbell's *World's Columbian Exposition Illustrated.*[7]

During the early period of construction, Arnold did not possess the absolute monopoly on photographic production that he was later given. With special permission from the Chicago board, several independent professionals also provided some of the official photographs. Frances Benjamin Johnston had been approached in July 1891 by H. C. Demorest to write an article for his magazine, and she received special permission to photograph on the Exposition grounds in November.[8] It was during this trip that she met Arnold, who provided her with some photographs she requested, and later she often corresponded with him. A request by Johnston in June 1892 to photograph at the Exposition was denied, however, because the policy of using only photographs produced by the official photographer had begun to be put in place.

Arnold worked in a range of formats, including foldout panoramas for many of the construction photographs, making a succession of images on a daily or monthly basis that showed the progress of the work. The captions inscribed on the negatives carefully oriented the viewer with respect to compass direction of each photograph, and his practice of dating the negatives by month and day made the progression of the individual images clear. The initial rationale for such a comprehensive photographic record was Daniel Burnham's plan for

FIGURE 4.1   Charles D. Arnold, who had initially been hired to photograph the construction of the Exposition's buildings, was one of two photographers appointed to be in charge of the official commercial concession, called the Department of Photography. (Halftone photograph; Johnson, *History of the World's Columbian Exposition,* 3:354; courtesy of the Rush Rhees Library, University of Rochester)

a visual as well as a written final report of the Bureau of Construction. This was not a conventional published report but rather a set of eight individual volumes of original typescript departmental reports supplemented with relevant photographs.[9] The text of the report was technical, descriptive, and comprehensive in depicting the nature of the work—describing the buildings' decoration, engineering, and electrical systems—while the photographs functioned as a visual overlay that was carefully integrated with the text. The formats ranged from full-page single 20″ × 24″ platinum prints, like that shown in Figure 4.2, to images placed within the text and groups of ten photographs on a single page in albumen and aristotype.

Later, many of these construction photographs were combined with general architectural views and used for other official and semiofficial purposes. Two large albums, designated Exhibit A and Exhibit B, were assembled at the request of the director general of the World's Columbian Commission to accompany reports being prepared in December 1893.[10] A twelve-volume

FIGURE 4.2   View of the Manufacturers and Liberal Arts Building, August 15, 1892, one of the many C. D. Arnold made that were later incorporated into the *Final Report* of the Bureau of Construction. (Platinum print, 50.2 cm x 65.5 cm, by C. D. Arnold; from Burnham, "Final Official Report," 2:54; courtesy of the Art Institute of Chicago)

collection of similar platinum prints in the Chicago Public Library, with a comprehensive inventory of subjects and a chronological arrangement of the prints, appears to have served an administrative or reference purpose.[11] Assembling these photographs and others for elaborate presentation albums tended to cause Arnold's official photographic work for the bureau to overlap with the commercial work he later did for the Department of Photography, which was also under his direction. Such albums were either purchased or presented to individuals associated with the Exposition. The three-volume set of Exposition photographs belonging to the Art Institute of Chicago, about which Peter Hales has recently written, was originally in the possession of a railroad industrialist named Van Horn who later moved to Canada.[12] Levi Zeigler Leiter, for example, a leading Chicago businessman, acquired one of the elaborate portfolio-style albums of large platinum prints, which he presented to his son-in-law, Lord Curzon of Kedleston.[13] Among the fifty hand-numbered and titled prints by Arnold was the view from the Electricity Building shown in Figure 4.3. The photograph, taken from the second-floor portico to enhance the spectacle of the architecture itself with its unifying cornice and style, looks past the

FIGURE 4.3   A view from the portico of the Electricity Building looking south to the obelisk on the South Canal. This is the
kind of photograph Arnold made to show off the architectural
features of the Exposition's buildings and monuments. (Platinum print, 49 cm × 68 cm, by Charles Dudley Arnold; from a
presentation album, Lord Curzon of Kedelston from L. Z. Leiter; courtesy of the Harry Ransom Humanities Research Center,
the University of Texas at Austin, Gernsheim Collection)

MacMonnies fountain on the right and the Column of
Victory to the Obelisk at the end of the South Canal.
This photograph epitomized Arnold's ability to replicate
the celebratory rhetoric and style of representation espoused by the Exposition's officials and architects.

The arrangement and quality of these fine platinum
prints are in striking contrast to that of the mass-produced, consumer-oriented versions available to the general public from the Department of Photography. They
created an official view of the Exposition that served the
aspirations and ideals of the Exposition's promoters and
architects, not the general public. No real debate had
taken place on the question of whether there should be a
multiple photographic viewpoint because the Exposition's administrators had never had any intention of
opening the field to competition. By May 1891, the
Exposition board had in place its projected plan for
incorporating both official and commercial photography
under its control. The albums demonstrate the continuity of photographic representation from the construction phase through the completed Exposition by
producing a seamless image from beginning to end. Similarly, there had been no contest in the appointment of
an official photographer because the main purpose of the
administrators was to a ensure a controlled viewpoint.
To maintain this viewpoint for official photography, the
Exposition board appropriated its own photographer and
attempted to incorporate all other photographic operations into its system of regulations.

The Commerce of Official Photography

The decision to include the commerce of official photography as part of the activities of the Exposition board was a significant departure from previous international expositions, where the main photographic concession had been awarded as the result of open competition. At the international exhibition of 1876 and the New Orleans Cotton Centennial of 1885, for example, an open bidding process ensured some degree of competition. In contrast, the tactics Edward Wilson used at the Cotton Centennial, where he edged out local competitors, met with stiff criticism from other members of the photographic community.[14] The decision to incorporate commercial practices had significant effects on amateur photography, as we will see in chapter 5. The regulations included the purchase of a two-dollar permit for a camera that used negatives not larger than 4″ × 5″. Stereo cameras and tripods were totally banned.

The lucrative possibilities of the photographic concession made it a highly desired plum at the Exposition. As early as April 1891, George Eastman, on behalf of the Kodak Company, wrote to the Chicago board about the possibility of the company sponsoring the photographic franchise. He pointed out Kodak's position as the "largest plant for manufacturing small photographs in the world," with facilities "much greater than could be organized for the Fair business alone."[15] Eastman put forward a cooperative plan that would be more profitable to the board in dividing the franchise between several parties as follows:

> We believe with our facilities we could make these small pictures at a lower price to the public (and still allow a fair percentage on the gross sales for the privilege) than any other concern. We believe that if the franchise is split up in the manner we suggest that the party undertaking the large work will concentrate his energies on it and do more business than if he combined the small work with it and the amount your organization would receive from us would be just so much clear gains over the other plan, which was, we understand followed at the Centennial.[16]

This plan to divide the business into two parts, with negatives under 5″ × 8″ to be furnished by Kodak, played to the company's strengths in the small-photograph market while leaving intact the "large work" for the board to exploit commercially. Eastman must have known of the large-format photographic work already underway by the Bureau of Construction and was attempting to steer clear of any hint of interference or competition with it.

This suggests that plans for the Chicago board's photographic concession were under consideration even at this early date. By designating a maximum 5″ × 8″ format for itself, Eastman was seeking to include the new larger Kodak models that were of a folding rather than a box design and thus more compact. Not surprisingly, Eastman's bid for the Exposition's photographic concession, like others, was unsuccessful.[17] In fact, rather than promoting his own cause, Eastman's enthusiasm for the potential of the small-photograph market may have alerted the Chicago board to the potential for competition from amateur and commercial photographers. This would have strengthened its resolve to incorporate the whole commercial enterprise under its own jurisdiction.

The Department of Photography did not actually appoint the official photographer until April 1893, just two months before the Exposition was to open. But as the photographer for the Bureau of Construction, Arnold had in fact been doing the department's work for some ten months prior to his appointment as official photographer. There was an important link between his appointment and the establishment of an official Department of Photography, and Arnold played a key role in securing this link. The young Harlow D. Higinbotham, son of the president of the Exposition board, was also appointed to the position of official photographer—Arnold and he held the position jointly.[18] The disparity between them in age and photographic experience, however, ensured that Arnold would direct the operations. Under the appointment, both men were to receive salaries of $2,000 and 10 percent of the profits. They were not financially responsible for constructing the photographic building or providing the materials and staff for it. The Chicago board provided all of this, which was a very generous arrangement compared to previous expositions. At the Centennial the photographic concessionaire had been required to provide facilities, labor, and materials, and to pay the Centennial board a substantial fee and a percentage of the gross earnings.

The unpretentious building that housed the Department of Photography was located just behind the Horticulture Hall and was erected at a cost of $6,000. Here the department produced its commercial photographic prints, lantern slides, and albums at a level that required a substantial work force. Beginning in late 1892 with six employees, the department's staff increased to thirteen positions in February 1893 and to forty-five for the May opening. It peaked at 108 workers in August.[19] This pattern was quickly reversed with the closing of the Exposition.

A number of capable professionals were among the department staff, including Otto Scharf and F. Dundas Todd, who had recently arrived from Scotland and who would become editor of the *Photo Beacon* a year later.[20] Salaries were based on the specialized skills of printers, lantern-slide makers, and photographers and ranged between sixty and seventy-five dollars a month. Women employees were paid a substantially lower wage,[21] a condition that inspired a fictionalized melodrama depicting a "hand camera" romance between two photographic retouchers at the Exposition, George Sage and Maude Cook. In it, Maude works in a photographic factory known as "the prison of Brutus" after its owner, who rules it with an iron hand. Her forced abduction by Brutus is foiled by Sage, Brutus's estranged brother. The melodrama ends with the marriage of the two retouchers, who eventually inherit the factory.[22] Though not high drama, the play is an illustration of the kind of popular interest in conditions in the new factory work open to women in photographic businesses.

Understandably, there were problems in overseeing the work of such a large number of temporary employees. The work required special administrative, technical, and social skills, but the editor of the *American Amateur Photographer* described Arnold as having little "tact and business ability in dealing with and directing assistants."[23] The same writer noted the poor performance of both Arnold and the Department of Photography and lamented that "many valuable photographic records will be lost, as there will be no talent or time to make them. If he [Arnold] would gather around him the best expert professional and amateur photographers, appoint them his assistants, and proceed in a broad liberal spirit, the photographic record of the fair would be a grand success." The fact that photographic productions from the department were not of a consistent quality is an indication that the operation had in fact moved beyond Arnold's control.

The financial stakes in regard to photography were clearly high, and the board placed substantial pressure on producing a large profit. The running cost of such an operation was substantial; the Department of Photography spent more than $37,000 over the period from July 1892 through May 1893.[24] In the end, the board earned a substantial return on its investment, with reported net receipts from the department of $90,577.64 from the sale of prints, lantern slides, and commissioned photographs. At the time Arnold was appointed official photographer, the elder Higinbotham announced that it was the intention of the management to award a concession that would both "yield the stockholders of the World's Columbian Exposition a fairly substantial revenue" and at the same time provide "artistic photographs to be sold at prices that would be entirely satisfactory to the public."[25] These two goals were not necessarily incompatible, but the priority of the former was clear. Arnold's lack of management skills and the pressure for volume sales did not augur well for quality commercial production. To produce large amounts of inexpensive photographs, it proved necessary for the department to make multiple use of certain views, as well as recopying negatives rather than making originals in different sizes.

Lantern slides came under particular criticism from the general photographic community. The editor of the *American Amateur Photographer* even claimed that "amateurs of ordinary skill consider them only good enough to be washed off and used as cover glasses."[26] This situation presented a potential problem for the department, as it was not the sole producer of lantern slides. The Eastman Company, the Carbutt Company, and the McAllister Lantern Company, as well as William Rau and Samuel Castner, all marketed their own slides of the Exposition. The great popularity of the lantern slide, shown in Figure 4.4, which was fostered through the American Lantern Slide Interchange, ensured a high expectation among members of the general photographic community about the quality of such images.[27] The extensive range of views available from the Department of Photography was intended to cater to a well-established and discerning amateur and commercial market.

There were also problems with a lack of consistent quality among the department's ordinary process prints. Each 8″ × 10″ photograph sold for fifty cents, and each 4″ × 5″ for twenty cents, which were not considered competitive prices from the amateur's standpoint.[28] The process of marketing the department's photographs was enhanced by Arnold's promotional dealings, including his endorsement of the cameras provided by the American Optical Company.[29] His practice of copyrighting his personal and official work ensured that he could maintain control over the use of the image. The Copyright Law, in effect since July 1, 1891, required that the creator of the photograph register each photograph for a fee of fifty cents and submit a title and two copies of the original.[30] Arnold sent off packets of albumen photographs covering every aspect of the Exposition to the Library of Congress several times a month. From November 1892 to 1896 he registered more than a thousand

FIGURE 4.4   Lantern-slide presentations with accompanying
lectures re-created the Exposition for audiences around the
country. (From the *Scientific American* 69 [Jan. 20, 1894]: 39)

photographs, which is indicative of the degree of control
he exercised over the "artistic" side of the production.
The general commercial print work carrying the department's imprimatur and Arnold's name, however, was not
of consistently high quality, a point that becomes clear
when one examines any large collection of the department's commercial work. While Arnold's name was attached to the photographs produced in the department,
this did not necessarily ensure a quality print for the
ordinary consumer.

Photographs from the Department of Photography
were published in a variety of forms, ranging from the
products of less expensive halftone processes to the high
quality of fine photogravures. In his commercial work,
Arnold did not attempt elaborate interpretive strategies
but instead repeated pictorial formulas he had already
established for his architectural patrons. These the department selectively repackaged and sold in small, inexpensive popular formats to a large audience of consumers. One of the key Exposition buildings featured in

souvenir publications by Arnold and other photographers was the striking, glass-domed Horticulture Hall.
Covering some five acres, it was designed by W. B.
Jennings, with sculptural work by Lorado Taft. Arnold
made a number of photographs of the building, and
many of them appeared in various publications, including a photogravure in *Official Views of the World's Columbian Exposition,* an aristotype frontispiece for *Anthony's
Photographic Bulletin,* and a zinc halftone engraving in
Portfolio of Views.[31] While all these photographs were
different, all were taken from the same vantage point on
Wooded Island, just east of the building. The viewpoint
from a small bay at the end of the bridge was the one
guidebooks suggested for making "artistic" views. Here,
one guide noted, "the dome of the Horticultural Building
has a charming effect"; if the "water be in a suitable
condition, its beauty will be enhanced by the reflections."[32] None of Arnold's other views of the building
came as close to this ideal as did his 1892 photograph of
the building. Even though it was unfinished in this view,

the photograph was reissued successfully as a commercial print (see Fig. 4.5). Its appeal came from the perfectly reflected image of the Horticulture Hall's 113-foot glazed dome. The similarity between this view and others by both commercial and amateur photographers is striking. The pervasiveness of the "charming effect" formula testifies to the existence of a popular and marketable "artistic" photography.

Considering how carefully Arnold had controlled the photographs made in the department, it is not surprising that he was reluctant to turn the negatives over to Daniel Burnham for use in his publication at the close of the Exposition. Burnham then hired William Henry Jackson to provide a master set of prints and negatives for his own projected publication. The haste with which

Jackson was hired necessitated that his equipment be sent on from Denver, and it arrived on October 31, only a day after the formal close of the Exposition.[33] Burnham's action was a complete reversal of his position of the previous year, when he justified Arnold's monopoly as a way of ensuring that only "pictures as shall do credit to our work" would be produced.[34] The hiring of a photographer with a reputation like Jackson's was as much an acknowledgment of the failure of official policies as it was a public relations gesture aimed at the photographic community. Granted that it was a very late accommodation to the criticism of the Exposition's monopolistic practices in photography, it did attempt to address the demand for justice and also to acknowledge that there were skilled hands other than the official ones of Arnold.

FIGURE 4.5   Arnold's photograph of the uncompleted Horticulture Building, taken from a point on the Wooded Island later recommended to, and frequented by, many amateur photographers, represents the kind of "artistic" photograph that was both popular and marketable. (Albumen print, 18.5 cm x 22.5 cm; courtesy of the Chicago Historical Society; Prints and Photographs Department, ICHI-23464)

FIGURE 4.6   This view of the sixty-foot Statue of the Republic was one of the photographs that the Exposition board commissioned William Henry Jackson to make following the close of the Exposition and that were later reproduced in a variety of mass-produced publications. The statue was located at the end of the basin of the Court of Honor, and Jackson photographed it against the backdrop of the forty-eight-columned peristyle and the arch surmounted by the sculptural group representing the approach of Columbus. (From Jackson, *The White City (As It Was)*, pl. 6; courtesy of Charles Rand Penney, World's Columbian Exposition Collection)

Because Jackson's views were made in just ten days, their highly concentrated "look" was more coherent or apparent than Arnold's, which he had been able to express over a three-year period and on a far wider range of subjects. In Jackson's view of the Statue of the Republic (shown in Fig. 4.6), he has managed to position his raised viewpoint to convey the central idea of subordination in the relationship between the sculptural group that features the approaching Columbus above the arch and the figure of the Republic, which is usually represented as dominating the scene. Because the Exposition was closed and the waters of the basin were calm, such viewpoints were much more accessible to Jackson for this kind of carefully constructed image. Comparing the kinds of photographs Jackson and Arnold made of similar sites, Peter Hales concludes that there was a sense of "disjunction and surprise" in Jackson's images of the Exposition that was lacking in Arnold's.[35]

FIGURE 4.7   In his magazine *Sun and Shade,* which was known for its quality reproductions, Ernest Edwards displayed an unusual sense of design in the page layout of these Exposition photographs. Here the view of the massive Manufactures and Liberal Arts Building and the ornate sculptured pillar is relieved by focusing attention on the simple curved form of the gondola, which is repeated in the close-up below. (Photogravure, 15.5 cm x 19 cm, 6.5 cm x 11 cm; *Sun and Shade* 6 [December 1893], n.p.; courtesy of the George Eastman House, International Museum of Photography and Film; Library Collection)

Jackson's hundred views did not remain the exclusive possession of the Chicago board. In true entrepreneurial style, he sold a second set of negatives to Harry Tammen for $1,000. Tammem published the images in a large pictorial format after adding human figures, boats, and details to relieve the nearly deserted post-Exposition scenes Jackson had produced. Another edition of the Tammen material, *Jackson's Famous Pictures of the World's Fair,* was put out by the N. D. Thompson Company of St. Louis.[36] The firm also included several unattributed Jackson views in its other publication on the Exposition, *The Dream City,* which was part of its Educational Art Series.[37] Such publications illustrate how photography was developing rapidly in this period due to the new, inexpensive halftone reproduction process. The complicated lineage of such photographs suggests that there were few rules about how publishers could use this material to suit their needs and that photographers had little control over the use of their work once they had sold it.

A number of other talented professional photographers, perhaps lesser known but no less important, produced some excellent work on the Exposition without any such fanfare or patronage. Ernest Edwards, the editor of *Sun and Shade,* published a portfolio of exceptional photogravures for the special December issue of his unusual fine-art and photography journal.[38] There he demonstrated his skill in laying out images on the page and including hand-drawn details in some of the photogravure plates. In the example shown in Figure 4.7, note the tightly composed view taken from the Machinery Building, incorporating as it does the pillar with its ornamental prows in the foreground to balance the heavy horizontal facade of the immense Manufactures and Liberal Arts Building and the horizontal sweep of water in the main basin of the Court of Honor. Almost unnoticed is the small gondola approaching the balustraded pier, repeated in the magazine in a similar image below that focuses the spectator's viewpoint in a cinematic way.

The general commercial work of Thomas Harrison, a local Chicago professional photographer, showed a noticeably consistent production superior to that available from the Department of Photography.[39] The photograph in Figure 4.8, also made from the Machinery Building but toward the North Canal along the length of the Manufactures and Liberal Arts Building, retains its sharpness and clear tones even today, with no muddiness or yellowing deterioration, which indicate poor-quality

processing. Harrison, like most enterprising professionals, including F. Dundas Todd, marketed individual prints as well as published work in mass-produced souvenir publications. Such efforts are noteworthy because they were the work of independent professionals and were made under less-than-ideal conditions, probably without the aid of elaborate equipment, tripods, or large-format cameras.

Providing the press with photographs of the Exposition was one of the responsibilities of the Department of Photography because official restrictions initially prohibited outside photographic press work on the Exposition grounds.[40] In a period when the technology of inexpensive illustration was expanding rapidly, photographs were in great demand as feature material in illustrated journals and newspapers. The department was expected to furnish photographs on a special commission basis to newspapers, but this process did not run smoothly. Moses Handy, the Exposition's director of publicity and a prominent Philadelphia journalist, reported that there were "complaints from publishers everywhere regarding their treatment by Mr. Arnold."[41] The uneasy relationship between Arnold and the press dramatized the struggle over the administration's control of photographic practice. Not surprisingly, Arnold was targeted for his "autocratic" role, as in the cartoon shown in Figure 4.9. Public sensitivity to the issue of monopolistic power was very strong in the 1890s, and Arnold's dealings were of great interest to an audience whose popular tastes had been shaped by the muckraking press. The photographic journals were also incensed over Arnold's "created" position as official photographer, a situation that caused deep resentment in a photographic community well aware that such procedures had not been followed at previous events.[42]

Arnold's arbitrary dealings with the press were the subject of a May 1893 investigation by the Committee on Photography of the World's Columbian Commission, the national administrative branch in Washington. The committee's report concluded that the complaints were well founded. Arnold's dealings with the press, the report went on, were "unfair, unjust and practically prohibitive in their effect."[43] It was further recommended that all information on Arnold's contract and operations be forwarded to the commission in Washington for review. The absence of cooperation between the national and local Exposition administrators was reflected in the powerful and uncritical support the Chicago board wielded in favor of Arnold. The well-known illustrated

FIGURE 4.8   Thomas Harrison, a professional photographer in Chicago, produced consistently good commercial prints like this view from the Machinery Building looking north toward the North Canal along the Manufactures and Liberal Arts Building. (Aristotype print, 11 cm x 16.3 cm; courtesy of the Chicago Historical Society, Prints and Photographs Department, ICHI-23463)

publications *Harpers, Leslie's Illustrated Weekly, Youth's Companion, The Illustrated World's Fair, World's Columbian Exposition Illustrated, Graphic,* and the *Inland Architect* were granted permission to use cameras without charge but were required to apply daily to the photography concessionaire for a permit. H. L. Aldrich of the *Scientific American* was not treated as fairly: four times during May he unsuccessfully applied to Director Davis for permission for his photographer to use a camera larger than 4″ x 5″ on the grounds, a permission subsequently granted to other illustrated publications.[44] Davis did not give Aldrich permission until August 5 despite directives to do so from the national commission and from Oscar R. Hundley, a representative from Alabama and head of the national committee. The policy of restricting photographs to a single official source was simply unacceptable to the press, which demanded diversity as well as access. Their response was immediate, vocal, and effective in removing the restrictions imposed by the officials of the Chicago board.

Individual Commercial Concessions: Competing Imagery

While the Department of Photography controlled the major production of photographic prints and lantern slides for commercial distribution at the World's Columbian Exposition, it chose not to offer products in several other photographic formats. This was another departure from previous exposition concessions, which had provided the full range of stereographs, prints, lantern slides, and passbook portraits. Since concessions were the major source of income for the board, maximizing their sales was in its best interest, although it was still necessary to protect its own photographic department from significant competition.

Stereographs, whose popularity had generally declined in the 1880s, once again become popular in the final decade of the century. They had regained their sense of visual novelty and offered a wider range of subject matter than general photographic prints. Further, their captions contributed significantly to their popular appeal since they were often viewed in a parlor or living room. Their three-dimensional images were well suited to representing the displays in the various buildings, special events, and general scenes of spectators. As a result of the mass production and marketing techniques introduced in the 1880s and 1890s, the industry was both thriving and highly competitive.[45] As a specialty item, the Department of Photography had made some stereographs in 1892, but it decided it would be better to sell the concession. The successful bid was that of the B. W. Kilburn Company, a New Hampshire firm, although the bid of its closest competitor, Underwood & Underwood, was not far behind.[46] The firm—owned by Benjamin W. Kilburn (Fig. 4.10) and his brother Edward—employed about a hundred assistants to do its developing and printing in a four-story factory in Littleton, which was capable of producing more than five million photographs a year. Kilburn used a camera from the American Optical Company and a Henry Clay stereo camera for handwork during the Exposition. Kilburn's enterprising agent, James Davis, was responsible for the purchase of the concession.[47] The purchase agreement called for Kilburn to pay $17,000 in cash and return a percentage of the gross profits—a far cry from the $5,000 James Wilson and his colleagues had invested in similar concessions in 1876 and 1885.

FIGURE 4.10   Benjamin W. Kilburn, whose firm paid a high price for the stereograph concession at the Exposition, had the exclusive right to produce stereographs of the Exposition, but in practice he could not prevent numerous professional photographers from marketing commercial stereographs. (Photogravure, 17.5 cm × 18.8 cm, by Kimball; *Photographic Times* 23 [May 19, 1893]: front.; courtesy of the George Eastman House, International Museum of Photography and Film; Library Collection)

FIGURE 4.9   In this editorial cartoon, Director General Davis triumphs rather easily over the autocratic Charles D. Arnold. The cartoon reflects Arnold's unfavorable relations with the public, especially the press. (From Pierce, *Photographic History of the World's Fair*, 434)

Kilburn's stereo views were to be sold exclusively through the Department of Photography at a fixed price of two dollars a dozen. With 1,400 to 1,500 titled views, each of which had three or four duplicate negatives, Kilburn's output was prodigious. According to William Darrah, however, the quality of his stereos had suffered by the 1890s because of his use of dryplates, which tended to reduce the tonal contrast in the prints and decrease the impact of the stereo effect.[48] Each stereo view was made up of two albumen prints pasted on a card, with a printed caption that included a number, a title, and a copyright statement. In making stereographs, most photographers employed a formula that relied on emphasizing a dark foreground feature and enhancing diagonal lines to increase the three-dimensional appearance of the image. Louis H. Melander used this style of selecting dark foreground features in a number of views for a series of 125 stereos on the Exposition

FIGURE 4.11 One of the most popular of Kilburn's stereo-graphs, this photograph of the opening day of the Exposition has the apt title *The Surging Sea of Humanity*. (Albumen print, ster-eograph no. 7929, 7.7 cm x 7.7 cm; courtesy of Charles Rand Penney, World's Columbian Exposition Collection)

copyrighted in March 1894. They show the sites after the closing of the Exposition when the fountains were empty and spectators had departed.[49]

Kilburn's Exposition views, in contrast, did not ex-ploit this device to nearly the same extent. His crowd portrait, *The Surging Sea of Humanity* (Fig. 4.11), made on opening day, was a key image of the Exposition. Opening day, with its attendant crush and excitement, drew numerous photographers, though conditions were certainly less than ideal. One eyewitness noted that three photographers were present with "cameras mounted on poles" above the heads of the crowd, who at first seemed intrigued with what they were doing but then made fun of them.[50] In Kilburn's stereograph the viewer can identify directly with the physical experience of the Exposition, especially the pushing crowds of on-lookers, momentarily caught during their rush. Tom Heseltine speculates that, based on the number of ex-tant copies available, this view may have been used as a premium or gift.[51] The crowd theme was also used by other commercial stereo makers, like Strohmeyer and Wyman, and by the lantern-slide maker T. H. McAllis-ter.[52]

The spectacular fire at the cold-storage building on July 10 (Fig. 4.12)—a tragedy in which fifteen firemen were killed—was the only commercial disaster image to result from the Exposition. The building housed perish-able goods and the Exposition's ice-making machinery, and its upper floors had a restaurant and a novelty ice-skating rink. The fire began at 1:30 in the afternoon in a dome section of the tower housing the machinery. The fifteen firemen who were killed had proceeded to the tower balcony to put out the blaze but were trapped by a second blaze that erupted from below, and only two were able to slide down ropes to safety.[53] Caroline Barrett White, one of the witnesses to the tragedy from the roof of the Manufactures and Liberal Arts Building, wrote that they were unaware that "the pieces of charred debris falling, were human beings falling or jumping into the seething pit below."[54] The impact and unique-ness of the tragedy was such that most of the major Exposition pictorial publications carried at least one photograph of the fire.

Another subject treated in the stereo format was the popular theme of celebratory nationalism associated with the Exposition. Patriotic views featured the Ameri-

FIGURE 4.12 Kilburn's stereograph of the burning of the cold-storage building in July 1893, in which fifteen firemen lost their lives, was the only disaster subject represented in connection with the Exposition. (Albumen prints, stereograph no. 8232, 7.9 cm x 7.9 cm; courtesy of American Antiquarian Society)

can flag as seen from the Administration Building and included such captions as "Long may it wave in peace, never in war."[55] The centrality of the American flag in views like that shown in Figure 4.19 repeats the composition device and viewpoint that was used by Arnold, Jackson, Kilburn, and others and reproduced in different versions in nearly all the pictorial publications. The school-flag movement and Francis Bellamy's newly written Pledge of Allegiance, intended to honor the Columbian anniversary, reinforced the popularity of this view.[56]

The similarly popular idea of the Exposition as a dream world had been successfully promoted by several writers. Charles Robinson, for example, called the Exposition a "Dream City," a place where "the dreamer is a magician with limitless power."[57] Photographers sought to capture this elusive theme in their stereographs, but they were much less successful since the conventional understanding of photography was that it created an illusion of visual reality rather than of the creative imagination. Nevertheless, several of Kilburn's stereographs did evoke this theme and had captions like "I dream of the Beautiful," "Fairy Land," and "Enchanted Dream."

Kilburn's stereo concession was officially protected by the regulation that banned other stereographic cameras from the grounds of the Exposition, but in practice this did not prevent either commercial productions by other photographers or their copyrighting of such productions. The firm of Underwood & Underwood had proved that it was technically as well as commercially possible to make stereos from two conventional 4" x 5" camera images set side by side, and even amateurs were given advice about how to do this at the Exposition. Using such a simple approach, Underwood and a number of other commercial firms produced their own sets of stereos, including such leading firms as Strohmeyer & Wyman of New York, J. F. Jarvis of Washington, D.C., H. H. Bennett of Wisconsin, and Webster & Albee of Rochester, New York.[58] Still other commercial stereograph companies simply refused to comply with the prohibition of stereo cameras. In response, Kilburn brought at least one civil suit against his competitors, and this was against his formidable rival Underwood & Underwood.[59] The suit—*Kilburn & Davis* v. *Underwood*—was argued in U.S. District Court in New York, and it pitted the two leading stereo firms in the country against each other.

FIGURE 4.13 One of James J. Gibson's official photographic passes, in this case for an assistant in the model kitchen of the Woman's Building. (Albumen print, 4 cm diameter, by J. J. Gibson; courtesy of Charles Rand Penney, World's Columbian Exposition Collection)

The Underwood bid for the stereo concession at the Exposition had been just $2,000 short of Kilburn's, but the administration's restrictions banned the firm from publishing its prints. The suit was resolved in favor of Kilburn and Davis.

The number of photographic companies that made Exposition photographs indicates that the administrators' efforts to control and incorporate commercial photographic practices at the Exposition were futile. The determination of professional photographers was fueled by a consumer public that was oblivious to the Exposition administrators' efforts to manipulate the commercially available photographic products. One important example of this enterprising and entrepreneurial branch of professional photography that has not previously been noted by historians derived from the concession to provide photographic passes of the kind shown in Figure 4.13. The passes were considered necessary for identifying staff members and ensuring orderly admissions, but the Department of Photography did not provide this service, probably because it was considered too tedious and repetitive. James J. Gibson, however—a Canadian portrait photographer who was then working in Ann Arbor, Michigan—transformed it into a thriving and

substantial business. Gibson had initially contracted to do the photographic-pass work for free with the understanding that additional portraits that visitors ordered would reimburse him for his services.[60] Unlike Arnold and Higinbotham, he was required to erect his own studio building, located at the 62d Street entrance to the Exposition, just east of the Department of Photography. Before its completion he used one of the galleries of the Horticulture Hall for his work.

Gibson's financial arrangement with the board was modified once the realities of his workload became apparent. The Department of Admissions eventually reimbursed him ten cents per negative for the production of more than 79,000 photo passbooks. Gibson's staff included two operators, two printers, two retouchers, a finisher, and two receptionists, as well as his wife, May Clark Gibson, as manager. On Gibson's death from tuberculosis ten years later, his wife took over the operation of the successful studio. Photo passbooks were issued to the majority of those admitted free, including the top administrators, foreign commissioners, exhibitors, employees, and concessionaires, although not everyone acquiesced easily to having his or her photograph made for this purpose. There were those who felt it "an indignity to be compelled to identify himself by a photograph to enter the grounds."[61] The work began in March 1893 and preceded at a rate of twenty to fifty photographs a day. By April this had increased to three hundred to nine hundred a day, and it later reached a daily rate of fifteen hundred portraits. Three copies of each portrait were required, with one to be attached to the passbook and the other two for use by Exposition officials. There was no cost to the individual, although people could purchase additional commercial prints from their portraits. The board permitted this as part of the original agreement provided that the extra portrait work did not interfere with the primary service.

It was Gibson's outside portrait work that gave him a real opportunity to demonstrate his talents as a photographer. His clientele included not only the employees and officials previously noted but also exhibitors and visitors to the Exposition (Fig. 4.14). Sylvester R. Koehler, curator of graphic arts at the Smithsonian, for example, ordered an additional six photographs for $1.50 along with his passbook photographs, with the assurance that they would be forwarded to him within a week, although they still had not arrived a month later.[62] Gibson advertised his "first-class" portraits as the "finest souvenir you can take home," and attracted dignitaries like the Duke of Veragua and his son, whose portraits he copyrighted. The special focus of Gibson's commercial portrait work, however, were the members of the various countries represented on the Midway Plaisance, the arm of the Exposition devoted to entertainment concessions and displays of various national groups. Collections of these portraits by Gibson were published in *The Chicago Times Portfolio of the Midway Types* and in J. W. Buel's *The Magic City*.[63] This was a period when foreign nationalities were often perceived, and represented, as stereotypes and when popular journalistic writing catered to the less-than-tolerant prevailing attitudes. To Gibson's credit, his portraits—especially those of the different national groups represented on the Midway— were distinctively individual, empathetic, and dignified in their portrayal. His portrait, for example, of an Algerian dancer, one of the performers of the controversial "danse-du-ventre" on the Midway Plaisance (Fig. 4.15), was devoid of any reference to the exotic, sensual, or physical aspects of the dance, aspects that were of-

FIGURE 4.15 James Gibson's graceful and dignified portrait of an Algerian dancer differed from the more stereotypical representations by other commercial photographers of the many nationalities working on the Midway. (Halftone reproduction, 12.5 cm x 19 cm; *The Chicago Times Portfolio of the Midway Types*, pt. 2; courtesy of the Chicago Historical Society; Library Collection)

FIGURE 4.14 An unidentified member of the Columbian Guards posed for this photograph, an example of Gibson's commercial portrait work, which he conducted in conjunction with the thousands of passbook photographs his staff produced. (Albumen print, 14 cm x 10 cm; courtesy of the Chicago Historical Society; Gibson Collection, folder 2, ICHI-23459)

ten exploited in journalistic accounts.[64] Gibson's photographs of these subjects also contrasted sharply with the conventional representations of Middle Eastern women that overseas commercial firms constructed and produced through the lens of colonialism for the tourist trade. The widely reproduced photograph *The Dancers of Cairo Street*, for example, lacked all the positive features of Gibson's portraits, instead feeding the rhetoric that dismissed the women as being as "graceless as stall-fed bovines."[65] Gibson was by no means the only professional photographer to photograph people who appeared along the Midway. Place and Coover, another Chicago photographic firm, produced an extensive collection of Midway portraits that provided the major part of the photographs for a popular portfolio whose more informative text was provided by F. W. Putnam, head of the Anthropology Department.[66]

In addition to the major photographic concessions, it was possible to obtain permission to sell prints or souvenirs on the grounds of the Exposition by applying directly to the Ways and Means Committee of the Chicago board. Registration required giving the board a percentage of the receipts from such sales, but permission was regularly granted throughout the life of the Exposition. A number of requests were submitted for permission to sell photographs of local sites in various state buildings, including those of Kansas, Michigan, Washington, and Montana. These included requests like that from Ida J. Burgess, a Chicago artist, to sell, in the Illinois Building, photogravure albums of the celebrated decorative frieze in the Woman's Building reception rooms.[67] Her request was granted, but she had to pay the standard 25 percent commission fee to the board. H. Jay Smith & Company of Minneapolis, which was responsible for creating the cliffdwellers display shown

in Figure 4.16, requested permission to sell souvenir photographs at its popular attraction. The sixty-five-foot-high exterior structure, made of staff, building paper, and iron, was a re-creation of Battle Rock Mountain in southwestern Colorado. Inside were displays of original artifacts and reproductions of prehistoric Indian rock tombs and ceremonial and settlement complexes such as the Cliff Palace.[68] These models had been made to one-tenth scale from photographs and drawings the Smith Company had made at the time that the surveying and collecting of artifacts was being done at the site. The firm included many of them in its published catalogue and also sold them as prints. The income generated for the board from these small enterprises was negligible, but the restrictive effect on photography in general at the Exposition was significant.

Considering the detail in which such restrictions on photography were enacted, it is surprising that Arnold

FIGURE 4.16   The cliffdwellers re-creation outside the Anthropological Building proved profitable for its creator, H. Jay Smith & Company of Minneapolis, both from the admission fees it generated and the sale of photographs of the structure, the exhibits inside, and even reproductions of the prints and drawings used to create them. (Photogravure, 13.5 cm × 19 cm, by C. D. Arnold and H. D. Higinbotham; World's Columbian Exposition, *Official Views of the World's Columbian Exposition,* pl. 90, courtesy of Charles Rand Penney, World's Columbian Exposition Collection)

FIGURE 4.17   Because of the restrictions on the use of cameras, few photographers were ever permitted to work with large-view plate cameras of the type shown here. The unidentified photographer, possibly a foreign amateur, was presumably suffi-ciently important to be photographed doing just what others were forbidden to do. (Albumen print 17.3 cm × 25 cm, by C. D. Arnold; courtesy of the Chicago Historical Society; Prints and Photographs Department, Vertical File, ICHI-19617)

made available one of his own copyrighted views showing an unidentified photographer working with a plate camera and a tripod on the Midway (see Fig. 4.17). According to one report in May, only one permit had been issued, and that was by the president of the board, Higinbotham, to the Duke of Newcastle allowing him to photograph anywhere on the grounds with his 8″ × 10″ camera and tripod.[69] Clearly, in order to circumvent the system of controls on photography, it was necessary either to be somebody important or to be adept at defeating the system with ingenuity, which is what many professional and amateur photographers attempted to do.

The Federal Government's Exposition Photographs

The Chicago board's restrictions on photography and the inconsistent quality of the work by the Department of Photography were certainly factors that caused the Government Board of Management for the Exposition to set up its own Committee on Photography. The board had been appointed by the president from members of the nine government departments and was responsible for the displays located in the Government Building. Major Clifton Comly, the representative of the War Department, was chairman of the Government Board's Committee on Photography, with Lieutenant Henry L. Harris of the 1st Artillery as his assistant. According to Harris, the photography project was created to ensure "that the Government should have in its possession as complete a collection of views of the more important features of the Exposition—more particularly of course of the Government Exhibit proper."[70] More than 700 photographic negatives were made for the Government Board's Committee on Photography, including many in duplicate sizes. The committee ceased to exist following Comly's death in April 1894, although Harris continued the work of preparing photographic prints for use by the various departments in their reports.

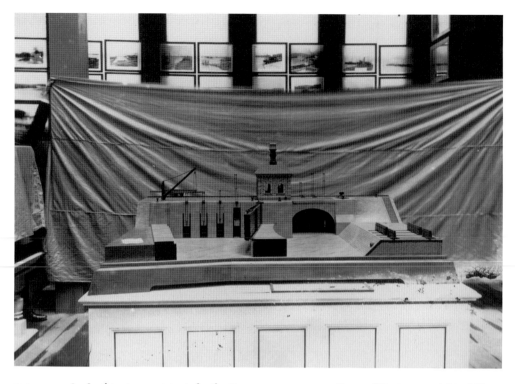

FIGURE 4.18   In this view, assistants for the Government Board's Committee on Photography hold up a backdrop to improve, modestly, the conditions for photographing a model of the Des Moines Rapids Dry Dock on the Mississippi River in the Corps of Engineers exhibit. (Albumen print, 15 cm x 20 cm, negative by the Government Board's Committee on Photography; RG 77E, 111-RB-3344, box 24, Records of the Office of Chief of Engineers, Still Pictures Branch, National Archives)

The work of making the negatives was a three-part collaboration among Thomas Smillie, Frances Benjamin Johnston, and Harris. Smillie, the Smithsonian photographer, had trained a number of other photographers, including amateurs and staff members of other government departments. Frances Benjamin Johnston was one of his students in 1888 and 1889.[71] Both Johnston and Smillie were professionals, while the extent of Harris's photographic experience is unknown. As a freelance Washington journalist and photographer, Johnston had done work for various government agencies, such as the Department of Agriculture, the Fish and Fisheries Commission, and the Treasury in preparation for the Exposition.[72] She had already completed one journalism assignment on the Exposition in 1892 for an article in *Demorest's Family Magazine,* which included a number of her own photographs along with portraits by other photographers and possibly some of Arnold's own views. She became a friend of Arnold's at this time, and exchanged a number of letters with him between December 1891 and June 1892. Johnston had also approached Moses Handy, the Exposition's chairman of publicity, on the feasibility

of supplying commissioners with camera outfits, probably on behalf of the Eastman Kodak Company, in January 1891.[73]

Smillie received his authorization to photograph at the Exposition in late September with the provision that "neither the negative, nor any prints there from, be sold or offered for sale," which was similar to the limitation placed on Grabill for work in the Anthropological Building.[74] Presumably, Smillie's work was done at the same time that Johnston and Harris were working together on views of the Indian school exhibits in the Alaska Gallery of the Government Building.[75] The three photographers must have followed a coordinated schedule to conduct the extensive photographic work required. This was no ordinary photographic record—it was composed of 62 20" x 24" negatives, 150 11" x 14" negatives, 427 8" x 10" negatives, and 95 6" x 8" negatives.[76] A number of these were repeated in different format sizes.

The representatives from the government departments were requested to specify the number of prints required and "to arrange the exhibits so designated with a view to their being photographed."[77] The Departments of State, Interior, Treasury, the Navy, and the Post Office, plus the Fish and Fisheries Commission, all requested such material. Not surprisingly, the largest number of photographs was made for the War Department and the Smithsonian Institution.

Photographing the exhibits in the Government Building was technically difficult because of uneven lighting conditions, especially because some displays had been located adjacent to windows that did not have sufficient shutters. Harris noted the problems, particularly in dealing with reflections and cross-lighting, that he had encountered during his work with Johnston at the Alaska Gallery. To minimize these conditions, the photographers had assistants hold up special backdrop cloths or set up backboards, especially in photographing the Corps of Engineers' technical models, discussed in chapter 3. An example of the limited utility of the backdrops is shown in Figure 4.18. In preparing the images to be used for the departmental albums and prints, the figures holding the cloths were generally cropped out, leaving just the image of the individual models.

The second type of photograph made for the Government Board's Committee on Photography was of the Exposition's prime locations and buildings. These photographs were executed in a large format using 20″ × 24″ or 11″ × 14″ negatives. They were generally printed on platinum paper, with the work being done by Johnston, who was in charge of such printing. The collaborative

FIGURE 4.19 Thomas Smillie made this dramatic view of the Court of Honor from the balcony of the Administration Building. It incorporated much of the celebratory nationalism of the Exposition as a whole, and it was repeated by the official photographer. (Platinum print, 51.8 cm × 51.8 cm, negative by the Government Board's Committee on Photography; cat. no. 3320.c, Division of Photographic History, National Museum of American History, Smithsonian Institution)

FIGURE 4.20   One of a series of views Frances Benjamin Johnston made of the entrance to the Transportation Building, which was designed by Louis Sullivan. This photograph was part of the work Johnson did for the Government Board's Com-mittee on Photography. (Cyanotype print, 28 cm x 35.5 cm; RU 70, box 64, folder 3/6, neg. no. 12317; Smithsonian Institution Archives)

nature of the project has made any identification of the authorship of individual negatives provisional except in a few cases. Only 10 of the 62 20″ x 24″ prints have been located. Six carry Smillie's name, including one taken from under the balcony of the Administration Build-ing.[78] Using this viewpoint, which required consider-able climbing, was permitted only by special arrange-ment because, following the disastrous fire at the cold-storage building, the public was not allowed onto the balcony. The dramatic sweep looking out onto the Court of Honor and the Statue of the Republic, seen in Figure 4.19, was enhanced by the lengthening shadows from the west, which created just the necessary degree of foreground darkness. This photograph was a visual rep-

resentation of the rhetoric of celebratory nationalism that was so much a part of the Exposition and that was, not surprisingly, repeated in versions by both Arnold and Jackson. It is no. 46 in the series listed in the catalogue of prints Harris forwarded to the secretary of war in October 1894 as part of the War Department's official Exposition report. Other views also attributed to Smillie and now in the Smithsonian's Division of Photography include two of the ship *Illinois* made from the top of the Government Building, a view of the Machinery Building from the colonnade of the South Canal, and another of the Administration Building and the basin.

Some of Johnston's photographs can be authenticated because of their use as illustrations in a book on the work of Connecticut women at the Fair.[79] While these were only small halftone reproductions, the original 11" × 14" plates are impressive and striking. The images included a succession of views, taken minutes apart, of the striking obelisk in the south basin colonnade and the spectacular gilded entrance of the Transportation Building (Fig. 4.20). A variant view taken minutes before or after the exposure shows a group of ducks in the foreground, and Johnston made a second series of photographs farther back from the bridge to the wooded island. This viewpoint, from the back corner of the Mines Building, was similar to that Dundas Todd recommended for "artistic" work by photographers, especially amateur photographers.[80] But it was its scale and Johnston's careful working style which distinguish this image. Her practice of making successive exposures, sometimes only minutes apart, to obtain variations of the same scene ensured that she would have a quality choice for later use.

Following the completion of the photographic work at the Exhibition, the government negatives were removed to Washington and eventually came under Harris's control. Harris and Johnston jointly undertook the work of preparing the prints for albums and reports. Harris had his laboratory and studio in operation by mid-December of 1893 at the Ordnance Department Arsenal on Governor's Island in New York. He was assisted by Charles J. Hanson, also of the 1st Artillery, who had been seconded to work with the Exposition material since November 1893.[81] Johnston, working in her Washington studio, assumed responsibility for printing the 20" × 24" negatives. She also completed numerous orders for platinum prints, because Harris had little skill with this printing process.[82]

Their photographs provided the illustrations for the government departments' reports to the Government Board. The War Department's report, "with accompanying sub-reports and photographs," prepared by Harris after months of work, was finally submitted in October 1894.[83] No trace remains of the original report, or that of the Corps of Engineers, which also included a large number of photographs. A set of eight albums, with many photographs with titles identical to those included in the above reports, originally belonged to the Treasury and War Departments.[84] These albums were assembled as a group and include both general views and photographs of displays executed on platinum, aristotype, and albumen papers in 8" × 10" and 11" × 14" formats. In addition to this collection, the National Archives also holds a large selection of duplicate Committee on Pho-

tography material, possibly made from the original negatives at a later date.

Photographs made for the various government departments included those showing the display of the Army Medical Museum. A total of 346 photomicrographs were featured in the display, several of which were in frames on the walls.[85] Arranged by Dr. William M. Gray of the Army Medical Museum, this display appeared in the Army Medical Building, which was adjacent to the Government Building, where apparatus of its anthropometric work was also included. This exhibit would have been of interest to visitors who had seen the working laboratory in the Anthropological Building, discussed in chapter 3.

The Signal Corps exhibits concentrated on the full-size diorama of the Arctic explorations of 1881 through 1884. This diorama was a composite of events showing Lieutenant Adolphus W. Greely formally shaking hands with Lieutenant Lockwood, who reached the farthest point north but who later died with others while waiting for supplies.[86] Also on view were photographic enlargements from the Arctic negatives as well as large oil paintings of, and artifacts from, the expedition. Absent from the photographs and the diorama were the realities of the disastrous expedition: the starving condition of Greely and the other seven survivors, and the frozen bodies of Lockwood and other members of the expedition. The sensibilities of viewers were protected from such realism by the artificial construct of the diorama and the careful editing of photographs. The staged or recreated historical event was so popular that, after closing in Chicago, the diorama was forwarded to the 1894 Mid-Winter Exhibition in San Francisco.

Popular interest in three-dimensional displays extended to exhibits like the large reproduction of the Battle of Gettysburg at Panorama Place and the reconstruction of the Civil War–era Libby Prison in Richmond, both feature events just outside the Exposition grounds.[87] In addition, the War Department's National Military Parks prepared an extensive display of photographs of Civil War battlefields. These were placed in various sections, with topographical models of Chickamauga, Chattanooga, Gettysburg, and Vicksburg. On the walls were exhibits of statistics and framed photographs of the sites, as shown in Figure 4.21.

The stunning nature and quality of the general-view photographs of the Exposition, like that reproduced in Figure 4.22, prompted Harris to propose that a portfolio be produced that would feature them.[88] His proposal was

FIGURE 4.21   The display of photographs of Civil War sites by the National Military Parks was one of many responses to the public's interest in this historic event. Here photographs of the Chickamauga and Chattanooga battlefields accompany a large to-pographic model of the area. (Gelatin print, 18.5 cm x 23 cm, negative by the Government Board's Committee on Photography; RG 111-RB-3324, box 23, Still Pictures Branch, National Archives)

not taken up, however, most likely because after Comly's untimely death Harris was forced to take on the responsibility of preparing the extensive written report of the War Department, which severely limited his time for photography. Nearly all the large-format 20″ x 24″ negatives would have been ideal for the proposed portfolio. They were also useful in "pictorial" view albums, which were in demand for official and semi-official purposes. Harris received numerous individual orders from government departments for the large-format prints. Most were printed by Johnston in platinum, and several were made into albums of 11″ x 14″ print-size. Among others, an order from Major General Howard for 250 11″ x 14″ prints and another 120 20″ x 24″ prints is a tantalizing suggestion of the existence of additional photographic

material not yet located.[89] Certainly the extent and quality of the large collection of surviving photographs from the Government Board's Committee on Photography testifies to the professionalism of the photographers involved.

The negatives from the project were government property, and Harris was scrupulous in maintaining control over their use. He did allow Johnston and Smillie to make lantern slides for their own use, and Johnston seems to have interpreted the policy somewhat liberally, acquiring her own collection of negatives at the same time that she executed her government contract. With respect to outsiders, Harris expressed concern over the possible pirating of the government material,[90] which may in fact have occurred in connection with the Chi-

FIGURE 4.22   One of the excellent photographs produced by
the Government Board's Committee on Photography, in this case
a corner of the Manufactures and Liberal Arts Building from the
Wooded Island. (Original negative, 19 cm × 25 cm; Smithsonian
Institution, Photo No. 12155)

cago firm responsible for processing some of the negatives. Harris hired S. E. Norton, of the firm of Bolton & Company, in early November 1893 to make prints from the negatives, and some of them were apparently copied or reused before being returned.[91] Given the financial instability of some photographic businesses and the opportunities for publishing such material, it is not surprising that at least one eager photographic company would take advantage of the situation.

The individual government departments were to receive the negatives related to their own exhibits as part of their agreement to share the $1,000 cost of the photography project. The U.S. National Museum of the Smithsonian was especially insistent on the transfer of its negatives, and in any case Harris realized the value of the negative collection, especially the general Exposition views, and suggested that the National Museum would be the best repository for them.[92] The existing collection of 11" × 14" and 8" × 10" cyanotype contact prints in the Smithsonian Archives indicates that many of the original negatives were in the institution's collection until recently. Indeed, some of the original 8" × 10" Exposition negatives are held in the Smithsonian's Office of Printing and Photographic Services, although the location of a number of 11" × 14" negatives copied in a 4" × 5" format in 1973 is unknown.[93] None of the larger 20" × 24" negatives of the general Exposition views have been found. They may be part of a group of large-format Exposition negatives held in the Smithsonian's Division of Photographic History and unavailable at the time of this study.

Clearly, the Government Board photographers were not part of the conflict between official and commercial photography at the Exposition. They were not subject to restrictions on their work that were designed to favor official over commercial practice and to protect the investment made by the Exposition's administration. Nevertheless, the photographs made for the Government Board and those for the Chicago board served similar functions in providing records for eventual use in official reports of the Exposition as well as pictures for various official and semi-official presentation albums. The main difference between the two projects was the complete lack of commercial exploitation of the government photographs. These photographs never entered the large visual pool that formed the public memory of the Exposition. The photographs that did fulfill this purpose came from the mass of diverse images produced commercially—and independently—for a general audience. Whether as stereographs, lantern slides, portraits, or souvenir publications, these images provided the necessary complement to the narrowly focused commercial work of the official Department of Photography.

5

MAKING ALTERNATIVE IMAGES
Amateur Photography at the Exposition

And as I sit in my easy chair thinking of the benefits of photography to stay-at-homes, as well as to visitors, I cannot help wondering what kind of a photographic representation the Fair would have had without the efforts of amateurs.
                                                                    M. Y. BEACH in *American Amateur Photographer*[1]

There is no question that amateur photography was more adept at representing the ephemeral event that was the Exposition than were the official, government, and commercial photography discussed to this point. The amateurs provided a new stylistic element, a wider range of content, and a more diverse use of formats. Both the newly emerging photographic industry and the rapidly developing consumer culture had dramatically accelerated the growth of amateur photography. In a period when the individual was being incorporated into powerful industrial and social processes, so too was the amateur photographer being swept by the same tide in the industrialization in its own practices.[2]

While the presence of amateur photographers was not a recent phenomenon at major public events, their presence at the Exposition was pervasive. They were not, however, a homogeneous population. The term *amateur* was like "a certain robe which covers a multitude of sins," and according to Catharine Barnes, a spokesperson for the amateurs, there were "species" of amateurs just as there were of professionals.[3] Ward never accepted the growing polarization into factions among the different groups of photographers, especially that between professionals and amateurs. The most recent and largest amateur population consisted of the photographic consumers, who were a conscious creation of the photographic manufacturers. These photographers did not need to possess any great knowledge of technique, chemistry, or art since most camera manuals were written without lengthy technical instructions. In journals, ad-

vertisements, and books, members of the new breed of photographer were often labeled "push button amateurs," "snappers," "kodakers" or even "camera fiends."[4]

Another species of amateur photographer, and the traditional backbone of the photographic community, consisted of the self-trained, loyal participants in the local photographic societies. These societies had a life of their own, extending even to the formation of "type" behaviors among their members. There was the "pot-hunter," who sought only the medals and trophies of competition, the "investigator," who dabbled in the newest inventions, as well as the "Faddist," the "Base Imitator," and the "Punster."[5] The societies' exhibitions, lectures, and discussions provided a form of training in which it was possible, as well as desirable, to produce a popular form of "artistic" photography. Supported as they were by the photographic journals with articles on picture-making techniques, the societies popularized the notion that amateurs could apply artistic techniques to photography through proper study and practice.[6] These photographers were "men and women of means and leisure," according to Horace Markley, with both a "professional and artistic temperament" and "keen judgment in matters pertaining to art."[7]

The third species of amateur, only beginning to be formed in this period, attempted to go beyond the popular artistic formula to the "aesthetic" mode, which derived from current trends in the fine arts. These photographers, who identified themselves as "capable amateurs" or "serious workers," were seeking to transform a technique into a craft. Their attempt to distance themselves from both the consumerism and the popular artistic photography of the two former groups was producing a serious fracture in the practice of amateur photography that would have repercussions for the next two decades. These were the amateurs who had been prominent at the May 1893 Exhibition in Philadelphia, and their absence from the displays of photography at the Exposition was an important indication of their rejection of the industrial, commercial, and popular aspects of photographic practice.

Set down in the midst of this fracturing of amateur photography was the contest of strength with the Exposition's administrators over the imposition of restrictions on the practice of photography. Taken as a whole, the various amateur groups—the created consumers, the traditional amateurs, and the aspiring aesthetes—represented a significant number of individuals drawn from a broad spectrum of the general public. What prevented them from forming a useful and effective alliance in opposition to the heavy-handed tactics of the administration was the lack of a coherent social or political focus for their activities. They were unprepared for the contest, which required coordination with professional photographers and manufacturers because administration officials refused to distinguish between amateurs and commercial photographers, who were considered a threat to the success of the board's own official photographic concession. Nevertheless, though placing restrictions on photographers may have been a technical victory for the corporate-thinking administrators, it did not dampen the enthusiasm of the ingenious, enterprising, and individualistic amateur practitioners.

Regulating Photography: The Exposition at Two Dollars a Day

Exposition rhetoric sought to promote the image of "The Fair as Educator," which for photography was a challenge that it be not just a pictorial entertainment but a tool for illustration, information, and recording. Some members of the photographic community saw the photograph as analogous to the pencil and notebook traditionally used by travelers and students for these very purposes, and as the amateur photographer C. D. Irwin said, people simply believed they had the right to photograph at the Exposition.[8]

In the early summer 1892 the impending regulations regarding camera size and fees caused considerable consternation among interested amateurs. The American

Photographic League, successor to the American Photographic Conference, drew on a national network of amateur societies for support in its protest. In August 1892 a petition with 3,261 signatures from forty-eight clubs and societies in the United States and Canada, as well as eighteen British and French organizations, was presented to the Ways and Means Committee of the Chicago board.[9] Further, the international nature of the Chicago event drew protests from overseas participants, including the British Photographic Convention, which passed a resolution opposing the restrictions, and the commission member from Great Britain, Sir Henry Trueman Wood, who was a keen amateur photographer.[10] This mobilization of public opinion resulted from the efforts of individuals like F. C. Beach, one of the founders of the Society of Amateur Photographers in New York and editor of the *American Amateur Photographer*. Just as Wilson had done during the Centennial, Beach badgered, bullied and agitated for public support. Throughout 1892 and 1893 he called on amateurs "to make it hot for the officials," and in late 1892 he orchestrated moves—through the Honorable John Boyd Thatcher, an amateur photographer and a New York State member on the national commission in Washington—to remove the restrictions.[11] The lack of agreement between the Exposition's national commission in Washington and the board in Chicago demonstrated once again the basic struggle between the two groups. Even Director General Davis was not fully aware in February 1893 that the licensing system for cameras then in effect was to be extended for the term of the Exposition.[12] Because of Davis's position on the World's Columbian Commission, many amateurs still hoped that the Exposition would take a more liberal stand in regard to photographic practices. The restrictions on newspaper publishers were eventually lifted, though only after much agitation, as discussed in chapter 4. But efforts in behalf of amateurs were totally unsuccessful. The Chicago board was carefully insulated from public pressure, and without political or economic pressure from professionals and manufacturers it was impossible to force a change.

The regulations stipulated a payment of two dollars per day for a permit to photograph on the grounds of the Exposition (which was four times the daily admission charge); a prohibition of cameras that used negatives larger than 4″ × 5″; and a complete ban on stereo cameras and tripods. This meant that the cost of a camera pass for the entire season would be as high as $350, although with mounting pressure on the officials, the fee was apparently reduced considerably in August to fifteen dollars a month.[13] Still, even this fee was effective in barring some visitors from bringing their cameras to the Exposition. It was reported, for example, that a "country school teacher" had had her camera taken away at the gate because she could not afford the fee.[14] There was nothing new in the imposition of fees for photographic privileges at such events, but in 1889 at the Paris exposition the charge for the season was reasonable and carried no restrictions regarding the size of the camera or the use of a tripod.[15]

Further, the Exposition required that each day the registrant present his or her camera for inspection at the Department of Photography, adjacent to the 62d Street entrance, and pay the fee. Visitors at other entrances had to be escorted by a guard to this point, to purchase the permit. A dated permit tag was to be attached to the camera or worn by the operator to indicate that the camera met the required specifications. This was a tedious and cumbersome system and did not always run smoothly, due to its reliance on the staffs of two diverse departments, the Columbian Guards and the Department of Photography, and encounters with the officials sometimes required photographers to use ingenious deceptions. Fred Felix, for example, repeatedly had to persuade Exposition officials of the authenticity of his permit. While he was climbing up the still-unfinished Administration Building to secure an "imposing" view, Felix was stopped by an officer and told to leave his camera and return to the gate for a new permit. Having done this, Felix was told that all permits had been declared void. Fearing that his camera and plates would be seized, he left immediately.[16] F. Hopkinson Smith, a well-known artist acting on behalf of the architect for the Art Building, C. B. Atwood, described his experience in attempting to enter at the 57th Street entrance with his "sketch-trap," an easel used by painters. He was immediately seized by "the agent of the Society for Fostering Fine Arts in America," better known as the Columbian Guards, who accused him of violating the tripod rule. The whole incident drew a crowd of spectators, who participated in the encounter on both sides of the question.[17]

Beating the System: The Ingenious Amateurs

The restrictions noted above were to ensure that amateurs were not able to use large-plate cameras on tripods and thus possibly to compete with the photographs being sold commercially by the Department of Photography.

The rule, however, failed to take account, first, of the ingenuity of amateur practitioners, and second, of the wide diversity and overall excellence of the new hand-camera technology. The revolution in hand cameras in the 1890s had a significant effect on the kind of imagery produced, and hand cameras were available in a number of makes from various manufacturers. It is important to realize, however, that their size and weight, which ranged from three to four pounds fully loaded, still made them a substantial and bulky article to carry around the Exposition compared to the lightweight, compact cameras of today.

Beyond the cameras themselves, access to a darkroom for loading film was a necessity at this time. Local photographic societies usually made them available, as did some hotels and railway companies—but not the Exposition. In March, just three months before its opening, when criticism by the photographic press was mounting, a demand for the public "convenience" of darkrooms was put forward.[18] This demand overlapped with attempts by the Eastman Kodak Company and the Gustav Cramer Dry Plate Company to obtain a joint concession at the Exposition for their goods, and not surprisingly, they had included provision for free darkrooms. The board might have resisted pressures from amateur photographers, but combined with those from two leading manufacturers in the field, the demand could not be ignored. George Eastman went to Chicago in March 1893 and again in May to present his application for a concession and accompanying darkroom facilities personally. Finally, on May 16, well after the opening of the Exposition, Eastman was able to write: "I have just received a telegram from a representative of the Gustav Cramer Co. saying that our concession contract has been signed by the World's Fair authorities. . . . We are to share the expense and the accommodations evenly. Cramer has the exclusive concession for selling glass plates and we have the exclusive concession of selling Kodaks and films and renting Kodaks."[19] A month later the building had been constructed and the darkroom concession was operating. Eastman concluded that even with the $1,500 cost of the building and the requirement to return to the Board 25 percent of the receipts from sales and rentals, it would be possible to make it pay. If not, he believed it would be money well spent for advertising. The delays that Eastman and Cramer experienced in obtaining this concession reflected both the Exposition's inefficient administration and its persistent reluctance to encourage independent photographic practice.

The Kodak and Cramer building was located close to the Department of Photography at the back of the Horticulture Hall on a street lined with souvenir booths. It contained eighteen stalls for the convenience of customers wishing to change their film and a showroom where people could rent Kodak cameras (and replacement cameras for any nonfunctioning Kodak machines) and buy rolls of film for several Kodak models.[20] There are no figures on the number of cameras rented, but at a fee of two dollars a day plus a ten-dollar deposit, it was an activity open to a relatively select group. Still, camera users came in all ages and types, and the Eastman Company catered to all tastes with its popular box cameras, including the No. 2 model, with its characteristic 3½″ round images, and the No. 3 and No. 4, with their rectangular print formats (Fig. 5.1).[21] The company even temporarily renamed one of its standard models the "Kolumbian Kodak" and, to encourage photography by amateurs, manufactured a special Columbian spool that held 200 exposures, double the regular number, along with the advertising slogan, "To get value received the amateur must take a large number of pictures in a day."[22] This message encouraged the proliferation of the snapshot, a style of photography that was relatively rapid, serial, and instantaneous, in contrast to the individual plate exposures and carefully constructed tripod images that had characterized both amateur and professional photography to this time.

One of the Eastman Company's Exposition advertisements featured two "young ladies" as "the Kodak girls," shown carrying the latest camera, although parts of the apparatus were adapted graphically to fit in with the design (see Fig. 5.2). In addition, framed copies of views of the Exposition featuring a "Kodak Girl" were supplied as promotions to some of the leading journals, like the *Photo Beacon*.[23] These were all products of the firm's marketing strategy, initiated in 1890, that was designed to encourage women to use Kodak cameras. George Eastman had even engaged Frances Benjamin Johnston to prepare an illustrated article on "ladies who use the Kodak," featuring prominent society women.[24] Women amateurs constituted a fast-growing segment of the photographic population and were encouraged by writers like Catherine Barnes, who urged women to study photography because it was a more "satisfying occupation than most of what are called feminine accomplishments," and because it provided a "mental and moral tonic, and a strong aid to general culture." "It is invaluable," she concluded, "to those who have learned its

FIGURE 5.1 A range of cameras with carrying cases like the ones shown here was available from the Eastman Company's concession for use by amateurs of all ages. The Eastman and Cramer concession building provided film, plates, replacements and rental cameras for hire and purchase. (Albumen print, 11.5 cm × 9.5 cm; photographer unknown, "Kodak snapshot album"; courtesy of the George Eastman House, International Museum of Photography and Film; album cat. no. 89:1507:146)

power." This message was eagerly taken up by the "new woman" amateurs who were present at the Exposition in the guise of the ubiquitous "'Kodak' fiends." The caption for a photograph titled *The Ever Present "Kodak" Fiend*, for example, reads: "The fiend in this picture was very lovely and pleasing and the two men sitting by the Javanese village had no horror of being 'took'. Long live the 'Kodak.'"[25]

Other photographic manufacturers besides Kodak also saw the Exposition as an opportunity to promote the use of their products. The Photo Materials Company, also of Rochester, New York, produced a promotional booklet (Fig. 5.3) detailing a trip across the Atlantic from Europe to the Chicago Fair with one of its new Trokonet cameras, which was on display in the photographic section.[26] It was, the company proudly announced, a camera "for the tourist not wishing to be bothered with an adjustable instrument," thus making a virtue out of a fact. Packages of thirty-five exposures in either cut or roll film were available for fifteen dollars. The pamphlet's writer took photographs with the Trokonet while en route on the Guion Line mail steamer to New York City, and then by steamship up the Hudson River to Albany, by Empire Express to Rochester to visit the company's headquarters, and finally on to Chicago by train. Just introduced in June 1893, the Trokonet was a prominent display piece for the company in the photographic section of the Manufactures and Liberal Arts Building.[27] The E. & H. T. Anthony Company, the Blair Camera Company, and John Carbutt's Keystone Plate Works all offered versions of the "free darkroom" for changing film at their respective display booths in the same building. This was, however, not a central location and was some distance from the crowds who frequented the Department of Photography to purchase souvenir photographs.[28] Outside the grounds of the Exposition, the Columbian Visitors' Association provided darkroom

FIGURE 5.3 The Photo Materials Company took the opportunity to promote its new Trokonet camera at the Exposition both in a display in the Manufactures and Liberal Arts Building and in this pamphlet, which outlined a route for traveling to Chicago. (Courtesy of the George Eastman House, International Museum of Photography and Film; Technology Collection)

FIGURE 5.2 Women amateurs were a fast-growing segment of the amateur population, and the Eastman Company targeted them in their use of the "Kodak Girls" theme for their advertising for the Exposition. (Drawing by T. Perara, Advertisement Files, Corporate Archives, Eastman Kodak Company; courtesy of the Eastman Kodak Company)

facilities at its nearby South Shore Hotel, which had erected a special addition forty-eight feet long and twelve feet wide with stalls for individual use, cooled running water, and electricity specifically for the purpose of making prints.[29] Two of the leading photographic journals, the *American Amateur Photographer* and the *Photo Beacon,* shared office space here and maintained a registry for both professionals and amateurs. They also provided information on "methods and ways of photography in the Fair grounds and about the city."[30]

While hand cameras were used prolifically, a tripod was sometimes crucial to ensure a steady support for longer exposures or unsteady angles. As a result, amateurs employed a number of ingenious contrivances to circumvent the official ban. One confidently noted that there were plenty of places for resting a camera, such as "on a railing or the piazza of a building," an extendible cane at an eight-foot height, a borrowed carpenter's horse, or even a portable camp chair, as in Figure 5.4.[31] Some amateurs went so far as to carry their own stepladders around to get a better vantage point on sites of special interest to them.

Amateur photographers found similar ways to beat the restriction on making stereographs on Exposition grounds. Using two single cameras to obtain dual exposures, or working with another person who had a similar camera, it was possible, with careful positioning, to approximate the technical setup of a double-lens stereo apparatus. The two exposures were normally made by placing the lenses three inches apart, preferably with the same camera, although it was possible to use two different cameras if the two had the same type of diaphragm, shutter speed, and plate sensitivity.[32] The means that amateurs used to get around such limitations showed the same kind of enterprise that commercial photographers had used to obtain their photographs of the Exposition.

Making Amateur Photographs at the Exposition

When amateurs made photographs at the Exposition, especially those in the category of artistic photography, they adhered to specific conventions or formulas whose logic and structure were influenced by a number of

FIGURE 5.4   Because tripods were not allowed on the grounds of the Exposition, amateurs devised ingenious methods of achieving the same results, as with this device, which attached to a folding chair. (Wood engraving; *Scientific American* 69 [Aug. 12, 1893]: 99)

factors, technical as well as artistic. Many amateurs were overwhelmed by their first impressions of the Exposition. For some, the initial experience of the Exposition was one of "aimlessness," with "no beginning or ending," no "clear, guiding thought and method in his pursuit."[33] Such an experience required some structuring, and there was no shortage of advice designed to guide the amateur in making sense of this visual confusion. W. A. Morse, secretary of the Chicago Lantern-Slide Club, advised amateurs not to take their cameras with them on their first visit to the Exposition. The notebook, he said, was a more important tool to "study and jot down the desired pictures." Surveying the Exposition for possible "picture views," he said, was like sketching before the final work, and selecting lighting and viewing positions for potential photographs with a reliable handbook was a day's work. Morse was quick to point out that it was not possible to "enjoy the grand sights within the buildings" and photograph them at the same time. While he recommended that visitors take a month to see everything properly, this was certainly not an option for most.[34] Instead, amateurs had only limited time and needed to assimilate quickly the approaches and techniques necessary for photographing a diverse array of events and architectural sites.

When not at work in the Department of Photography building in his capacity as a professional photographer, F. Dundas Todd prepared material for an article that outlined a photographic walking tour of the Exposition specially for the amateur. The article, which noted key "picture points," guided amateurs through the Exposition like tourists following a standard travel text. Todd directed visitors to begin at eight in the morning (in order to make best use of the light) and proceed to make a sequence of a half dozen photographs of key buildings from a series of four points on a circular route around the Wooded Lagoon. For the Woman's Building he advised that the best lighting and view should be "from the edge of the lagoon at a point in front of the doorway of the Illinois State building" but not after ten o'clock. From the Woman's Building near the doorway, he suggested that the Illinois State Building be taken. After passing the west end of the Illinois building, there should still be enough time "to get the art palace in prime condition as regards light for a view from the edge of the lagoon." Todd also suggested picture points for the Transportation Building, the first a northern angle from the walking bridge to the Wooded Island.[35] Todd used this position himself in his photographic souvenir publication, as did

FIGURE 5.5   Three amateur photographers share a vantage point on the Wooded Island for their photographs of the Fisheries Building. (Albumen print, 20.2 cm x 25.5 cm, copyrighted by C. D. Arnold; private album, Lot 10984, Pentland Collection, Prints and Photographs Division, Library of Congress)

amateurs like Mrs. Anna C. Ball, whose photograph was reproduced in the December 1893 issue of the *Photo American*.[36] The other approach to the Transportation Building that Todd featured was the spectacular "Golden Arch" doorway Louis Sullivan had designed into the building. This view was to be from the back of the Mines Building, an angle again used by many professionals, such as Frances Benjamin Johnston (see Fig. 4.20). But these walking-tour picture points were different from the professionals' structured viewpoints designed to create an architectural image of the Exposition, with its carefully laid out vistas, which were often shared by more than one photographer (Fig. 5.5). The official and commercial photographs were made from predictable sites on the second-floor porticos of the Court of Honor, along the South Canal, and from the roof of the Manufactures and Liberal Arts Building. Yet commercial and traditional amateur practitioners agreed on what constituted a good picture in the artistic sense. Obtaining it was simply a question of following certain established rules. The Exposition, however, presented technical conditions for the photographer that were to some extent restrictive.

One of these was that, despite the dazzling possibilities for photographs at the Exposition, with pictures at hand everywhere, the average "ambitious hypos" were unaware of the problems of photographing architectural subjects. Instead, as Archibald Treat, a California law-

yer and amateur photographer, said, they just went around "pointing their cameras at architectural details, their boxes off the level from ten to forty degrees."[37] The process of reducing grand architectural vistas to the scope of the camera lens was complicated by intruding objects and the severe limitations of the equipment, such as the lack of tripods and larger plate cameras with rising fronts to accommodate the distortion of verticals that occurs in photographs. There was also the question of light. "Imagine a clear, crisp atmosphere," wrote Harold Serrell, setting the scene, "a bright crystalline sky and brighter sunlit white buildings, and the intelligent amateur will be able to grasp the problem at hand." Yet, he soberly observed, the "efforts of so many amateurs had been fruitless."[38] Louis C. Bennett, for example, noted that he had lost three-quarters of his negatives from overexposure, a problem he solved by using rubber bands to get a faster shutter speed on his Triad camera.[39] While manufacturers lauded hand cameras as simple and easy to use, even the experienced amateur found that success was not guaranteed, and a substantial loss of photographs often occurred. The amateur's general lack of understanding of optimal lighting conditions was one factor. One amateur who found only rain and mud and no sun said that he had "only exposed the film twenty times, having no idea that I could get any pictures at all, but I find now, when they are developed that I have just as many perfect pictures."[40] As Horace Markley pointed out to readers of the *Cosmopolitan*, there was an advantage in waiting for overcast days because such conditions "took away the glare and lent a softer shading to the picture, giving less contrast and greater beauty of detail." Markley noted that the "effects of clouds in the sky added much to the artistic value of either land or water views."[41]

A characteristic feature of amateur photographers who were not attempting to be artistic was the serial quality of exposures, made possible by the relative technical ease of using hand cameras. A series of exposures created a type of cinematic reproduction of the viewer's experience. To cite one example of this effect, during his

FIGURE 5.6 The versatility of hand-held cameras made it possible for amateur photographers like Walter Hubble to record activities like this excursion along the North Canal on the Exposition's electric launch. (Albumen/solio prints, 9 cm diameter; courtesy of the George Eastman House, International Museum of Photography and Film; Photographic Print Collection, Lyndon Wells Collection, no. 81:1684:66, 67, 02)

FIGURE 5.7   Night views of the spectacular lighting of the Exposition buildings were a special interest of amateurs like Dr. George Bartlett of Buffalo, New York. His photograph of the Court of Honor using a three-minute exposure was one of many he made of the subject. (Bromide print, 19.7 cm × 23.5 cm; courtesy of the Chicago Historical Society; Prints and Photographs Department, Vertical File, ICHI-23461)

May trip to the Exposition, George Eastman was accompanied by three close friends, Walter Hubble, his lawyer; Frank Seamon, his advertising designer; and Sidney Colgate, a business friend from New York City. Both Hubble and Eastman made a large number of snapshots at the Exposition, although only those by Hubble have been located.[42] One of the series showed the group together on the electric launch, a popular guided tour that initiated the spectator to the buildings and the overall design of the Exposition. Hubble photographed the route in a sequence north along the canal and the Manufactures and Liberal Arts Building toward the Art Building. These images, three of which are shown in Figure 5.6, present the serial effect of passing under the bridge, looking backward and forward en route, and anticipating the final destination. "They are excellent" recalled Colgate, referring to the photographs Eastman had sent him, "and recall vividly our pleasant trip together to the windy city and the great exhibition."[43]

One of the technical challenges for the ambitious amateur was to capture the spectacle of the night illuminations. Outlining and ringing buildings and the Court of Honor with electric lights, transforming electric fountains with colored lighting, and sweeping the sky with powerful German searchlights atop the Manufactures Building created a memorable visual event. Official photographers had not paid much attention to this subject, although Kilburn had featured it in several of his stereographs. Amateurs, however, were especially interested in the effect and devised several ways to photograph it successfully. Among the several hundred photographs made by Thomas and Charles Gilbert Hine of the Newark Camera Club were two night illumination scenes—one of the Administration Building and the other of the basin in front of it—that were published in the special issue of the *Cosmopolitan* on the Exposition.[44] The Hine exposures were made from the southern end of the roof of the Manufactures and Liberal Arts Building, one of

FIGURE 5.8   Strange conjunctions were often present in amateur photographs, as with this view of a woman beside the Mac-
Monnies Fountain, part of a series of photographs made by an
unidentified amateur and collected in a personal album.

(Cyanotype print, 8 cm x 10.8 cm, in a dispersed album, a gift
of Rutgers University; photo courtesy of the Chicago Historical
Society; Prints and Photographs Department, Vertical File,
ICHI 23465)

the key positions for western views. Hine had a keen
interest in the subject and put together an extensive
collection of night views by his fellow amateurs. His collection would certainly have included at least one of the
many photographs made by Dr. George F. H. Bartlett, a
physician and historian and founder of the Buffalo Camera Club in 1888.[45] Bartlett made several versions of the
view of the Court of Honor and Administration Building
shown in Figure 5.7, and they testify to his technical and
artistic skills. The dazzling effect of the lighting and the
brilliant reflections on the water were beautifully caught
in the image and were enhanced by the rich blacks of the
print.

Other Exposition images by amateurs fulfilled no pro-
grammatic function, artistic or technical. Though often

they are buried in the private memorabilia of anonymous
visitors, lack traditional framing and posing, and are
repetitive in subject matter, they express their own
powerful visual impact, surviving the loss of both authorship and context. One such image, shown in Figure
5.8, captured a female spectator whose position next to a
sculpture in the empty MacMonnies fountain inadver-
tently created a heightened sense of dislocation and con-
tradiction.[46] The appeal of this type of imagery, with its
unconscious disjuncture in the subjects portrayed and in
the role of the viewer, did not go unrecognized by commercial publishers. The Lee & Laird Company was
quick to exploit it for a number of inexpensive souvenir
publications, including *Glimpses of the World's Fair*.[47] In
Figure 5.9, looking over the shoulders of the crowd,

listeners hear "the harangue of the specimen scout as he talks of the specimen red man," and the viewpoint of the photographer and the spectator merged. The commercial adaptation of this style of imagery signaled the popularity and appeal of photographs, which were direct, immediate, and able to convey some of the ambivalence of the spectator's own experience of the Exposition.

Photography and the Midway Plaisance

The mile-long stretch of land that originally connected Washington and Jackson parks in Chicago—referred to locally as the "midway" between East 59th and East 60th streets—was the site of the popular Midway Plaisance. The juxtaposition of the Midway concession, with its reconstructed Egyptian sites and temples and the imposing Ferris wheel, offered a sharp contrast to the newly erected buildings of the University of Chicago just outside the gates (Fig. 5.10). Looking east from the height of the Exposition's Ferris wheel, a ride taken by nine out of ten visitors, the view at the first of the wheel's six stopping positions revealed half of the Midway, looking east toward the main part of the Exposition. This view also showed the Midway's random order, the false fronts on its buildings, and its milling crowds, a striking contrast to the orderly architectural vistas of the main Exposition.[48]

Set side-by-side were an array of concessions, entertainments, and living-people displays. This arm of the Exposition provided an uneasy balance between entertainment and instruction. Following the extraordinary success of a similar entertainment section at the 1889 Paris exposition, where several colonial displays had attracted wide popular attention, the Midway combined business, pleasure, with the opportunity for real financial success. As Eric Sandweiss has pointed out, however, while classed as concessions, many of these were formally sponsored by the nations represented.[49] People came to walk, visit the free displays (like the Model Workingman's House[50] and the military campground that served as the base for the ascent of a captive balloon), attend the various concert halls, and sample the offerings of the international cafes. Not all such enterprises were a success. The Aztec Village, for example, was open only during the last two months of the Exposition. According to Denton Snider, a contemporary observer, it failed due to "public disinterest," a lack of general knowledge about it, and the fact that "ethnology was Greek" to most spectators.[51] The Midway as a

whole, however, was overwhelmingly popular because, Snider observed, it offered relief from "the tension and earnestness of our Occidental World." Contemporary life, he continued, offered "little or no place for caprice," and "we are a people almost without holidays and festivities, without real amusement, for which we go to the Oriental, or even to the Europeans in the Plaisance."[52] The Midway provided spectators with a visual counterpoint to the Exposition, and a psychological catharsis as well. It was in this landscape that the photographer, especially the amateur photographer, was most clearly and intensely at home.

A traditional form of popular theatrical attraction, combining color, sound, and light with visual effect, was present in a number of entertainment concessions located on the Midway. Most were very successful financially, including a kaleidoscopic room of mirrors in the Moorish Palace, a painted panorama of the Alps around Bern, and a panoramic painting of the great Hawaiian volcano Kilauea. The painting of Kilauea showed a simulated eruption, with flowing lava enhanced by more than 300 lights. It was so realistic, said one visitor, that "observers could easily imagine they had been transported to that interesting but dreadful place."[53] While not as commercially successful as these large-scale traditional painted concessions, the Electric Scenic Theatre, shown in Figure 5.11, also exemplified the attraction that these visual entertainments had for the Exposition's visitors. The show opened at dawn with light just beginning to play on a painted scene of the Alps and Mt. Blanc, moved through the atmospheric changes of the day from morning mists to a thunderous lightning storm, and ended with a re-creation of evening, with moonlight and stars. The visual drama produced by the theatre's electric lighting was enhanced by the music of Tyrolean singers and musicians.[54]

Given the number of visual attractions on the Midway, it is not surprising that the competition for customers was intense. The Zoopraxographical Hall (Fig. 5.12), located halfway down the Midway and next to the Persian Theater, was begun with apparent optimism by Eadweard Muybridge, the photographer, celebrated lecturer, and promoter of the study of animal locomotion by means of photography. In the 1870s, after an initial career as a landscape photographer in San Francisco, Muybridge worked for Leland Stanford in photographing racehorses. The results were published in 1881, and Muybridge also presented them in series of popular lectures in Europe. He continued his work at the Univer-

FIGURE 5.9 Photographs made with hand-held cameras (in this case a No. 4 Kodak) emphasized the less formal and more immediate viewpoint of the spectator, which was often exploited for commercial publications. Here the spectators are shown listening to "The Noble Red Man and Oratorical Scout"—hawkers who were drawing visitors to their nearby concession, a practice which was common throughout the Midway. (From *The Vanishing City*, n.p.)

sity of Pennsylvania beginning in 1884, extending its scope to include human subjects. The culmination of the project came with the publication in 1887 of the encyclopedic volume *Animal Locomotion,* which contained nearly 20,000 photographs printed in collotype on 781 plates. Zoopraxography was the name Muybridge gave to the visual presentation of his movement studies in a machine he had devised from a projecting lantern and a rotating slotted disk, a device that was similar to the visual effect produced by the popular handheld phenakistoscope.[55] The individual single-motion photographs were transferred to circular glass disks for use in the projector. Each rotation, which lasted only a few seconds, represented a movement sequence. These brief photographic images of individual people and animals in

motion had been transcribed from photographs Muybridge had made during his ten years of work at the University of Pennsylvania.

The instructional tone and content of the images and the less-than-theatrical presentation did not cater sufficiently to the pleasure-seeking audiences of the Plaisance, so it failed to attract the anticipated crowds.[56] Muybridge lacked the modern technology for his images that was then being developed for popular entertainment by Thomas Edison with his kinetoscope, which was slated for display in the Electricity Building. The kinetoscope was an arcade machine with an eyepiece for viewing a fifty-foot loop of film on a popular subject. Edison had given his secretary, A. O. Tate, the right to market the machines, and Tate signed a contract with the mechanic James Eagan to produce them for display at the Exposition.[57] By May 1893, however, only one prototype was available for the first commercial showing to the press at the Brooklyn Institute, so it is unlikely that the kinetoscope was available for the concession in Chicago.

Muybridge could have stimulated interest in his display with the presentation of his dramatic lectures, which had drawn interested audiences in Europe, but it is unclear whether he did so. Two proposed lectures appeared in the special publication *Descriptive Zoopraxography,* which was sponsored by the United States Bureau of Education for the Exposition and which also included a chapter on his studio and working methods while at the University of Pennsylvania.[58] Muybridge also produced fifty illustrated disks for use in the handheld phenakistoscope in his publication and probably similar to those shown in the Zoopraxographical Hall (see Fig. 5.13). The book and the portfolio of disks were both available for purchase at the hall.

Despite these commercial efforts, the Zoopraxographical Hall was soon closed, as were many concessions following the early weeks of the Fair, during which business was so slow that many feared bankruptcy and were forced to leave. Muybridge's building was taken over for yet another painted panorama. This one, depicting Pompeii, was by the celebrated Neapolitan painter Count Antonio Coppola. Showing the customs and life of the ancient city destroyed in 79 A.D. by the eruption of Mount Vesuvius and with a second view of the site as was in the 1890s, it proved a great success, producing $19,505 in gross earnings compared to the meager $350 that Muybridge received for his efforts.[59] Clearly, exhibitors like Muybridge had something to learn from the promotion of the painted volcanic events, dramas of history, and landscape views that were successfully packaged on the Midway for the visual entertainment of spectators.

The Reconstructed Image: The Streets of Cairo

The concession adjacent to the Zoopraxographical Hall proved to be the most spectacular financial success of all. The Streets of Cairo exhibit was based on the popular Rue du Caire at the 1889 Paris exposition, and both were designed by Max Hertz. Like its predecessor, the Streets of Cairo attempted to represent a reality—the colonial world—within the format of the exhibition. As Timothy Mitchell has argued, the displays of Middle Eastern countries at such expositions were themselves a kind of picture representation or tableau, complete with a single viewpoint, recognizable symbols, and conventionalized images designed for a viewing audience.[60] The relatively drab entrance to Cairo Street, shown in Figure 5.14, masked the sense of dislocation the spectator confronted in encountering the spectacular sounds, smells, and colors of another world. Cairo Street was a "copy" of one of the most picturesque streets of old Cairo. Complete with lattice-windowed buildings and projecting second-story balconies, there were about sixty shops, a mosque with a reenactment of daily prayer, characteristic Egyptian donkeys, camel rides, snake charmers, water carriers, and fortune-tellers (Fig. 5.15). Many Egyptians could be found behind the doorways and operating some of the booths, of course, but there were also college students from Otterbein University in Ohio, selling souvenirs.[61]

The appeal of Cairo Street derived from its successful combination of skillful reproduction and the popularity of vicarious travel. A large audience already existed for

FIGURE 5.10 The Exposition's Ferris wheel seen from outside the fairgrounds, with the University of Chicago's Foster Hall on the right. The Ferris wheel had a series of six stopping points so that the riders in its thirty-six roomlike cars could make their own photographs. (Solio print, 11.5 cm × 16 cm, by William Franklin Johnston, private "Kodak" album; courtesy of Charles Rand Penney; World's Columbian Exposition Collection)

FIGURE 5.11   The Electric Scenic Theatre on the Midway featured a stage setting in which the changing atmospheric effects of an alpine scene from dawn to evening were created by the set of 250 incandescent lights. The lights were controlled from the front of the stage in full view of the audience. (Albumen print, 35.5 cm × 28 cm; cat. no. 293.320.1891, Division of Photographic History, National Museum of American History, Smithsonian Institution)

the genre of pictorial travel albums, like H. H. Ragan's grandly titled *Art Photographs of the World and the Columbian Exposition: An Album of Rare Photographs of the Wonders of the Universe,* which promoted the "delights of travel without its discomforts." The reliance of such albums on what Ragan called "the infallible camera," which "speaks the truth, nothing but the truth," was crucial to persuading the reader of the authenticity of the description.[62] Tourist photographs provided both the rationale and the technical means for the Streets of Cairo concession, which was essentially a combination of living-people display and diorama. Ragan's book included a section on the Exposition, but in some cases he substituted views of the original sites—the Temple of Luxor, for example, as well as Blarney Castle and an Arab wedding procession.[63] The reader required no explanation for this interchangeability of images of the original sites and their reproductions, which demonstrates the easy acceptance of this transposition. The effect of being on Cairo Street, according to one popular

writer, was to "feel that we are indeed in the land of the Nile, all the full current of Egyptian life flowing about us."[64]

The underlying ambivalence of the Streets of Cairo experience was often revealed in the photographs amateurs made of the sights and entertainments offered there. On entering "the liveliest, jolliest place," where donkeys were ridden by children and "giggling girls or grinning men," the young Philip Rodman, one of the fictional characters in Tudor Jenks's *Century World's Fair Book for Boys and Girls,* proceeds to photograph what he experiences.[65] Armed with a rented No. 4 Kodak camera and a mind "agog with eagerness," Rodman's adventures as a snapshot photographer epitomize the experience of amateurs at the Exposition, even to the theft of his camera. On the Streets of Cairo, Rodman, like many others, is charged an additional dollar to take his camera into the concession. The Egyptian concessionaires recognized the commercial value of their own images, as well as the insatiable demand of amateurs for "snaps" of

FIGURE 5.12 The Zoopraxographical Hall was the site of Eadweard Muybridge's concession, which showed projections of his studies of animal and human movement. (Cyanotype print, 9 cm × 12 cm, by Joseph E. Hartman; courtesy of the Chicago Historical Society; Prints and Photographs Department, Hartman Collection, ICHI-23705)

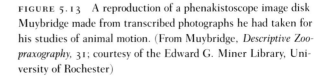

47. COLUMBIAN EXPOSITION SPEEDWAY.

FIGURE 5.13 A reproduction of a phenakistoscope image disk Muybridge made from transcribed photographs he had taken for his studies of animal motion. (From Muybridge, *Descriptive Zoopraxography,* 31; courtesy of the Edward G. Miner Library, University of Rochester)

FIGURE 5.14   The entrance to the Streets of Cairo was where
spectators purchased their tickets to this popular entertainment.
The musician with his drums and riding a camel was part of the
colorful reenactment of an Arab wedding procession performed
daily. (Solio print, 11.2 cm x 16.5 cm, by William Franklin
Johnston, private "Kodak" album; courtesy of Charles Rand Penney, World's Columbian Exposition Collection)

their own entertainment. Rodman "captured a view or
two of the picturesque 'donkey boys'—who were stal-
wart grown men," which was a subject of great interest
to other amateurs as well.[66]

The most popular of all the photographic subjects on
Cairo Street were, in the words of Denton Snider, "the
great nodding camels docilely following their tiny boy
leaders," with their women riders giving "shrieks of
dismay" on their "amusing" dismounting. The camel, he
wrote, "must be ridden, particularly by the American
girl" because of the pluck and resolution required.[67]
This was a subject easily exploited by the serial format of
the snapshot, with its succession of exposures fixing
each stage of the zig-zag movements of the lurching
camels. Compared to the stiff and conventionally posed
commercial tourist views used in souvenir publications,
these serial images conveyed a convincing impression of
the original chaotic ride as well as the incongruities of an
intercultural experience.

Another concession adjacent to and accessible from
the Streets of Cairo was the Temple of Luxor, an attraction that drew on the popular interest in Egypt produced
by dramatic archaeological finds that were then so much
in the spotlight.[68] Here was a large-scale replica of the
Egyptian temple from the Eighteenth and Nineteenth

dynasties, from 1800 to 1480 B.C. More educational in its
organization than the other commercial operations on the
street, the interior contained display cases with decorated replicas of the tombs of Thi from 3800 B.C. and the
Sacred Bull Apis from 260 B.C., as well as wax mummies
of figures from 1700 to 1070 B.C.[69] The display was produced by a group of Egyptologists and entrepreneurs with
the assistance of John M. Cook, managing partner of the
Thomas Cook & Son Company, organizers of the earliest
publicly advertised trip from Cairo to the First Cataract
of the Nile in 1869 in connection with the opening of the
Suez Canal. For its display in the Transportation Building, the company also built a model of the Ptolemaic
Temple of Edfu and added photographs of their offices
around the world, model boats, and sites on their tours.[70]
Before leaving the temple complex, visitors could have
souvenir tintypes made of themselves standing in front of
the edifice or posed on a donkey by the photographers in
the shop shown in Figure 5.16. For many spectators, this
reproduction of an Egyptian tour, complete with photo

FIGURE 5.15   The Streets of Cairo were filled with activities,
including the popular camel ride, and crowds of spectators.
Shops like that of the photographer G. Lekegian, which specialized in Egyptian views, were popular among souvenir collec-
tors. (Platinum print, 7 cm x 8.8 cm, courtesy of the Chicago
Historical Society; Prints and Photographs Department, Vertical
File, ICHI-22843)

FIGURE 5.16   The Temple of Luxor replica, made with the assistance of the Thomas Cook travel agency, housed a number of Egyptian archaeological facsimiles. Note the tintype concession on the right. (Albumen print, 24 cm x 18.5 cm; courtesy of the Chicago Historical Society; Prints and Photographs Department, Vertical File, ICHI-02432)

FIGURE 5.17   Amateurs generally had to negotiate to photograph the various subjects on the Midway. Here a Turkish guard strikes one of the customary poses that visitors favored. (Albumen print, 9 cm diameter; World's Columbian Exposition Kodak #2 Series, courtesy of Mike and Gladys Kessler)

opportunities, was their first and only contact with a world far removed from their own in time and space.[71]

Commercial photographs of original Egyptian sites, including the popular seventy-five-cent albums of photographs by the Egyptian photographer G. Lekegian, were also available at the Temple salesroom and at Lekegian's own shop a few doors away (see Fig. 5.15).[72] Here it was possible to purchase a selection of commercial views of the five different ethnic groups represented in the living-people displays on Cairo Street. A keen businessman, Lekegian saw many of his Exposition photographs reproduced in various pictorial publications that issued from the Exposition. Among these were his photographs of the Boushareens (Nubians), whom Lekegian photographed both in street and studio settings and who were, in fact, often photographed because Westerners considered them an especially handsome people.

For the amateur, photographing members of the living-people exhibits on Cairo Street and elsewhere involved an extra charge, arrived at following an interchange between photographer and subject to negotiate a proper fee. Philip Rodman's fictional adventures typified those of the amateurs. He visited the "huts of the Soudanese" to see the dances of the featured performer, the "Dancing-Baby only eighteen months old!" who was able

to mimic the warlike dance of the men, who also performed. Rodman's account of his attempt to photograph the child was a classic example of the bargaining process. After attempting to lower the price from a dollar to fifty cents, a compromise allowed Rodman to "take her into the sunshine" for a photograph.[73] The negotiation process required to make such photographs ran counter to the generally held assumption that, in the photographic sense, people were there for the taking. It also marked a clear distinction between commercial and amateur practice. Hired subjects often assumed one of the conventional poses or postures that they had found pleased amateur photographers, as the Turkish guard is doing in Figure 5.17. In another example, the amateur photographer Carl Koerner, on paying twenty-five cents to photograph two Turkish sedan-chair bearers on the Midway, noted that they immediately adopted a pose of "standing with heads and shoulders erect, with one foot a little in advance of the other as if in the act of walking."[74]

Encountering the Other: Photographs Along the Plaisance

It was along the mile-long open thoroughfare of the Midway Plaisance itself that the spectators, ethnic groups, living-people displays, and picture-takers merged. Here the crowd—with its mixture of human types, juxtaposition of cultures, and fluctuation between observer and observed—moved in a succession of picture subjects, as in Figure 5.18. Here, in the words of one writer, you "rubbed elbows with Laplanders and Arabs, with Dahomeyans and Japanese, with New Englanders and Turks, until you felt that you yourself were an unusual exhibit."[75] The amateur photographer, the "camera-fiend with his weapon," was encouraged to "collect" images from the Midway, and the cameras were designed to do this with a minimum of effort. This was a unique opportunity, Carl Koerner wrote, to "be able to add to my album photos of these different nations clothed as they are in their exact national dress . . . a far more interesting souvenir than photographs of the Exposition buildings."[76]

FIGURE 5.19   These three men entering the South Sea Island concession produced an incongruous image when caught outside their living-people display. (Albumen print, 9 cm × 11.2 cm; courtesy of the Rochester Museum and Science Center, Rochester, N.Y.)

FIGURE 5.18 While the streets of the Midway Plaisance offered an opportunity to rub shoulders with a great mixture of
humanity, the camera fixed the deeper isolation of individuals in
the experience of the crowd. (Aristotype, 7.5 cm x 10 cm, photographer unknown; Series G 1984.477; courtesy of the Chicago
Historical Society; Vertical File, Prints and Photographs Department, ICHI-22843)

FIGURE 5.20   Not all the people on the Midway were willing subjects for the camera, so capturing a subject from behind avoided a possible cultural confrontation. These two subjects were unwillingly, or at least unknowingly, "collected" by an amateur photographer on the Midway Plaisance. (Albumen print, "Kodak snapshot album," cat. no. 89:1507:119; courtesy of the George Eastman House, International Museum of Photography and Film; Photographic Print Collection)

For an experienced photographer like Horace P. Chandler, the men and women of the Plaisance were "truly 'nature's noblemen,'" who owed much to the camera, for without "its faithful work they might have come to us and gone away forever, leaving no trace for the treacherous memory of the sightseer to recall."[77] But not all of "nature's noblemen" shared this belief, nor were they all cooperative in front of the lens even for payment, and photographers did not always understand their reluctance. An amateur photographer, in remarking on his experience in the Dahomey Village, noted that it was "odd to still find people who are afraid of the photographic camera."[78] During Koerner's first attempt in the Javanese Village, he pointed the camera at two "frightened-looking beings" standing "as if spell-bound, not daring to move a muscle," which left him wondering "what these odd little fellows imagined I was doing to them."[79] Frederick Putnam argued that the popularization of anthropology with the living-people displays would produce tolerance of different cultures, but the reality was a different matter. While fairgoers made some connection with the nationalities they encountered, there was always, according to Curtis Hinsley, a "psychological exit" in which the other was "roped off."[80] There is an inherent barrier between the spectators and participants in the living-people displays which was integral to the Exposition's structure. Sometimes, though rarely, the barrier broke down, and produced incongruities of the kind shown in Figure 5.19.

Amateur photography was essentially a photography of collecting, in which individuals became objects rather than human beings in portraits, impressions rather than living subjects. One well-dressed Arab spectator attempted to explain to a photographer that "his people believe a camera to be 'an evil eye'" and that creating their facsimiles made "it impossible for them to enter heaven."[81] This did not deter amateurs from approaching their subjects from behind, as in Figure 5.20, and even recording the withdrawal of unwilling subjects from the view of the camera's eye itself. The captured subject receding before the threatening camera was an image that had a profound resonance. This was not photography as replicated in the commercial or official imagery of the Exposition. The camera in the hands of the amateur was clearly not a neutral machine; it gave the person behind the lens power. The "horror of being took" was in many cases as much a response to the enactment of this power as it was a cultural confrontation. If amateur images sometimes revealed complex cultural motivations, there were also occasions that what the eye saw fleetingly, the camera possessed forever. These were the unnegotiated images, often not fully observed by either the photographer or the subject, lacking both artistry and convention. These brief but alert images carried a message not found in the scripted or paid-for photographs associated with other work done by amateurs who were collecting images on the Exposition Midway.

One's role was the key to success at the Exposition, as in life. Marina Van Rensselaer, writing in *Century Magazine,* advised the potential visitors to play the role of experimenter—just stay in bed one day, she suggested, or go to a completely unknown section.[82] This would be a corrective for the distinctly American desire for self-instruction. For Van Rensselaer the model spectator at the Exposition was the flâneur, the person who liked to "idle in the city," the hero of modern French life, the anonymous observer, seen but never interacting.[83] At the Exposition this would be a person who "keeps himself purely receptive to the city [which] prints each instant a fresh picture on his brain"—a role not unlike the one suggested for the photographer. She further urged her readers to "go to the fair wholly conscienceless, not like a painstaking draftsman but like a human kodak, caring only for as many pleasing impressions as possible, not for analyzing their worth." This was an apt metaphor for the spectator as camera, the "human Kodak." The observer who was solely intent on absorbing the impressions of the Exposition, receiving the light of experience like the passive lens of the camera—this was also an apt view of the amateur photographer. The box with the eye had been endowed with a significant power—technological, mechanical, and acquisitive. But the idea that there could be such a thing as a "conscienceless" image that had nothing to do with power, economics, and culture was as much an illusion as was the Dream City itself.

6

CONCLUSION

Nothing was transparent or neutral about photography at the World's Columbian Exposition; it was scripted and orchestrated. As a stage both contrived and complex, the Exposition was the setting for a struggle among the various groups that made up the photographic world. The administration sought to control the kind of photographs that would be shown to the world, even the type of photographs that would be made, but the dynamics of the photographic world could not easily be suppressed. The differing positions of the photographic practitioners—official, commercial, and amateur—and those of the photographic manufacturers proved an important determinant of photography's presence at the event. For all the rhetoric of the Exposition extolling the progress of industry and technology, there was no guarantee that photography, or for that matter any other endeavor, would be fully represented. When the role of other disciplines at the Exposition, such as anthropology, education, and engineering is studied in detail, we will no doubt see how pervasive this situation was. The representation of American artists at the Exposition, for example, was determined by the competitive nature of the jury system employed by the Fine Arts Department, which favored professional artists and experienced exhibitors.[1] As a means of display as well as an image-making process, photography was engaged in a series of contests at the Exposition which required constant negotiation about the terms of its function and practice.

For the generation who had experienced the Centennial, with its separate photographic hall, the Exposition had to be disappointing. Whereas at the Centennial the photographic manufacturers, amateurs, and professionals had functioned together to make the presence of photography a success, now there was a growing fragmentation. There had been significant changes in the groups since 1876, and the photographic section of the Exposition mirrored them in its uneven representation. The favoring of industry over art in the Exposition as a whole guaranteed that the strongest presence would be among the photographic manufacturers. This was in direct contrast to the pragmatic accommodation between the professionals and manufacturers at the annual professional photographers' convention and exhibition held just outside the grounds in the very summer of the Exposition. Further, the Exposition's emphasis on the industry and commerce of photography failed to provide an exhibition environment compatible with the newly emerging "aesthetic" photographers in the United States, though this was not the case among foreign participants, as seen in the comprehensive loan collection of works by the leading British pictorial photographers. This contrast reflected on the situation in the United States, where entrepreneurship took precedence over national representation. The same ambivalence toward defining a national culture could be seen in the derivative styles of the Exposition's own architecture.

Even in the speculative area of the proposed applications of photography, England took the lead with the proposals at the Auxiliary Congress of Photographers by H. Snowden Ward and Jerome Harrison. Ward's international union of photographic practice and Harrison's photographic survey were not nostalgic attempts to restore the unity of the past or quaint efforts to regionalize the world into an album of images. They were evidence of the deeper strain of visionary and utopian ideals that formed a common ground between the photographic practitioners and their productions. Such proposals were, however, in direct conflict with the realities of the severely factionalized photographic world. The fragmentation among photographic practitioners in this period would become a schism that has not yet been completely healed—witness the specialized histories that feature the technology, art, or economics of photography but not photography as a whole. The one exception to this trend is the recent work of some social historians who have sought to integrate the production, function, and meaning of photographs into the broader processes of society and culture.

Crucial to the success of the Exposition, as with any public exhibition, were the objects of its displays. That photography provided so much imagery for those displays—dramatically exceeding that of the Centennial—should come as no surprise. Photographs fed the public's imagination by providing the links between the objects on display and the contexts from which they had been removed. Without photography there would have been no replicas like the cliffdwellers' homes, the Yucatán monuments, or even life groups for the Smithsonian's displays. Standing in for the absent structures, populations, and experiences of educational institutions from all over the United States, photographs provided a visual encyclopedia of their endeavors. While this was also true to a lesser extent for the social-service institutions, in neither case were the photographs deemed important enough to retain for later reference. In contrast, as tools of investigation and research, photographs were valued in archaeology and the newly emerging fields of physical anthropology and psychology, fields with aspirations to a new scientific precision. Further, the government recognized the value of photographs for advertising and persuasion in its strategy for promoting trade with Latin American countries, just as they were employed by other countries in their attempts to enhance their image among potential investors. Finally, in the growing consumer culture of the 1890s, photography was beginning to be recognized as a tool for advertising goods and services, and the international stage of the Exposition offered a unique opportunity to attract a new market of immense diversity and size.

The appropriation of photography to serve a complex network of meaning was not unique to the Exposition. As a microcosm of the world, the Exposition showed how deeply woven photography was in the fabric of society. The spectator was at ease in the world of the Exposition, where photographs so richly studded the displays and where the reality of ideas, objects, and people was conveyed in an interweaving of purposes. That the Exposition was regarded as almost a photographic exhibition should not be surprising in the least.

The administration's attempt to gain control over the practice of photography at the Exposition with its regulations and its incorporation of commercial photography within an official department ultimately proved futile. Such policies produced only an official imagery that was overly conventionalized and of varying quality in its commercial forms. Official photographs matched the Exposition's inflated rhetoric of celebration and progress but revealed little of what the Exposition meant as an experience. Architecture provided the logo for the Exposition and was extolled in the official photographs, but the stunning architectural views so often reproduced in the popular souvenir albums (and historical publications today) were only a small part of the much larger and richer image produced by photographers at the Exposition. The independent commercial photographers' alertness to the possibility of exploiting other popular photographic formats produced a wealth of additional material, including both stereographs and souvenir portraits. The commercial imagery of the Exposition, driven by the expanding consumer market, was certainly more diverse than researchers have acknowledged, and the consumer public provided the market for these diverse forms of imagery.

Amateur photographers, too, created a vast quantity of new photographic material. Working under the same restraints on their practices as were the commercial photographers, they produced some conventional images, but they also evolved new strategies for making pictures. It was not the ornate architecture that dominated the ordinary spectator's camera but the Midway Plaisance, with its spectacle of the living peoples of the world. On the Midway the enigmas deeply embedded in the Exposition experience were uncannily, sometimes unconsciously, caught in the camera's lens. The visitor without a camera was, in the popular terminology, just "not in it."[2] Subverting official controls, amateur photographers created new images of their experience of the Midway Plaisance, versions of a reality both real and imagined.

While historians now see the Midway Plaisance and

the Court of Honor as metaphors for the gulf separating low culture from high culture in American society, for the Exposition's spectators they were two parts of an integrated experience. Reactions to the Exposition varied, but one graphic representation was the drawing *A Nervous Man's Impression of the Fair*.[3] Here a man is shown seated askew in his chair, overwhelmed by endless walls of paintings, tilting architectural facades, fast-approaching trains, and massive crowds of foreigners. Coping with the visual chaos that was the multilayered experience of the Exposition was the problem of the spectators as a whole, not just the nervous ones, and photography provided amateurs with a tool for doing this. The world through the viewfinder was a precise, bounded, often controlled instant in time before the world dissolved again into the confusion of everyday life.

If there is a last word to be said about photography at the World's Columbian Exposition, it belongs to the aged veteran photographer Abraham Bogardus. When given the task of summarizing the Exposition for his photographic colleagues, he wrote: "Write up the World's Fair? As well attempt to dip up the Atlantic Ocean with a four ounce graduate and keep a record of measurement. . . . To do it thoroughly, a writer must needs have his 'three score and ten' duplicated, and then he would say his time was too short to finish the work."[4]

Reference Material

APPENDIX

United States Exhibitors in Group 151 with Photographs and Photographic Apparatus in the Manufactures and Liberal Arts Building or the Woman's Building

Catalogue Number	Company	Location	Type of Product
X357[a]	Albertype Company	New York, N.Y.	Albertypes
719-WB[b]	Albright, Mrs. I. L.	Albuquerque, N.Mex.	Collection of photographs
358	Albright, Franc Luse	Albuquerque, N.Mex.	Amateur photographs
X361	American Aristotype Co.	Jamestown, N.Y.	Photographs on aristopaper
X363	Anthony, E. & H. T., & Co.	New York, N.Y.	Photographic apparatus and supplies
X364	Appleton, J. M.	Dayton, Ohio	Photographs
365	Aune	Portland, Ore.	Photographs
X366	Baker's Art Gallery	Columbus, Ohio	Photographs
X	Bellsmith, R. P.	Cincinnati, Ohio	Photographs
X370	Blair Camera Co.	Boston, Mass.	Photographic apparatus
X373	Breese, James L.	New York, N.Y.	Carbon portraits and reproductions
X403	[Carbutt, J.] Keystone Blue Paper Co.	Philadelphia	Photographic and drawing papers
X404	[Carbutt, J.] Keystone Dry Plate & Film Works	Philadelphia	Photographs, dryplates, and specialties
720-WB	Carter, Alice R.	Chatham, Pa.	Photographs of women and places in Chester County
X375	Chicago Photogravure Co.	Chicago, Ill.	Photogravures
X	Clark, Mr.	Little Rock, Ark.	Photographs
376	Clark, D. R.	Chicago, Ill.	Photographs
379	Cox, George	New York, N.Y.	Photographs
X380	Dana, Edward C.	New York, N.Y.	General collection of photographs
382	Davis & Sandford	New York, N.Y.	Photographs and photogravures
X	Dawson, R. W.	Little Rock, Ark.	Photographs
721-WB	Dock, Mira L.	Harrisburg, Pa.	Photographs
X384	Eastman Kodak Co.,	Rochester, N.Y.	Kodaks and accessories
X	Electro-Tint Engraving Co.	Philadelphia, Pa.	Halftone engravings
387	Elliot, J. M.	Columbus, Ohio	Photographs
388, 722-WB	Farnsworth, Emma J.	Albany, N.Y.	Amateur photographs
X	Gannaway, J. M.	Fort Springs, Ark.	Photographs
723-WB	Garrity, Miss	Chicago, Ill.	Photographs

Catalogue Number	Company	Location	Type of Product
X390	Geneva Optical Co.	Chicago, Ill.	Magazine cameras, improved photomicrographic cameras, etc.
X391	Gramm, Carl T.	Keokuk, Ia.	Photomicrographs
X392	Gundlach Optical Co.	Rochester, N.Y.	Photographic lenses, microscopes, and accessories
X394	Gutekunst, F., Co.	Philadelphia, Pa.	Photographic portraits and halftone engravings
396	Harrison, Thomas	Chicago, Ill.	Photographs
397	Hatton, M. F.	Princeton, Ind.	Photographs
398	Heimberger, C., & Son	New Albany, Ind.	Photographs
X400	Inglis, James	Chicago, Ill.	Bromide enlargements in black and sepia
401	Jackson, W. H., Photograph & Publishing Co.	Denver, Colo.	Photographic landscape views
X724-WB	Kendall, Mrs. Marie H.	Norfolk, Conn.	Photographs
X	Kennedy, Mr.	Hot Springs, Ark.	Photographs
405	Klein, George J.	Chicago, Ill.	Photographs
X	Kunz, G. F.	New York, N.Y.	Portraits of mineralogists
X	Kurtz, William	New York, N.Y.	"Azaline" photographs
X406	Landy, James	Cincinnati, Ohio	Portraits and genre photographs
X407	Levy, Max	Philadelphia, Pa.	Engraved photographic screens
408	Long, Mrs. J. G.	Chester, Pa.	Amateur photographs
X410	McAllister, T. H.	New York, N.Y.	Magic lanterns, stereopticons, and accessories
X412	McMichael, H.	Buffalo, N.Y.	Photographic studies
725-WB	Millay, Mrs. Jerry	Phoenix, Ariz.	Album of photographs
X	Montford & Hill	Burlington, Ia.	Photographs
X413	Morison, William M.	Chicago, Ill.	Photographs
726-WB	Otis, Miss Gertrude	Boothwyn, Pa.	Photographs
X416	Pach Bros.	New York, N.Y.	Photographs, portraits, groups, and landscapes
X	Perrings, W. J.	Pine Bluff, Ark.	Photographs
X	Photographic Publishing Co.	Denver, Colo.	Landscape photographs
X417	Photo Materials Company	Rochester, N.Y.	Bromide enlargements, photographic apparatus, and supplies
418	Place, Frank A.	Chicago, Ill.	Photographs and portraits
420	Radam, William	New York, N.Y.	Microphotographs
421	Randall, H.	Ann Arbor, Mich.	Photographs
X422	Rau, William H.	Philadelphia, Pa.	Photographs and lantern slides
728-WB	Richards, Miss Annie L.	Boston, Mass.	Amateur photographs
X426	Root, W. J.	Chicago, Ill.	Photographs and portraits
X	Rothberger, H.	Denver, Colo.	Photographs
X427	Savage, C. R.	Salt Lake City, Utah	Photographic views
428	Scholl, J. B.	Chicago, Ill.	Photographs
X429	Schumacher, F. G.	Los Angeles, Calif.	Photographs
X430	Scott, O. P.	Chicago, Ill.	Photographs
X729	Scull, Sarah A.	Washington, D.C.	Photographs
431, 730-WB	Slade, Elizabeth	Albany, N.Y.	Amateur photographs
X434	Steckel, George	Los Angeles, Calif.	Platinotypes and albumen prints
X435	Stein, S. L., & Rosch	Chicago, Ill.	Portraits and genre and architectural views
X436	Strauss, Julius C.	St. Louis, Mo.	Photographs

Catalogue Number	Company	Location	Type of Product
731-WB	Titus, Mrs. Lillie B.	Boston	Photographs
X	University of Pennsylvania	Philadelphia, Pa.	Photographs illustrating animal locomotion
723-WB	Wellman, Miss. M. B.	Uplands, Pa.	Amateur Photographs
733-WB	Wells, Miss Kate	Salt Lake City, Utah	Tinted photographs
X	Western Coated Paper and Card Co.	Chicago, Ill.	Sensitized paper for photography
734-WB	White, Mrs. C. E.	Butte, Mont.	Photographic views of Butte
X	Williams, Brown & Earle	Philadelphia, Pa.	Parvin telephoto lenses
X	Williams & Shepard	San Francisco, Calif.	Flash photographs
X438	Willis & Clements	Philadelphia, Pa.	Platinotype photographs
439	Woodbridge, Mrs. L. D.	Chester, Pa.	Amateur photographs
735-WB	Wright, Mrs. J. O.	New York, N.Y.	Amateur photographs
440	Yates, Arthur P.	Syracuse, N.Y.	Bromide prints

Note: Information and catalogue numbers are from World's Columbian Exposition, *Official Catalogue of Exhibits*
[a]An *X* preceding the number indicates that the name also appears in the *Index to Awards*.
[b]The letters *WB* following the number indicate that the exhibit was in the Woman's Building.

NOTES

Abbreviations

CHS   Chicago Historical Society
GEH   George Eastman House, International Museum of Photography and Film
MDLC   Manuscripts Division, Library of Congress
NA   National Archives
RG   Record Group
RU   Record Unit
SIA   Smithsonian Institution Archives

Introduction

1. Loy, "A World's Fair Dream," *Poems of the White City*, 77.

2. For a useful discussion of the idea of the exhibition and its dislocation of objects, see Kirshenblatt-Gimblett, "Objects of Ethnography," 388–90, 394–97, 410–16.

3. James Gilbert has characterized this period as one in which "kaleidoscopic changes in behavior and culture" were underway; *Perfect Cities*, 3.

4. Badger, *Great American Fair*, 127.

5. Benedict, *Anthropology of World's Fairs*, 6.

6. "Introduction: Museums and Multiculturalism," in *The Poetics and Politics of Museum Display*, ed. Ivan Karp and Steven Lavine, 1.

7. For a more detailed discussion of these functions in relation to photographs see my dissertation, "Versions of Reality: The Production and Function of Photographs in Colonial Queensland, 1880–1900," 1–5.

8. George Brown Goode, "Recent Advances in Museum Method, II," Smithsonian Institution, U.S. National Museum, *Annual Report*, 1893, 57; George Brown Goode, "Draft of a Classification for the World's Columbian Exposition," in U.S. National Museum, *Annual Report*, 1891, 654.

9. Rydell, *All the World's a Fair*, 44.

10. Charles H. Gould, "The Photographic Exhibits at the World's Fair," *American Amateur Photographer* 5 (May 1893): 258.

11. Haraway, "Teddy Bear Patriarchy," 21.

12. Tagg, *Burden of Representation*, 118–19, 156.

13. Trachtenberg, *Incorporation of America*, 230.

14. Charles Erhman, "The Columbus of Photography," *American Annual of Photography and Photographic Times Almanac* (1894), 28–32.

15. Vidal was a professor at the National School of Decorative Arts in Paris and wrote widely on photography. The Auxiliary Congress of Photographers, where Vidal presented his paper, is discussed in chapter 1. Léon Vidal, "Present and Future Possibilities of Photography, Read Before the Photographic Congress at Chicago," *Photographic American* 4 (Oct. 1893): 341–47, reprinted from the *St. Louis and Canadian Photographer*.

16. W. Jerome Harrison, in the introduction to his 1887 history of photography, calls photography "an evolutionary science" that, in relation to its future potential, was then "as a little child"; *History of Photography*, 5–6.

Chapter 1. Photography for the Public

1. For an excellent discussion of the rise of the industrial institutes and their respective fairs in the United States, see particularly Sinclair, *Philadelphia's Philosopher Mechanics*, 1–18, 100.

2. Both the American Institute and the Franklin Institute had been founded in the 1820s to promote scientific technology in its applied forms for industry through annual fairs, educational lectures, and research publications. "The American Institute Its Past—Present—Future," in American Institute of the City of New York, *Catalogue of the 40th Exhibition*, i–ix; Wile, *A Century of Industrial Progress*, vi–xi.

3. The U.S. Sanitary Commission had far-reaching effects in its investigations into morale, living conditions, and medical treatment for soldiers in the field. Maxwell, *Lincoln's Fifth Wheel*, 224.

4. A *Record of the Metropolitan Fair in Aid of the United States Sanitary Commission*; Stillé, *Memorial of the Great Fair for the U.S. Sanitary Commission*. The E. & H. T. Anthony Company's and Bierstadt Brothers' stereographs are in the Robert Dennis Collection, Prints and Photographs Division, New York Public Library.

5. The Photographic Section of the American Institute, formed in 1867, was the continuation of the American Photographic Society, founded in New York City in 1859. The orientation of the section was more scientific than social, and the group staged several important exhibitions at the institute throughout the second half of the nineteenth century. "The Photographic Section of the American Institute," *Humphrey's Journal* 19 (April 1867): 357–58.

6. Foner, *Reconstruction*, 553–87.

7. Dr. H. Vogel, "Photographic Sketches from the Centennial Grounds," *Philadelphia Photographer* 13 (July 1876): 213.

8. Edward Wilson, "Views Abroad and Across IV," *Philadelphia Photographer* 11 (April 1874): 119. Wilson began his career in the studio of Frederick Gutekunst, where he worked as a cashier and bookkeeper. With capital of a hundred dollars and working principally at night, M. F. Benerman and he founded the *Philadelphia Photographer* in January 1864. In 1865 Wilson opened his own photographic supply business in partnership with John G. Hood and moved the magazine, now under his sole control, to their store offices. Wilson visited both the Paris Exhibition of 1867 and the Vienna Exposition of 1873, covering the latter as part of an extended trip through Great Britain, France, Germany, and Italy, which he described in detail in his articles. Brey, *John Carbutt*, 8.

9. International exhibitions organized objects first by group and then by class. For the Centennial Exhibition, photography was in Group 27, devoted to the plastic and graphic arts, and was divided into subclasses: 430, for photographs on paper, metal, glass, etc.; 431, for prints from photorelief plates; and 432, for photolithographs. Prior to 1876, photography at international expositions was placed as follows:

London, 1851: Machinery: Philosophical Instruments and Processes

Paris, 1855: Group 7: Furniture and decoration, fashions, industrial design, printing, and music. Class 26: Drawing and modeling applied to industrial pursuits, type printing and engraving, and photography

London, 1862: Group 2: Including machinery, civil engineering, naval architecture, and philosophical instruments. Class 14: Photographs and photographic apparatus

Paris, 1867: Group 2: Materials and their application in the liberal arts. Class 9: Photographs and photographic apparatus

Vienna, 1873: Group 12: Graphic arts and industrial drawings, including book printing, lithography, and photography.

Reports of the Commissioners of the United States to the International Exhibition Held at Vienna, 1873, 1:37, 46, 49, 53, 59.

10. The Art Advisory Board did not consider the matter of a separate hall for photography until mid-October, and the official decision was not made until December, well after the fundraising activities initiated by Wilson had begun. John Sartain to William Whittridge, December 14, 1875, Letterpress Books, 1875–1876, John Sartain Papers, Historical Society of Pennsylvania.

11. A partial list of subscribers to the ten-dollar shares was published at various intervals in 1876 before the exhibition. The Centennial proved to be financially successful, and each investor in the Photographic Hall earned $1.75 a share, with interest. "Photographic Hall," *Photographic Times* 5 (October, 1875): 233; "The Photographic Hall Fund," *Philadelphia Photographer* 14 (October 1877): 289.

12. The register included the name, address, nationality, kinds of display materials, space required, and approximate location. Nos. 28, 100, 2421, Registration Album, U.S. Centennial Commission, "International Exhibition, 1876, Philadelphia: Art Department Applications for Space," 1:A606–P53149, Free Library of Philadelphia.

13. Carbutt had emigrated from Sheffield, England, in 1853 and was listed in the Chicago photographic trade directories by 1861. His friendship with Wilson began with the publication of several of his photographs in Wilson's

journal. In 1870 he left a very successful professional business to move to Philadelphia to supervise the commercial operation of the Woodbury process in his American Photo Relief Company. Because of the strong competition from other, less-expensive photoreproduction processes, such as collotype, the company survived only six years. Carbutt finally achieved real business success in 1879 with the first commercial production of gelatin-bromide dryplates in the United States. Brey, *John Carbutt*, 2–8, 81–107.

14. For listings of exhibitors, see: "No. 104, Photographic Exhibition Building," in United States Centennial Commission, *International Exhibition, 1876: Official Catalogue*, 137–45.

15. Dr. H. Vogel, "Photographic Sketches From the Centennial Grounds (Conclusion)," *Philadelphia Photographer* 13 (September 1876): 284–85. Hermann Wilhelm Vogel studied chemistry and physics in Berlin. In 1864 he was appointed to the chair of photochemistry at the academy, which became the Technische Hochschule, and in the same year he founded the publication *Photographische Mitteilungen*. Sipley, *Photography's Great Inventors*, 32.

16. Vogel, "Photographic Sketches From the Centennial Grounds, II," *Philadelphia Photographer* 13 (August 1876): 234–35.

17. Edward Wilson, "Photography in the Great Exhibition, II," *Philadelphia Photographer*, 13 (July 1876): 197, 201. John Kent used a composite form of printing from several large negatives for his 101.9 cm × 69.8 cm portrait photographs, including one entitled *Making a Call*. The single female seated portrait he made with multiple negatives at the George Eastman House, International Museum of Photography and Film (hereafter GEH) may also have been present at the Centennial, as Pedzich has noted. Pedzich, "John Howe Kent," 1–10.

18. James Ryder was a leading photographer from Cleveland who organized the second convention of the National Photographers' Association in 1870 in that city. His Centennial display included a number of other genre scenes, including the prints *He Could Get Up and Dust*, and *Civil Rights Bill*, as well as straightforward records of events and a copy of the celebrated chromo by the artist A. M. Willard entitled *Yankee Doodle—The Spirit of '76*, which is now in the collection of the GEH. Ryder's outspoken criticism of the restrictions placed on photography at the Chicago Exposition is discussed with respect to official photography in chapter 4.

19. Edward Wilson, "Photography in the Great Exhibition," pts. 2 and 3, *Philadelphia Photographer* 13 (June, August 1876): 185, 231. Landy, born in New York City, was apprenticed to S. A. Holmes in 1850 and ran the Meade Brothers gallery in New York before establishing his studio in Cincinnati in 1861. Descriptions of him as "the Salomon

of the West" in the 1870s were based on the wide reputation of his work, mainly in portraiture and staged pieces. A more detailed discussion of Landy's Shakespeare series appears in chapter 2. GEH Interactive Catalogue and Biographical File; Welling, *Photography in America*, 235; "Cincinnati Correspondence," *Philadelphia Photographer* 8 (May 1871): 140–41.

20. Broadrim [pseud.], "Centennial Sights: Sunlight and Shadow," *St. Louis Practical Photographer* 1 (January 1876): 8–9.

21. In 1864 Root had published *The Camera and the Pencil*, the earliest history of photographic practice in America, a rambling anecdotal account from firsthand experience. Its later use, as Robert Taft has pointed out, has been limited by Root's failure to cite the sources of his information. Taft, *Photography and the American Scene*, 475 n. 148; Carson, "The Eclipse and Rediscovery of Robert Cornelius," 20.

22. "Scattered Photography in Our World's Fair," *Philadelphia Photographer* 13 (August 1876): 245.

23. The official catalogue gives very detailed descriptions of individual displays, particularly those on education. See U.S. Centennial Commission, *International Exhibition*, 322–26.

24. Holtermann left Germany before being drafted into the army in 1858, emigrating to the Australian goldfields in search of fortune. The reef mine at Hill End in which he owned shares made a spectacular strike in 1872, ensuring his fortune. "Scattered Photography in Our World's Fair," *Philadelphia Photographer* 13 (August 1876): 245; Bernard Holtermann, *Gold and Silver*, 11–33; "The Largest Negative in the World," *Philadelphia Photographer* 13 (October 1876): 320.

25. *Official Catalogue of the British Section*, 75.

26. Goetzmann, *New Lands, New Men*, 407–9.

27. O'Sullivan's work for Matthew Brady and Alexander Gardner during the Civil War prepared him for the rigors of expeditionary photography. He served first with the Clarence King survey in 1868 and later with Wheeler. O'Sullivan was equipped with the latest apparatus, which cost some $1,000 (one-tenth of an entire year's survey expenses), and he received an excellent salary of $150 a month. He left the West in 1875 and died of tuberculosis in 1882. William Bell worked for Wheeler during the 1872 season. *Frank Leslie's Historic Register of the United States Centennial Exposition, 1876*, 101; Naef and Wood, *Era of Exploration*, 52–55, 125–36.

28. Hayden was a geologist with a keen interest in the monumental representation of the environment he was exploring. He employed the painters Thomas Moran and S. R. Gifford to render this scale and panoramic effect, which in turn influenced the work of Jackson. Jackson had

begun working with the survey in 1870 and was in the Yellowstone area in 1871 and 1872, shifting to south-western Colorado and the Mesa Verde plateau in 1874 and 1875. Hales's treatment of this period in his biography of Jackson is extensive; see particularly chapters 4 and 5. Goetzmann, *New Lands, New Men,* 409–12; Naef and Wood, *Era of Exploration,* 222–26.

29. *Frank Leslie's Historic Register,* 278–79; Ingram, *The Centennial Exposition,* 148–49.

30. Holmes later continued this type of model work at the United States National Museum on a more spectacular scale for the Columbian Exposition. The Centennial models were based on photographs made in 1874 and 1875. Some of the photographs Jackson made of these and other models are in the collection of the GEH. William N. Jackson, *Descriptive Catalogue of the Photographs of the United States Geological Survey of the Territories,* 72–73; Hales, *William Henry Jackson,* 126.

31. Powell had gained his reputation by descending the Colorado River in 1869, a trip he repeated in 1871–72. His interest in the geological formations and methods of erosion that had created this natural wonder was paralleled by his interest in the people who inhabited the arid lands adjacent to it. Powell's surveys in the 1870s combined these interests and relied heavily on the photographic work provided by J. K. Hillers. Hillers, who had been born in Germany, emigrated in 1852 and settled in New York City, where he worked as a clerk before enlisting in the Union Army during the Civil War. Fowler, *Western Photographs,* 15–18.

32. It was during the Powell trip to the Kaibab Plateau in the fall of 1872 that Hillers was given the name of "Myself in the Water" by the Indians to describe the mirroring process of the photograph. The photograph entitled *The Arrowmaker and His Daughter* is reproduced in Fowler, *Western Photographs,* pl. 20; see also Fowler, 44–54.

33. Hillers made the 1873 trip with the painter Thomas Moran, whose influence on his style was similar to that of Jackson's in the same period. The photograph of the Paiute mother and children is reproduced in Fleming and Luskey, *North American Indians in Early Photographs,* pl. 5.39; see also Fowler, *Western Photographs,* 50.

34. Miner, "Government Building at the Centennial," 209.

35. Notman was a very successful photographer in Canada, with branch studios in Boston and New York in this period. Brey states that the group paid $15,000 for the concession, but the *New York Tribune* noted that the fee was $3,000. Considering that the Roller Chair Company paid $18,000 for its concession, and Centennial Guide Book Company $5,000, it is probable that the $3,000 figure is incorrect. Brey, *John Carbutt,* 100; "The Centennial Exhibition Value of Business Privileges, Concessions Granted

by the Centennial Board of Finance," February 12, 1876, *New York Tribune* scrapbook, Centennial Series International Exhibits, n.p., Library Company of Philadelphia.

36. For a description of the studio setup and printing techniques, see Gihon's account in Wilson, *Wilson's Photographics,* 190–91.

37. J. S. Ingram, *The Centennial Exposition,* 329–30.

38. In addition to the fifty-two-page pamphlet catalogue *Centennial Photographic Company's Catalogue, International Exhibition, 1876,* there was another listing entitled *Wilson's Catalogue of Selections of the Centennial Photo. Co.'s Views of the International Exhibition.* It was distributed by Wilson and Benerman, and it claimed to reproduce "the real gems of the collection" and a warning that copies by unscrupulous photographers were being marketed. Centennial Collection, Historical Society of Pennsylvania.

39. "A Large Photograph of the Exhibition Buildings," *Anthony's Photographic Bulletin* 7 (December 1876): 375–76. Gutekunst had made his reputation early with his portraits of Civil War generals, and he was one of the original members of the Philadelphia Photographic Society. For a detailed description of the making of the panorama, see Gutekunst entry in Brey and Brey, *Philadelphia Photographers.*

40. "Proceedings of the National Photographic Convention," *Philadelphia Photographer* 5 (April 1868): 140.

41. The National Photographic Association conventions were held in the cities of Boston in 1869, Cleveland in 1870, Philadelphia in 1871, St. Louis in 1872, Buffalo in 1873, and Chicago in 1874. Moves to revive the association in 1878 and 1879 led to the new name of the Photographers' Association of America, which held its convention in Chicago in August 1880, with James Ryder as president. "The Chicago Convention," *Anthony's Photographic Bulletin* 10 (November 1880): 325–27.

42. George B. Ayers, "Concerning the Annual Exhibition," *Philadelphia Photographer* 10 (July 1873): 202. Ayers made these assessments in the context of a critique of exhibitions generally, and they were similar to those by W. J. Baker regarding proposed changes for the next association exhibit in 1874. W. J. Baker, "The Exhibition," *Philadelphia Photographer* 10 (May 1873): 155.

43. The demise of the organization had various causes, but the uncontrolled influence of "editors and self-seeking trades" was seen as opposed to the interests of practical photographers, who concluded that they needed an organization to serve "their own interests." The first meeting of the new organization took place in August 1880 in Chicago and drew some three hundred participants. "The National Photographic Association," *Anthony's Photographic Bulletin* 9 (October 1879): 316; "Our Convention," *Anthony's Photographic Bulletin* 10 (November 1880): 326.

44. One report on the convention gave an attendance figure of 400, which was half the usual number and which dropped to 100 in the later sessions. Information on the convention is taken from a number of accounts, including "The Chicago Convention of the Photographers' Association of America," *Photographic Times* 23 (August 4, 1893): 414–15. For information on the background of the association in the 1880s, see Sarah Greenough, "Of Charming Glens, Graceful Glades, and Frowning Cliffs: The Economic Incentives, Social Inducements and Aesthetic Issues of American Pictorial Photography, 1880–1902" in Sandweiss, *Photography in Nineteenth Century America*, 261–66.

45. "The P. A. of A. Convention," *Wilson's Photographic Magazine* 30 (September 1893): 388.

46. "The Thirteenth Convention of the Photographers' Association of America," *American Journal of Photography* 14 (September 1893): 390. Frank Place had begun his professional career in 1875 in Manchester, Indiana, and in 1881 he became president of the Tri-State Photographic Association in Fort Wayne. Shortly after this he moved to Chicago, and at the 1891 meeting of the association was elected vicepresident of the association. "Frank A. Place: President of the P. A. of A.," *St. Louis and Canadian Photographer* 11 (July 1893): 316.

47. The Photo Materials Company of Rochester offered prizes totaling $1,200 for work on its new "Kloro" paper. "The American and British Conventions," *Photo Beacon* 5 (August 1893): 253–54.

48. For a complete discussion of the "paper war" of 1893 to 1895 among the competing companies that were producing the new emulsion-based papers, see Jenkins, *Images and Enterprise*, 86–95.

49. "The Lessons of the Exhibition," *American Journal of Photography* 14 (May 1893): 198.

50. For a review of the first (1887) and subsequent joint exhibits, see Peterson, "Exhibitions of Photography in America, 1887–1917," 5–8.

51. The catalogue of the exhibition gives details on names, titles, and formats of objects on view; see Photographic Society of Philadelphia, *Sixth Joint Annual Exhibition*. For a very comprehensive background discussion and an excellent assessment of the roles of various photographic groups in Philadelphia during this period, see Panzer, *Philadelphia Naturalistic Photography*, 8–12.

52. Buerger, *Last Decade*, 2. Davison's work was also present at the Exposition in the British section, discussed in chapter 2.

53. Rather than pursuing the career in mechanical engineering he had originally intended, in 1882 Stieglitz began to study photography in Berlin under Dr. Hermann Vogel. After eight years of study, he returned to New York in 1890 and entered into a photo-engraving business with two partners. See Alfred Stieglitz, "A Plea for Art Photography in America," *Photographic Mosaics for 1892* (1893): 135–37; "Distinguished Photographers of Today; I: Alfred Stieglitz," *Photographic Times* 23 (December 1, 1893): 689–90.

54. Alfred Stieglitz, "The Joint Exhibition at Philadelphia," *American Amateur Photographer* 5 (May 5, 1893): 201, 203.

55. Alfred Stieglitz, "The Joint Exhibition at Philadelphia," *American Amateur Photographer* 5 (June 1893): 253. William Rau was a leading professional photographer in Philadelphia whose career had begun at nineteen with the U.S. expedition to photograph the transit of Venus in 1874. He married Louise Bell, daughter of William Bell, who, with O'Sullivan, was one of the Wheeler survey photographers in 1872. Rau's various trips for stereo and general commercial photographs (including one to Egypt with Edward Wilson in 1881–82) earned him a national reputation. He was the official photographer for the Louisiana Purchase Exposition in St. Louis in 1904. Brey, "William Rau's Photographic Experiences," 4–11; Panzer, *Philadelphia Naturalistic Photography*, 40.

56. "The Sixth Joint Exhibition," *American Journal of Photography* 14 (May 1893): 216–17. The catalogue included no mention of this display of photographic history.

57. In 1893 Sachse, whose father had been the subject of one of Cornelius's early portraits, attended the American Philosophical Society's sesquicentennial meeting, where he urged those with information on the earliest period to recollect details. Carson, "Eclipse and Rediscovery of Robert Cornelius," 21.

58. Alfred Stieglitz, "The Joint Exhibition," *American Amateur Photographer* 5 (May 1893): 207. Farnsworth's photographs that received awards were no. 918, *Orpheus*; no. 919, *Ode*; and no. 922, *Friends*. Farnsworth's *To a Greek Girl* (Fig. 1.6) was exhibited as a transparency with a text by Austin Dobsen: "Where 'er you go, where 'er you pass, There comes a gladness on the grass"; Photographic Society of Philadelphia, *Sixth Annual Exhibition*, 67, 98.

59. "The Photographic Display at the World's Fair," *American Amateur Photographer* 5 (March 1893): 74; Robert E. M. Bain, "Amateur Photography at the World's Fair," *American Amateur Photographer* 4 (March 1892): 108.

60. For descriptive reviews of the congress, see "Congress of Photographers, Chicago, Illinois, July 31st to August 5th," *American Amateur Photographer* 5 (August 1893): 375–77; "The World's Congress Auxiliary," *American Journal of Photography* 14 (September 1893): 398–403. For a list of the papers to be presented, see "Congress of Photographers, Programme," *Photographic Times* 23 (July 28, 1893): 408.

61. *Photographic Times* 23 (August 4, 1893): 417; *A Biographical History with Portraits of Prominent Men of the Great*

West, ed. John A. Campbell (Chicago: Western Biographical and Engraving Co., 1902), 64; *Photographic Times* 23 (March 17, 1893): 135.

62. J. F. Sachse, "The Photographic Congress Auxiliary," *American Journal of Photography* 13 (November 1892): 484.

63. Barnes had taken up photography in 1886 as an amateur but wanted to support herself by it. She came from a publishing family and turned to writing. In 1890 she joined the staff of the *American Amateur Photographer,* writing a column called "Women's Work" and eventually becoming an associate editor. After moving to England she became co-editor and publisher with her husband of *The Photogram* in 1894. Palmquist, *Catharine Weed Barnes Ward,* 5–12; Richard Hines, Jr., "Women in Photography, 1898," in Palmquist, *Camera Fiends & Kodak Girls,* 63–67; Gover, *Positive Image,* 49–52; Catherine Weed Ward, "Amateur Photography: Read at the World's Congress of Photographers, August 2, 1893," *American Amateur Photographer* 5 (August 1893): 358–63.

64. Gover, *Positive Image,* 108. Wade, like many women, had moved from photography as a form of recreation to photography as a paying vocation, using photographs to illustrate her own poetry and narrative or story subjects; Elizabeth Flint Wade, "Amateur Photography Through Women's Eyes, No. 2," *Photo-American* 5 (June 1894): 235–36. Main's work was available in the United States through the Platinotype Company of Philadelphia, which charged no commission, since the revenue from her work was all donated to charity; Gover, *Positive Image,* 67, 108. Several of her photographs were reproduced in the *Photographic Times;* see "Distinguished Photographers of Today," *Photographic Times* 23 (December 15, 1893): 732–33. Elizabeth Main, "Winter Photography in the Alps," *Photographic Times,* 23 (September 22, 1893): 535–36.

65. Ives's background as a printer and commercial photoengraver laid the basis for his successful development of the modern halftone screen in 1885. He moved to color photography and patented a process of composite, or additive, color photography in 1890. In 1892 his color camera and optical viewer, known as the "Kromskop," was presented to the London Society of Arts. Sipley, *Photography's Great Inventors,* 121–122; W. I. Lincoln Adams, "Photography in the Colors of Nature," *Frank Leslie's Monthly* 36 (August 1893): 249–51; J. E. Weller, "Color Photography," *Pacific Coast Photographer* 2 (December 1893): 465–66; Coe, *Colour Photography,* 36–42.

66. Mason had been an active member of the photographic section of the American Institute since the early 1870s. He had made a large number of flashlight photographs as illustrations for Helen Campbell's 1893 book *Darkness and Daylight,* dealing with slum conditions and

missions as well as rescue work in New York City. Ellerslie Wallace's paper noted the usefulness of chronometric techniques for the study of disease, referring to Eadweard Muybridge's work at the University of Pennsylvania. See O. G. Mason, "Photography for Illustrating the Practice of Medicine and Surgery in a Great Hospital," and Ellerslie Wallace, "Photography for Illustrating the Practice of Medicine and Surgery in a Great Hospital," both in *The World's Congress Auxiliary of the World's Columbian Exposition Congress of Photographers.*

67. Frederick Starr, "Photography in Anthropological Work," in *The American Annual of Photography and Photographic Times Almanac* (1893): 210–11.

68. Ward had begun his career in association with Percy Lund, from whom he learned the publishing business. His marriage to Catharine Barnes in July 1893 led to the founding of the important new journal *The Photogram,* for which they served as co-editors. "Henry Snowden Ward, A Short Biography," *Practical Photographer* 5 (January 1894): 8–10.

69. H. Snowden Ward, "Photographers' Effort at Union: A Paper Read at the World's Congress of Photography," *Photographic Times* 23 (November 17, 1893): 66. Ward reviewed some forty-three American associations and societies and noted an increase in state and local associations affiliated with the Photographers' Association of America. He also presented a short talk at the 1893 Photographers' Association of America convention on the situation of its counterpart in the United Kingdom. Ward, "Photographers' Efforts at Union: A Paper Read at the World's Congress of Photography," *Photographic Times* 23 (November 10, 1893): 644–46; Ward, "Photographic Conventions," *Photographic Times* 23 (August 11, 1893): 440–42.

70. The third congress was not held until 1900. It was held in connection with the exposition of that year. "International Photographic Congress at Brussels," *Wilson's Photographic Magazine* 28 (November 1891): 663–65.

71. H. Snowden Ward, "Photographers' Efforts at Union: A Paper Read at the World's Congress of Photography," *Photographic Times* 23 (November 17, 1893): 663.

72. W. Jerome Harrison, "The Desirability of an International Bureau Established (1) To Record, (2), To Exchange Photographic Negatives and Prints," in *World's Congress Auxiliary,* 1–5. Harrison's essay was reproduced in the *British Journal of Photography* 25 (February 1894). As vice-president of the Birmingham Photographic Society, Harrison had proposed a survey of the county of Warwickshire in 1889, and it was begun in 1892. According to Poignant, the British Association for the Advancement of Science was interested in tapping into the work of the photographic survey that was then being conducted for ethnographic purposes. Poignant, "Surveying the Field of View," 61–62; "A Biographical Sketch of the Author, by W.

I. Lincoln Adams" in Harrison, *History of Photography,* 134–35.

73. The committee formed at the Exposition included H. Snowden Ward as chairman and Gayton Douglass as vice-chairman, with John Carbutt, Shapoor Bhedwar of Bombay, Léon Vidal of Paris, W. K. Burton of Tokyo, Elizabeth Wade of Buffalo, and Dr. John Nicol. "Congress of Photographers, Chicago, Illinois, July 31st to August 5th," *American Amateur Photographer* 5 (August 1893): 376.

74. Sir John Benjamin Stone, as president of the Birmingham Photographic Society in 1889, had given impetus to the implementation of the Warwickshire Record Survey, and other societies adopted the survey techniques used in Harrison's project. In 1892 Harrison's proposal of a national survey plan to the Royal Photographic Society of Great Britain met resistance from the photographic establishment. Harrison's critical response to the powerful but "fossilized" society resulted in his withdrawal from the survey and his resignation from the Birmingham Photographic Society. In 1897 Stone founded the National Photographic Record Association, based on Harrison's methods and ideas. James, "Evolution of the Photographic Record and Survey Movement," 205–17. C. J. Fowler, "The Photographic Survey," *Photogram* 7 (May 1900): 130–35.

75. Léon Vidal, "Letter from France," *Anthony's Photographic Bulletin* 24 (December 9, 1893): 733. Work on the formation of the Musée, according to Vidal, listed thirteen separate societies and participating clubs. The Musée collected photographs showing a comprehensive view of French life and classified into such subjects as religion, law, philosophy, politics, and the natural sciences. Léon Vidal, "Exposé de la situation," 33.

76. Dr. John Nicol, "A Plea for the National Recognition of Photography: Read at the World's Congress of Photography," *Photographic Times* 23 (August 11, 1893): 437–38.

77. A detailed prospectus for Vogel's teaching curriculum is included as an appendix in London, Commonwealth Institute, United Kingdom Section, *Catalogue of the Special Exhibition of Photography, Imperial Institute.*

78. Recommendations for formal training in photography had begun with those by Marcus Aurelius Root in the 1860s and Edward Wilson in the 1870s. Wilson was authorized by the National Photographic Association in 1872 to approach Congress for a $30,000 grant toward the establishment of a photography institute. Marcus Aurelius Root, "A Heliographic School—Its Implications." *American Journal of Photography and Allied Sciences* 3 (July 1860): 41–42; "Wanted: A School of Photography," *Photographic Times* 23 (July 14, 1893): 358–59; "Photographic Schools of Instruction," *American Annual of Photography and Photographic Times Almanac* (1894), 357; "Convention Notes," *Photographic Times* 20 (August 22, 1890): 417.

79. Professional photography was becoming big business in this period, with large firms employing staffs to perform a variety of specialized tasks. Declining prices and increased competition from newer, cheaply run businesses were factors that led professionals to seek protection in association and new avenues of specialty work. Brown, "Versions of Reality," 1:27, 44.

80. Charles H. Gould, "The Photographic Exhibits at the World's Fair," *American Amateur Photographer* 5 (May 1893): 258.

Chapter 2. Exhibiting Photography

1. Walker, *World's Fair,* 40. Walker, who later became president of MIT, made a balanced yet critical assessment of the 1876 Centennial and noted that an international exposition was a "thoroughly practical matter, requiring the minimum of theory and politics, and the maximum of executive efficiency and responsibility" (p. 40).

2. George Brown Goode, "First Draft of a System of Classification for the World's Columbian Exposition," in the U.S. National Museum, *Annual Report,* 1891, 711–12. The 1901 Buffalo Pan-American Exhibition placed photography within the Division of Liberal Arts with educational exhibits, pianos, scientific apparatus. Pan-American Exposition, *Official Catalogue and Guidebook,* 114.

3. Aristarch [pseud.], "Photography at the World's Fair," *St. Louis and Canadian Photographer* 10 (April 1892): 151.

4. Catharine Weed Barnes, "Amateur Photography in America: Read Before the Photographic Convention of the United Kingdom in Edinburgh, Scotland, July 13, 1892," *Photo Beacon,* 4 (Aug. 1892): 270; reprinted in *American Amateur Photographer* 4 (Aug. 1892). Barnes advocated looking at the question from both sides rather than accepting the division as a fact. She took the view that the amateur had the time and resources to test new methods and their applications, and thus had something to contribute to the professional as a co-worker.

5. "The Twelfth Annual Convention of the Photographers' Association of America, Buffalo, July 14 to 17, 1891," *St. Louis and Canadian Photographer* 9 (Aug. 1891): 308.

6. No record of this committee, if in fact it was ever convened, has been found. The Photographers' Association of America had formed a standing committee on the Exposition with the following members: Dr. A. H. Elliott, chairman; W. I. Lincoln Adams; J. M. Appleton; A. Bogardus; W. H. H. Clark; W. G. Entriken; J. F. Ryder; C. T. Stuart; and H. McMichael. Elliott, Adams, Bogardus, Ryder, and Stuart served on both this committee and that of the Auxiliary Congress. Photographers' Association of America, Program of the Annual 1891 Convention, Chicago, August 17

[1892], Library Collection, GEH; World's Fair Notes, RG 48, 386, box 1, NA.

7. *Columbian Exposition,* 23.

8. Charles Melford Robinson, "The Fair As Spectacle," in Johnson, *History of the World's Columbian Exposition,* 1:300; for a fuller description of the section of the Manufactures and Liberal Arts Building used for the Group 151 materials, see 2:264.

9. An open letter from Peabody to photographers describing the space and hanging conditions appeared in several photographic journals during February and March 1893; see, e.g., Peabody, "The Photographic Exhibit at the 'Columbian Fair,'" *Wilson's Photographic Magazine* 30 (March 1893): 100. The March edition of the *American Amateur Photographer* included Peabody's letter to the editor, F. C. Beach, acknowledging that all the space had been allotted. "The World's Fair Photograph Display," *American Amateur Photographer* 5 (March 1893): 134.

10. Charles Gentile, editor, *The Eye,* to Frances Benjamin Johnston, Feb. 4, 1893, Francis Benjamin Johnston Papers, reel 4, MDLC.

11. "The Photographic Display at the World's Fair," *American Amateur Photographer* 5 (March 1893): 74.

12. John Boyd Thatcher, Chairman, Executive Committee of Awards, to George Brown Goode, April 18, 1893, RU 70, box 33, folder 6, SIA.

13. F. Todd, "Baiting the Lines," *Photo Beacon* 5 (Oct. 1893): 332.

14. Landy had been awarded the Blair Cup, with its cash award of $500 sponsored by the Blair Camera Company at the 1887 Photographers' Association convention in Minneapolis for his photograph *Hiawatha. J. Landy's Catalogue of Celebrities,* 6–7.

15. The names of the European judges are given in Vogel's reviews of the photography section. Dr. H. W. Vogel, "Letter from the World's Fair," *Anthony's Photographic Bulletin* 24 (Sept. 9, 1893): 539. Stuart's review of the photographic section was vague and lacked any critical substance; see C. T. Stuart, "Photography," in World's Columbian Exposition, *Report of the Committee on Awards,* 1365–66.

16. Jackson's career at this point was undergoing pressure from the changing nature of the occupation of photography, which was becoming less the work of individualists like himself and more that of entrepreneurial businessmen. Considering the other work on exhibit in the photographic section, Jackson's work did not appear as dated as Peter Hales has suggested; see Hales, *William Henry Jackson,* 144–50, 200–202.

17. Some of Jackson's prints were in a large panoramic format, measuring 17" × 91". [Dr. John Nicol,] "Photo-

graphs at the Fair: The American Exhibit," *Photo Beacon* 5 (Aug. 1893): 257.

18. The panorama is now in the Prints and Photographs Division of the Library of Congress. James Inglis prepared a 30' × 6' print of Jackson's photograph mounted on canvas for the B & O Railway; "World's Fair Jottings," *Photo Beacon* 5 (April 1893): 116. W. H. Jackson, "Cramer's Isochromatic Plates," *Wilson's Photographic Magazine* 30 (May 1893): 216; Jackson, *Time Exposure,* 260–62.

19. Hales, *William Henry Jackson,* 192–94. Jackson also displayed forty-eight scenic views, including several colored ones, in the California Building. California, World's Fair Commission, *Final Report,* 170.

20. Rau was present at the Exposition, where he took a number of photographs that he later made into lantern slides, now in the collection of the GEH. Brey, "On the Rails with William Rau."

21. These strategies were characteristic of expositions, according to Burton Benedict; Benedict, *Anthropology of World's Fairs,* 15–18.

22. For references on the actors, see Chapter 1, note 19. When Walker died in the early 1880s it was Landy who arranged for his funeral. Conteur [pseud.], "Interesting Facts Concerning a Photographer of Prominence in Early Cincinnati," *Cincinnati Enquirer,* Dec. 23, 1923.

23. Gray, *Souvenir, World's Fair, . . . Shakespeare Boiled Down.* During the nineteenth century the taste for Shakespeare had moved from a broad-based to more specialized audience as the small performing stock company was gradually replaced by entertainment theater. Levine, *Highbrow/Lowbrow,* 79.

24. Gustine L. Hurd, "Elaine," *St. Louis and Canadian Photographer* 9 (July 1891): 283. Both "Lancelot and Elaine" and "Lucile," a poem written in 1860 by Owen Meredith, the pen name of Edward Robert Bulwer-Lytton, focused on heroines whose own destinies were founded on unrequited love. The 1893 Grand Prize competition was won by the Indiana firm of Heimberger and Son. "The Chicago Convention of the Photographers' Association of America," *Photographic Times* 23 (Aug. 4, 1893): 415.

25. [Dr. John Nicol,] "Photographs at the Fair: The American Exhibit," *Photo Beacon* 5 (Aug. 1893): 258. Elliot operated a photography business from 1865 until his death in 1899, and the first fine art gallery in Columbus was part of his studio. His portrait of Jones, taken in 1879, was purchased by a New York firm for $13,000, and he had won medals for his portrait work at the Ohio industrial fairs of the 1880s. James M. Elliot Family Photographic Collection, Ohio Historical Society.

26. Charles H. Gould, "The Photographic Exhibits at the World's Fair," *American Amateur Photographer* 5 (May

1893): 259. McMichael had been president of the Photographers' Association of America in 1889 and served in other capacities for the organization during the 1880s and 1890s. "Leading Photographer Dies at Hospital," *Buffalo Evening News,* May 9, 1907, p. 1.

27. McMichael's "Elaine" series had been awarded only a diploma at the 1891 Buffalo competition, but many considered it superior to the prizewinning work. As recognition of the esteem with which his three pictures were held, they were reproduced as frontispieces in the September 1891 issue of the *Photo Beacon* and the December 1891 issue of *Wilson's Photographic Magazine.* "The 'Elaine' Pictures at the Convention," *Wilson's Photographic Magazine* 28 (Nov. 7, 1891): 577–80.

28. "Largest Photo in the World," *Wilson's Photographic Magazine* 30 (Aug. 1893): 262–63. Strauss, born in Cleveland in 1857, began his photographic career at the age of twelve by working in a tintype studio. He eventually opened an extensive and elaborate gallery in St. Louis and played an important part in the St. Louis exposition through his efforts to ensure that photography was well represented. Welling, *Photography in America,* 346.

29. Dr. H. W. Vogel, "Letter from the World's Fair," *Anthony's Photographic Bulletin* 24 (Nov. 11, 1893): 665–66.

30. "World's Fair Jottings," *Photo Beacon* 5 (April 1893): 116.

31. "Our Pictures," *Photo Beacon* 5 (Sept. 1893): 291–92. The young Steckel left Allentown, Pennsylvania, in 1884, having served an apprenticeship with E. D. Jeans, and opened a studio in Los Angeles in 1888 which grew to a substantial business by the turn of the century. His reputation was enhanced by awards gained at the Photographers' Association convention exhibitions first in 1889, again in 1891, and most recently gold and bronze medals in 1893 in Chicago. Steckel, "George Steckel of Los Angeles: Correspondence from Helen Giorgi," *History of Photography* 13 (Jan.–March 1980): 106.

32. It is not clear from the Exposition review whether the photograph was a figural group or a copy made from sculpture, a print, or a painting, but it was significant that a photographer of Breeze's caliber had participated in the photographic section. Breeze's successful Carbon Studio in New York City was maintained for a time in partnership with Rudolf Eickemeyer, Jr. "Photographs at the Fair: The American Exhibit," *Photo Beacon* 5 (Aug. 1893): 258; "Photographic Exhibitions," *Photographic Mosaics for the Year 1891,* 104–5; Welling, *Photography in America,* 393.

33. Dr. H. W. Vogel, "Letter from the World's Fair," *Anthony's Photographic Bulletin* (Sept. 9, 1893): 539–40.

34. "Photography in Natural Colors—An Accomplished Fact," *Wilson's Photographic Magazine* 30 (April 1893): 160–

62; Horgan, "Photo-Engraving Pioneers No. 6: William Kurtz"; Sipley, *A Half Century of Color,* 16–17. Luis Nadeau points out that Frederick Ives exhibited three color halftone blocks in the 1885 Novelties Exhibition in Philadelphia and that a Belfast firm had made a similar deal with the Vogels to use the new color halftone process. Nadeau, *Encyclopedia,* 2:447.

35. The three-plate halftone engraving of the still life with vegetables was reproduced as the frontispiece in the May 1893 issue of *Wilson's Photographic Magazine.* The journal had 6,000 copies of this issue printed to show the importance of this "first time" publication. Earlier, in March 1893, the *Engraver and Printer* reproduced the three-color fruit piece. Horgan, "Photo-Engraving Pioneers No. 6," 325.

36. "There has been no disposition to discriminate against amateurs," Peabody wrote, "but the applications from amateurs are few, if any." "The World's Fair Photograph Display," *American Amateur Photographer* 5 (March 1893): 134.

37. Kendall's maiden name was Marie Hartig. She trained as a nurse in New York City before marrying John C. Kendall, and in 1884 they moved to Norwalk, Connecticut, where she bought a camera and began a professional career that lasted until her death in 1943. GEH Interactive Catalogue and Biographical File.

38. See Chapter 1, note. 58.

39. Farnsworth was given a camera as a gift, and she later said that it was because her early efforts at photography were "utterly unsuccessful" that she became interested in it. In 1894 her work received international recognition in the two important art photography "salons," one by the Linked Ring in London and the other by the Photo Club of Paris. By 1898 she admitted that she rarely took pictures anymore, because it was such hard work. Richard Hines, Jr., "Women and Photography: 1898," in Palmquist, *Camera Fiends & Kodak Girls,* 81–82.

40. The Society of Amateur Photographers in New York City had a policy that was open to the admission of women amateurs. Slade was the first active "lady member" of the society, in 1887, and she was later joined by Catharine Barnes. Farnsworth was associated with the New York Camera Club. The two New York City amateur societies merged in 1897, becoming the Camera Club. F. C. Beach, "The Society of Amateur Photographers of New York," *American Amateur Photographer* 6 (April 1894): 163–64, 169; Catharine Weed Barnes, "Photography from a Woman's Standpoint, 1890," in Palmquist, *Camera Fiends & Kodak Girls,* 64; Clarence Bloomfield Moore, "Women Experts in Photography," *Cosmopolitan* 14 (March 1893): 57–58.

41. Despite the acceptance of her work for exhibit in the early 1890s it was rejected for the First Philadelphia Salon of Photography in 1898 because of its lack of aesthetic features. Panzer, *Philadelphia Naturalistic Photography*, 15–16, 48–49. The photograph *Marcus Hook Looking Northeast* is currently held by Janet Lehr, Inc., of New York City.

42. W. H. Jackson, "Cramer's Isochromatic Plates," *Wilson's Photographic Magazine* 30 (June 1893): 216. Cramer, born in Eschwege, Germany, in 1838, emigrated to the United States in 1859 and apprenticed himself to John A. Scholten, a leading St. Louis photographer. Returning to St. Louis after serving briefly in the Civil War, Cramer went into partnership with Julius Gross until the partnership dissolved in 1879. In December 1879 Cramer began a dryplate manufacturing business with Herman Norden, who retired in 1883. Cramer gave up his photographic practice in 1889 to concentrate on his manufacturing business. He began making orthochromatic plates in about 1890, adding certain aniline dyes developed by Vogel in 1873 and 1884. Sidonia E. Loehr, "Gustave Cramer: A Biographical Sketch," *Wilson's Photographic Magazine* 30 (July 1893): 292–94; "The G. Cramer Dry Plate Works," *St. Louis and Canadian Photographer* 9 (Sept. 1891): 466–67.

43. Stieglitz, "The Joint Exhibition at Philadelphia," *American Amateur Photographer* 5 (June 6, 1893): 253.

44. Carbutt, who had been the superintendent of Photographic Hall in 1876, was now a successful dryplate manufacturer. Brey, *John Carbutt*, 146, 149–51. For a full description of the Carbutt display, see "Notes of the Month," *Photo-American* 5 (Feb. 1894): 127. A photograph of the entrance is reproduced in Brey, *John Carbutt*, 150.

45. Newbury, "Photographic Proofs and Apparatus," 203; "Kodak Prizes," *Photographic Times* 23 (May 12, 1893): 253.

46. [Dr. John Nicol,] "Photographs at the Fair: The British Exhibit," *Photo Beacon* 5 (Sept. 1893): 293. In Class A, for prints made from plates not less than 14″ × 17″, the top three winners from among the thirty-two entries were G. M. Elton of Palmyra, New York; H. McMichael of Buffalo, New York; and Stein & Roesch of Chicago. In Class B, for prints of figural groups suitable for enlargement and made from plates not less than 5″ × 7″, the first-place winner from among fifty-nine entries was H. S. Squyer of Auburn. "Kodak Prizes," *Photographic Times* 23 (May 12, 1893): 253.

47. H. W. Vogel, "Letter From Germany: The Chicago World's Fair," *Anthony's Photographic Bulletin* 24 (Nov. 11, 1893): 668.

48. "Explorer Peary Kodaks Wonders of Greenland," *St. Louis and Canadian Photographer* 11 (Feb. 1893): 58–59, reprinted from the *Rochester* (N.Y.) *Democrat*. Peary, on leave from the navy, made a number of trips to Greenland in this period in search of a jumping-off point for his planned North Pole trek. The need to raise funds for these expeditions required keeping his name and feats in the public eye. Goetzmann, *New Lands, New Men*, 444–47; Memorandum of an agreement between R. E. Peary and the Ethnology Department of the Exposition, Jan. 20, 1893, F. W. Putnam Papers, Harvard University Archives, Pusey Library; advertisements entitled "The Kodak at the North Pole" and "Peary Pressed the Button," in Advertisement Files, Corporate Archives, Eastman Kodak Company.

49. McAllister's display included the Ethoxycon (a compact limelight apparatus), a small apparatus that ran on natural gas or hydrogen, and other apparatus that used electrical current. "Two Dollars A Day" [pseud.], "Photographic Apparatus at the World's Fair," *Photo Beacon* 5 (June 1893): 187.

50. *Columbian Exposition*, 3–5.

51. The Exposition catalogue was put together under Moses P. Handy's direction, and initially William Safford of the navy was his chief clerk. Safford was replaced by Paul Hull, and eventually the project employed a staff of thirty. The massive job of collecting the text from exhibitors (including overseas participants) and editing it was begun late due to disputes between the local and national Exposition agencies. Some 80 percent (28,000) of the entries in the second edition of the catalogue were new, and according to Handy, it was, in spite of the difficulties, as well done as the catalogue for "any previous international Exposition." Handy to Joseph Cummins, Law Department, World's Columbian Exposition, Aug. 12, 1893, Moses Handy Papers, box 26, folder 40, William L. Clements Library, University of Michigan; "Making a Catalogue: Major Handy's Big Job for the World's Fair" *Chicago Journal*, April 12, 1993, Moses Handy Papers, box 44, William L. Clements Library, University of Michigan.

Unless otherwise noted, the information on the international exhibitors is from World's Columbian Exposition, *Official Catalogue of Exhibits*, pt. 8, Dept. H: Liberal Arts. See also the *Index to Awards*, a copy of which is in box 2376, RG 43, NA. The GEH Interactive Catalogue, Biographical File, and Exhibition History File was used to locate information on U.S. and foreign exhibitors.

52. In 1893 the firm of Fratelli Alinari was headed by Vittorio Alinari, son of Leopoldo Alinari, who with his two brothers had founded the firm in 1854. Vittorio had recently taken over after the death of his uncle Giuseppe, who had originally opened the Rome studio in 1865. Vittorio initiated systematic photographic projects throughout Italy during his tenure to 1918. Domenico Anderson, the son of James Anderson (pseud. of Isaac Atkinson), the English watercolorist, succeeded his father in the business

of photographing works of art, and his sons continued the business. The collection was assumed into the Alinari Archives in the 1960s. *Italy: One Hundred Years of Photography,* 15, 185; Rosenblum, *World History of Photography,* 240.

53. The work of Naya's large studio was carried out by employed assistants under his direction, which, Janet Buerger notes, did not preclude the production of truly creative work. Following Naya's death, the firm was successfully run by Tommaso Filippi, the main cameraman, and then by Naya's widow until her death in 1893, when her second husband, Filippi, assumed control. Buerger, "Naya's Italy," 1–3; Naya, *Venice,* 18–30.

54. Primioli was a Roman aristocrat who, with his brother Giuseppe, photographed the social life of Rome and Paris beginning in the 1880s. Both brothers were included in the important juried Vienna exhibition of 1891. *Italy: One Hundred Years of Photography,* 189; Club der Amateur-Photographen, *Katalog der internationalen Ausstellung kunstlerischer Photographien,* nos. 350, 351; *Internationale Ausstellung von Amateur Photographien in der Kunsthalle zu Hamburg,* ii.

55. Charles H. Gould, "The Photographic Exhibits at the World's Fair," *American Amateur Photographer* 5 (May 6, 1893): 260.

56. In addition to his work as a specialist in medical photography, Londé was an active participant in the Société Française Photographique and founder of the Société d' Excursions des Amateurs. On his death in 1917, his collection of papers and photographs was donated to the Academy of Arts and Crafts. See Londé, *Photographie médicale;* Graver, "Photographie Medicale."

57. Bertillon, son of the anthropologist Louis-Adolphe Bertillon, began his career in 1879 as a clerk in the Paris Prefecture of Police. For information on Bertillon and the growth of his career from anthropology to criminology, see Rhodes, *Alphonse Bertillon,* 72–109.

58. Bertillon, *Signeletic Instructions,* vii–x, 239–48.

59. Sekula's argument sets Bertillon squarely within a larger context of work, including that done by Francis Galton. Galton employed photography, though in a less rigorous or systematic way than did Bertillon to produce composite images of social types to support his eugenics theories on hereditary features. According to Sekula, this produced "pictorial statistics," in which optical data was merged with statistical methods. Both Galton and Bertillon were part of a larger context of using photography to establish "social truth and social control." Sekula, "The Body and the Archive," 25, 48, 51, 55.

60. Sipley, *Photography's Great Inventors,* 105–6; Nadeau, *Encyclopedia,* 1:154; Coe, *Colour Photography,* 21–27.

61. The captions of the four-inch-square Lippmann specimens at the Exposition were: "photographs of the solar spectrum"; "four pieces of colored glass" (also called "stained glass," in yellow, green, blue, and red); "a branch of holly," and a "stuffed parrot." These were the same as those shown at the 1892 international photographic exhibition in the Champs de Mars and described in detail by Cameron Swan. The first portrait done with the process was shown at the 1893 Geneva exhibition of the Union Internationale de Photographie. "Professor Lippmann's Color Photographs," *St. Louis and Canadian Photographer* 10 (Sept. 1892): 352–53; Cameron Swan, "Lippmann's Color Process," *Pacific Coast Photographer* 1 (Oct. 1892): 156–57, reprinted from the *Times* of London.

62. Bogardus made these remarks at the Photographers' Association of America convention in Chicago in August. "Photographers' Association of America Convention," *St. Louis and Canadian Photographer* 11 (Aug. 1893): 358.

63. "Chicago Camera Club," *Photo Beacon* 5 (Sept. 1893): 323–24; "Photographic Wonders at the World's Fair," *Wilson's Photographic Magazine* 30 (Aug. 1893): 346. The dryplate manufacturers August and Louis Lumière had first become interested in color work in the early 1890s. They achieved a significant degree of success, obtaining patents on the use of organic salts for the formation of color compounds. They had produced the fine-grain emulsions and plates used by Lippmann and added their own improvements to his interference process. The Lumière brothers' later work with the production of autochrome plates in 1903 resulted in the development of the first successful direct color process. Sipley, *Photography's Great Inventors,* 125–26.

64. "Photographers' Association of America Convention," *St. Louis and Canadian Photographer* 11 (Aug. 1893): 350. Ives noted: "One of the landscapes was beautiful, although the foliage appeared to be that of autumn, while it was understood that the photograph had been made in early summer." Romyn Hitchcock of the Smithsonian Institution noted that he had seen the Lumière photographs at a display at the Chicago Academy of Sciences, where the specimens were "shown on a screen by the means of a reflecting lantern, and the exhibition was truly a revelation in photography." Frederick Ives, "The Lumiere Lippmann Color Photographs: A Communication to the Photographic Society of Philadelphia State Meeting, Nov. 8, 1893," *Journal of the Photographic Society of Philadelphia* 1 (March 1894): 49–51; Romyn Hitchcock, "Photography in Colors," *Anthony's Photographic Bulletin* 25 (Feb. 1894): 50.

65. H. W. Vogel, "Letter from the World's Fair," *Anthony's Photographic Bulletin* 24 (Sept. 9, 1893): 541.

66. S. R. Koehler to G. Brown Goode, Feb. 13, Sept. 30, 1893, RU 70, box 39, SIA. Sylvester Rosa Koehler had been the official curator of graphic arts since 1887 and had developed a print collection on printing through its indus-

trial and technological history rather than as a pure art form. Roese was very impressed with the unusual nature of the Smithsonian's graphic arts collection, which he considered an "original, one-sided, genuinely American" idea in showing technically "how man managed to make pictures multipliable." Smithsonian Institution, *Annual Report of the U.S. National Museum*, 1893, 125. Wright, "The Division, the Smithsonian, and the Mission of Art," 27.

67. Meisenbach developed the first commercially viable halftone process in 1882 and patented it with Josef Ritter von Schmaedel in England and Germany. The single-line screen initially used in the process was later supplanted by the Ives cross-line method. By 1891 Meisenbach had retired due to poor health, and the firm was continued by his son. Eder, *History of Photography*, 630–31; Nadeau, *Encyclopedia*, 2:327.

68. Buerger, "Art Photography in Dresden," 2, 4. The "aesthetic" movement in photography was fostered by the staging of a series of very large international juried exhibits held in Austria and Germany and later in Belgium, Holland, Russia, England, France, and the United States. *Internationale Ausstellung von Amateur Photographien*, 291.

69. Greenhalgh, *Ephemeral Vistas*, 58; see also MacKenzie, *Propaganda and Empire*, 122–26.

70. William McFarlane Notman assumed the responsibilities for the business on the death of his father and formed a partnership with his brother Charles in 1894. He had been assisted by another brother, George, during his earlier railway work. Triggs, *William Notman*, 69–74.

71. New South Wales included photographs of the recent Federation Convention in its own section. It had approached the government of neighboring Queensland to make a joint representation, but the governor, Sir Samuel Griffiths, after initially showing interest, decided against the plan and made arrangements with its agent general in London for space in the British section. Brown, "Versions of Reality," 1:62.

72. The Government Printing Office of New South Wales had a reputation for innovative work, and at the annual New South Wales Agricultural Exhibition in Sydney in 1895 it exhibited a 26' 3" × 3' 10" panorama on bromide paper and made from eight enlarged 15" × 12" plates. *Australian Photographic Journal* 3 (May 20, 1895): 225. For a view of the New South Wales exhibit, see Kilburn stereograph #8375.

73. Rev. F. C. Lambert, "Mounts and Frames," *Anthony's Photographic Bulletin* 25 (Jan. 1894): 13–18. An 1893 discussion following the presentation of Briant's paper at the Camera Club in London between the photographer Alfred Maskell, of the new "Salon" or aesthetic style in photography, and Rev. F. C. Lambert, representing the more established "artistic" position, revealed similarities as well as differences among these groups with respect to mounting and framing practices. Roland Briant, "Mounting and Framing" and discussion, *Journal of the Camera Club* 7 (Dec. 1893): 215–20.

74. Harker, *Linked Ring*, 104–8. Van der Weyde had been a painter before becoming a professional photographer in London. The general move among photographic societies toward reforming display practices was evident at the Exposition in the ruling body's coordination of the designs for catalogues and invitations, as well as in the emphasis placed on hanging individual prints rather than walls of framed objects.

75. "The Photo Corrector," *Photo Beacon* 5 (June 1893): 182–83; Henry Van der Weyde, "The Pictorial Modification of Photographic Perspective (Society of Arts)," *St. Louis and Canadian Photographer* 11 (June 1893): 257–60. Van der Weyde's device was a plano-convex lens with the convex side placed as near as possible to the plate, enabling the light from the image to pass through it and converge in proportion to the convexity of the lens. Several different lenses were required to accommodate the full portrait pose. His scheduled paper for the Auxiliary Congress, "Electric Lighting in the Studio," was not presented.

76. Charles H. Gould, "The Photographic Exhibits at the World's Fair," *American Amateur Photographer* 5 (May 6, 1893): 261.

77. "Sir Henry Trueman Wood," *World's Columbian Exposition Illustrated* 3 (Sept. 1893): 171; *Who Was Who, 1929–1940* (London: Adam & Charles Black, 1941), 1482.

78. Individual titles for photographs by some of the English exhibitors follow. Titles for those taken from the *Index to Awards* lists are indicated with an asterisk; the others are from various cited review sources on the Exposition:

Abney, William, *The Hoar Frost**

Bolton, Gambier, *The Young Bloods**

Byrne, W. J., *Cupid's Call, The Light of the World, Innocence, ABC (A-was-an Archer)*

Cameron & Smith, *Lord Tennyson and Friends*

Crooke, Joseph, *Professor Blackie, Paderewski*

Davison, George, *The Farm on the Marsh, Telford Bridge*

Diston, Adam, *A Rehearsal*

England, William, *View at Chamouni**

Gale, Joseph, *In Cressbrook Dale, Sleepy Hollow*

Hollyer, Frederick, *Dante's Dream**

Keene, Richard, *Old Morton Hall, Haddon Hall, In Cressbrook Dale**

Keighly, Alex, *Spring Time*

Lafayette, J., *The Sisters, Cupid, Lady at Organ, An Evening Zephyr*

Lord, R. H., *Neddy's Little Shoes*

Robinson, H. P., *The Rising Lark*,* *Gossip on the Beach*

Sawyer, Lydell, *Smokey Tyne*

Sutcliffe, Frank, *Water Rats**

Van der Weyde, *Invitation to Supper, Scene from Hypatia*

West, G., *Yacht Racing*,* *Mohawk**

Wilkinson, B. Gay, *Sand Dunes**

Robinson's *Gossip on the Beach*, with its original Exposition label as part of the British loan collection is currently held by Janet Lehr, Inc., of New York City.

79. Harker, *Linked Ring*, 83–90.

80. Lydell Sawyer came from a family of photographers in Newcastle-on-Tyne and began his own business there in 1885 after having studied chemistry and optics for the City of London Guild's examination. Between 1887 and 1892 he earned forty-eight medals and diplomas at various exhibits and was represented by nine photographs in the juried Vienna exhibition of 1891. His father's portrait painting, the writings of Joshua Reynolds, the paintings of David Wilkie, and the photographs of H. P. Robinson all influenced his work. "Distinguished Photographers of To-day, III: Lydell Sawyer," *Photographic Times* 24 (Feb. 1894): 69–73.

81. "Photographs at the Fair. The British Exhibit," *Photo Beacon* 5 (Sept. 1893): 291. Gale, a volunteer army officer and architect, had been a practicing amateur since the late 1850s. The photograph entitled *Sleepy Hollow* appeared as a key illustration in the 1890 popular version of H. P. Robinson's *Art Photography in Short Chapters*, demonstrating the principles of the balance of lines and tones. Harker, *Linked Ring*, 152.

82. Frank Sutcliffe, "How to Look at Photographs: Read by Title Before the Photographic Convention of Great Britain, July 14, 1892," *American Amateur Photographer* 4 (Aug. 1892): 363. Sutcliffe was closely identified with Whitby on the Yorkshire coast, where he had first set up a studio in 1876 to do portrait work. Eventually he began making views of the seaside area that were popular with tourists and that provided his staple income. Sutcliffe had participated in numerous photographic exhibitions, accumulating sixty-two awards between 1881 and 1905. He also served on juries and wrote on topics relating to photography. J. L. Hankey, "The Frank M. Sutcliffe Memorial Lecture," *Photographic Journal* 82 (Aug. 1942): 280–94; Michael Hiley, *Frank Sutcliffe*, 65–73.

83. [Dr. John Nicol,] "Photographs at the Fair: The British Exhibit," *Photo Beacon* 5 (Sept. 1893): 292. In his 1889 publication *Naturalistic Photography for Students of the Art,* Dr. Peter Henry Emerson had advocated a soft visual effect through controlled differential focusing because it

was faithful to scientific truth, which was essential to but distinct from its art, a position he repudiated a year later. Emerson was not associated with the Linked Ring group, because of his opposition to H. P. Robinson's traditional methods and his personal differences with George Davison. P. H. Emerson, "Appendix A: Science and Art, A Paper Read at the Camera Club Conference, 26 March 1889," in his *Naturalistic Photography*, 76; Keller, "The Myth of Art Photography," 23.

84. Davison, "Impressionism in Photography," 17. Through astute investments in the Eastman Photographic Materials Company, Ltd., Davison eventually became managing director, a position he held until 1913 when he failed to be re-elected to the board because of his Christian Socialist beliefs. Brian Coe, "George Davison"; Buerger, *Last Decade*, 2, 15; Arts Council of Great Britain, *Pictorial Photography in Britain*, 77.

85. [Dr. John Nicol,] "Photographs at the Fair: The British Exhibit," *Photo Beacon* 5 (Sept. 1893): 291.

Chapter 3. Appropriating the Image

1. Abraham Bogardus, "Summer-y," *St. Louis and Canadian Photographer* 11 (Aug. 1893): 329.

2. Charles F. Himes, "Photography as an aid to Education: World's Congress Paper by Prof. C. F. Himes," *Photographic Times* 23 (Aug. 25, 1893): 472. Himes, originally from Germany, held the chair of natural history at Dickinson College in Carlisle, Pennsylvania.

3. Captain William. L. Marshall to Captain John G. D. Knight, Corps of Engineers, Jan. 31, 1891, RG 77, box 42, no. 2279, NA.

4. Photographs serve the functions of illustration and information differently. In the former, the photograph is tied to the text through a caption; in the latter, the photograph is itself the data, the replica. Similarly, there are differences between the functions of recording and persuading, between the photograph as evidence of a specific moment in time and the photograph as a means of affecting the attitudes, behavior, and ideas of the viewer. Brown, "Versions of Reality," 1:75, 79, 83, 85.

5. Orvell, *Real Thing*, 75.

6. The catalogue and *Index to Awards* for Group 149 noted when individual displays included photographs, class work, books, and charts. World's Columbian Exposition, *Official Catalogue of Exhibits*, 18–22; *Index to Awards*, 325, 328–29.

7. The Van Norman Institute, founded in 1857 by D. C. Van Norman, LLD, was a boarding and day school on West 62d Street whose aim was "thoroughness, moral and social culture and practical education," with no emphasis on medals or prizes. Madam Van Norman, a Parisian, was one

of the teachers, and methods based on the work of Friedrich Froebel were used in the kindergarten. New York State Department of Public Instruction, Exhibits of Public School Students Work, vol. 2, Van Norman Institute, Series A0300, New York State Archives.

8. Johnson, *History of the World's Columbian Exposition*, 2:260.

9. Copies of 15,000 circulars giving the details of the plan for the Exposition's education exhibit were issued to the superintendents' section of the National Educational Association meeting in February 1892. Ibid., 2:252–56.

10. *The Catholic Educational Exhibit*, 4.

11. New York, Board of General Managers, *Report*, 465.

12. New York, Board of General Managers, *Report*, 460. The society's free kindergarten, founded in 1878 for tenement residents, was extended to other grades in the Workingman's School. In 1890 the school admitted a limited number of paying students. "Manuscript of Hand Book for World's Fair," pp. 2–3, Ethical Culture/Fieldston School Archives.

13. Massachusetts, New Jersey, and Pennsylvania acted to preserve their exhibits permanently. New York, Board of General Managers, *Report*, 465–67; Massachusetts, Board of Managers, *Report*, 101.

14. The archbishops of the United States had begun preparations for an exhibit of the Catholic educational institutions in 1891. The operation was placed under the direction of Brother Maurelian, president of Christian Brothers College in Memphis. It is unclear whether Mrs. Rothery (née S. E. Garrity) was responsible for creating the negatives as well as the reproductions. *The Catholic Educational Exhibit*, 1–10, 56, 247, 254.

15. The exhibit of the Catholic church at the Exposition was less controversial than the Columbian Catholic Congress, which dramatized the struggle among conservative and liberal forces in the United States and the church administration in Rome; see Dennis B. Downey, "Tradition and Acceptance: American Catholics and the Columbian Exposition."

16. Massachusetts, Board of Managers, *Report*, 113; see also 103–9, 111–12.

17. The English-born John William Draper was trained at the University of London before coming to the United States in 1833, where he continued his medical studies at the University of Pennsylvania. A number of photographs of the University of the City of New York's exhibit were made by Professor C. L. Bristol, who held the chair of biology. Trombino, "Astronomers on the Hudson," 3–4; Hyde, "John William Draper, 1811–1882"; Professor E. R. Shaw, "The University Exhibit at the World's Fair," *University Quarterly* 17, no. 1 (1893): 9.

18. During the 1870s Henry Draper made important discoveries concerning the solar spectra using photographs, examples of which were on display at the Exposition along with a photograph of the Orion Nebula. Trombino, "Astronomers on the Hudson," 5–6; New York, Board of General Managers, *Report*, 487.

19. The daguerreotype portrait was made during the spring or summer of 1840 with an exposure of sixty seconds. Hershel acknowledged its receipt with a letter dated July 28, 1840. For a reproduction of this correspondence, see Taft, *Photography and the American Scene*, 29–31; and Wood, "The Daguerreotype Portrait of Dorothy Draper."

20. Correspondence concerning the loan began in February 1893, MacCracken received the daguerreotype in April, and he returned it to the family in December 1893. In 1908 Daniel Draper sent "a copy of the photograph exhibited at the World's Fair" to MacCracken. It was probably one of the artotype prints. Daniel Draper to Rev. Henry M. MacCracken, Sept. 30, 1908, Henry M. MacCracken (Administrative) Collection, box 28, folder 1, New York University Archives; inventory of "Letters concerning the Daguerreotype portrait of Dorothy Draper in the possession of Mrs. E. D. Shorland, England," Spencer Museum of Art, University of Kansas.

21. Julius F. Sachse, "The Oldest Sun Picture of the Human Countenance: Persistent Efforts to Detract from the Honor due Philadelphia Scientists," *American Journal of Photography* 15 (Jan. 1894): 32–38. See also Julius F. Sachse, "Early Daguerreotype Days," *American Journal of Photography* 13 (July 1892): 241–43. George Gilbert has noted that Samuel F. B. Morse began experimenting with portraits of his immediate family in September or early October 1839, the same time that Joseph Saxton and Robert Cornelius were doing similar work in Philadelphia. Also identified as an early worker is Henry Fitz, a telescope maker from Massachusetts who made several self-portraits as early as November 1839. Draper made the first published statement on his success with portraits in March 1840, and this information had been incorporated into his entry in *Appleton's Cyclopedia of American Biography* in 1888. Gilbert, "Draper," 5–7; Trombino, "Henry Fitz," 3–4.

22. Newton noted that the portrait that Draper had identified as his earliest carried a distinctive image on the reverse not present in the Herschel daguerreotype. "Proceedings of Special Meeting of December 19, 1893," *Journal of Society of Amateur Photographers*, 1 (Feb. 1894): 10. The Draper daguerreotype returned to the Herschel family, but it continued to accumulate a history. Due to its deteriorating condition, it was submitted for restoration in 1934 by John A. Gear, but the restoration was unsuccessful. It was

subsequently sent to the photographic historian Robert Taft at the University of Kansas in 1939, who included a reproduction of the 1893 artotype in his 1938 book. A subsequent attempt to strengthen the image in 1970 was partially successful, but the image remains unsuitable for reproduction. Taft, *Photography and the American Scene,* 22; Enyeart, "Reviving a Daguerreotype," 338–44.

23. Following the completion of his duties in 1894, Putnam took over the newly established Department of Anthropology at the American Museum of Natural History in New York City. For details on Putnam's career, see Hinsley, "From Shell-Heaps to Stelae." For lists of exhibitors and items in the Anthropology Department see World's Columbian Exposition, *Official Catalogue of Exhibits,* pt. 12, pp. 1–33.

24. During fieldwork in 1882 with Charles Metz on the Indian mounds of the Ohio Valley, Putnam had established a careful regime for photographing material during excavation. The resulting glass-plate negatives were then used as illustrations for articles and books and for fundraising lectures to support this work. In advising a fellow researcher on the way to obtain material on the life and customs of Indians, especially from their burial grounds, Putnam noted that it was necessary to "photograph all the contents, before disturbing anything." He included the same information for those preparing materials for exhibit in the Exposition's Anthropology Department. For a detailed overview of the subject and resources on anthropology and photography, see Banta and Hinsley, *From Site to Sight,* 61, 76; F. W. Putnam to Mr. T. P. Nolgate, Newburgh, Ontario, July 7, 1891, in F. W. Putnam Correspondence, HUG 1717.2.12, box 32; World's Columbian Exposition Assets, Pusey Archives, Harvard University Archives Pusey Library; Johnson, *History of the World's Columbian Exposition,* 2:320, 323.

25. Jacknis cites Putnam's letter to the Exposition's administrators in March 1893 suggesting the sale of photographs, but no subsequent evidence indicates that this was done. Restrictions on the sale of photographs were just beginning to be imposed at this time. One guidebook did note that "handiwork of the natives and photographs of themselves and habitations are sold to visitors as souvenirs," which may be a reference to material and photographs sold at the cliffdwellers exhibit owned by H. Jay Smith, noted in chapter 4. Jacknis, "Franz Boas and Photography," 6, 55 n. 12; Flinn, *Official Guide to the World's Columbian Exposition,* 40.

26. Owens's sudden death in January 1893 came just after the expedition uncovered part of the sculptured "hieroglyphic" stairway whose later excavation was conducted and photographed by George Byron Gordon, who was the surveyor on the first expedition. Following the close of the Exposition, Saville moved to the Department of Anthropology at the American Museum of Natural History as assistant curator of archaeology under Putnam. Johnson, *History of the World's Columbian Exposition,* 2:328–29; Banta and Hinsley, *From Site to Sight,* 78.

27. Fagin, "Closed Collections and Open Appeals," 255–63.

28. Zelia Nuttall, "Archaeological Exhibits of Central America and Mexico," in World's Columbian Exposition, *Report of the Committee on Awards,* 323. The comparison was with the illustrations, some derived from daguerreotypes, Frederick Catherwood made during John Stephens's expeditions in 1840 and 1841.

29. Claude Joseph Désiré Charnay, a Frenchman, was a traveler, photographer, and writer whose expeditionary work in the Yucatán in 1858 and 1859 was the earliest systematic use of photography in archaeology, It marked the transition from descriptive travel accounts to the more scientific methods at the end of the century. The publication of large folio editions of his work and his later writings helped to create a popular interest in the Yucatán. Davis, *Désiré Charnay,* 35.

30. A mixture of woodash and flake white was sometimes painted on the sculptured ornamentation to enhance the surface contrast for photographing. The difficulties in obtaining a steady work force for clearing and preparing a site for surveying and photographing is described in Alfred P. Maudslay's accounts from the 1890–91 Palenque expedition. Maudslay, *Archeology,* 3:4–5.

31. Maudslay, *Archeology,* 3:4. Maudslay, a graduate of Cambridge University, had spent eight seasons between 1881 and 1894 in surveying Mayan sites in Mexico and Central America, During the Palenque expedition of 1890–91, Maudslay was assisted by Hugh Price, who did survey work while Maudslay photographed. In lieu of the large 12″ × 10″ plate camera, which had been misplaced before the expedition, all negatives were made on 8½″ × 6½″ plates. Maudslay, *Archeology,* 3:1–4, 4:1–5; Banta and Hinsley, *From Site to Sight,* 90.

32. F. H. Mead, "Massachusetts in the Department of Ethnology at the World's Columbian Exposition," in Massachusetts, Board of Managers, *Report,* 163.

33. Under Boas's direction, a group of Kwakiutl Indians formed part of the living-people displays, with their sculptured totems and wooden ceremonial building on display outside the Anthropological Building. Following the close of the Exposition, Boas stayed on for six months at the new Field Columbian Museum (where the bulk of the Department of Anthropology materials had gone), after which he joined Putnam at the American Museum of Natural His-

tory. Jacknis, "Franz Boas and Photography," 75–76.

34. Frederick Starr, "Photography in Anthropological Work," *American Annual of Photography and Photographic Times Almanac* (1893), 210–11; Erhmann noted that it was necessary to offer tobacco and candy to ensure the participation of the models. Charles Erhmann, "A Photographic Anthropological Excursion," *Photographic Times* 23 (Dec. 29, 1893): 777–78.

35. Boas continued to use the ethnographic "type portraits" of frontal and profile views, measurement techniques, and plaster casts in his 1894 and 1897 fieldwork. He devised ways to collect such images even from resistant natives and jail inmates. Jacknis has carefully studied the interrelationship between Boas's photographs and his later research work and has concluded that for him photographs were a supportive rather than primary form of evidence. For an extensive discussion of Boas's interest in photography, see Jacknis, "Franz Boas and Photography," 16–20.

36. Boas, "Remarks on the Theory of Anthropometry," 21; see also chapter 2 for Bertillon's work in the French exhibit.

37. Dudley Sargent was a physician and director of the Hemenway Gymnasium at Harvard College from 1878 to 1920. Boas was critical of Sargent's use of average measurements to produce these statues, which did not give as comprehensive a statistical rendering of the data as was possible. John D. Stoeckle and Guillermo C. Sanchez, "On Seeing Medicine's Science and Art: Cure and Care, Body and Patient," in Ambler, Banta, and Janis, *The Invention of Photography and Its Impact on Learning*, 74–75; Boas, "Remarks on the Theory of Anthropometry," 20; Massachusetts, Board of Managers, *Report*, 136–41.

38. J. S. Billings and Washington Matthews, "On Composite Photography as Applied to Craniology and on Measuring the Cubic Capacity of Skulls," *Thirteenth Memoir, National Academy of Sciences* (1886), 3:105–19. Because of the close association between the U.S. Medical Museum, founded in 1862, and the Smithsonian Institution, a number of composite photographs of Indian skulls are held in the Smithsonian's National Anthropology Archives, Photo Lot 6A. Alice Fletcher, of the Peabody Museum, employed the composite-portrait method as one of her research tools for work on Plains Indians in the mid 1880s. For a critical review of the English application of this photographic practice, see Green, "Veins of Resemblance," 3–16. Banta and Hinsley, *From Site to Sight*, 102–3; Hrdlička, *Physical Anthropology*, 66–67.

39. For an extended contemporary review of the development of the academic discipline of psychology, a technical explanation of new experimental work, and detailed descriptions of some of the exhibits of psychology tests on display at the Exposition, see Dr. J. Mark Baldwin, Professor of Psychology, Princeton University, "Historical and Educational Report on Psychology," in World's Columbian Exposition, *Report of the Committee on Awards*, 357–404.

40. The Clark University photographs included views of the faculty and of apparatus for the study of the physiology and psychology of vision, auditory sensations, and time perception. Copies are held in the Division of Mathematics, National Museum of American History, Smithsonian Institution. G. Stanley Hall was head of the Department of Psychology at Clark. Hrdlička, *Physical Anthropology*, 86–87.

41. Other views on display were captioned "Psychology Laboratory in Dane Hall 1892," "Studying the effects of sound and of attention in colors," and "Measuring reaction times." For a view of the interior of the psychology laboratory, see photograph no. H6324, 93–1, Photographic Collection, Peabody Museum, Harvard University.

42. Roy Lubove's discussion of the work of Lawrence Veiller, with a comparison to that of Jacob Riis, covers the background and changing attitudes about social reform with respect to the issue of housing; see Lubove, *The Progressives and the Slums*, 49–80, 117–49.

43. The catalogue listings of the bureau's exhibitors indicates whether photographs were included in the displays, and the state reports of New York and Massachusetts give more specific details on their own exhibits. World's Columbian Exposition, *Official Catalogue*, pt. 12, pp. 32–36; Massachusetts, Board of Managers, *Report*, 136–41; New York, Board of General Managers, *Report*, 444–46.

44. Maren Stange has offered an important critique of Riis's work in relation to his emotionally charged lantern-slide lectures, which promoted a vicarious rather than direct experience of the social issue for the middle-class audiences to whom they were presented; Stange, *Symbols of Ideal Life*, 17–18. Riis continues, however, to be cited for his artistic contribution in standard art historical surveys of social imagery, as in Lisa Peters's essay "Images of the Homeless in American Art," in Beard, *On Being Homeless*, 55–61. For a comparison of Riis's work with that of C. D. Arnold, the official Exposition photographer, see Hales, *Silver Cities*, 158.

45. World's Columbian Exposition, Department of Liberal Arts, *The Bureau of Charities and Corrections*, 13–14.

46. Nathaniel S. Rosneau to Charles S. Hoyt, Secretary, New York State Board of Charities, Feb. 15, 1893, in Correspondence, of the Secretary of the Board of Charities, A1977 38, D5/1, vol. 38, New York State Archives.

47. Oscar Craig was president and Charles S. Hoyt was secretary of the State Board of Charities, which was created in 1867 and its supervisory role constituted in 1895. It was intended to oversee both public and private institutions in the state. The cost of the board's exhibit was minimal.

The photographer, A. C. Hopkins, was paid seventy-one dollars, and preparing and displaying forty-two boards of photographs in winged frames cost about sixty-three dollars. Oscar Craig to Managers of Charitable, Correctional and Reformatory Institutions of the State of New York, Dec. 26, 1892, Secretary of the Board of Charities, Correspondence, A1977 38, D5/1, vol. 38, New York, State Archives; New York, Board of General Managers, *Report*, 595.

48. Charles Brace to Charles S. Hoyt, Secretary, State Board of Charities, Nov. 14, 1892, in State Board of Charities, Correspondence, A1977 38, D5/1, vol. 38, New York State Archives. Brace had initially founded the Children's Aid Society to care for orphan children through the operation of lodging houses and later a placing-out system that placed New York City children with Western families. Children's Aid Society, Children's Aid Society of New York.

49. "Report on the Charities and Corrections Exhibit," in New York, Board of General Managers, *Report*, 444–45.

50. "Report of the Committee on State Charitable Institutions" in Illinois, Board of World's Fair Commissioners, *Report*, 558–72. Frank Cassell has noted the strictly governmental representation of most of the exhibits in the appropriations made for the Illinois Building; "Welcoming the World," 236.

51. The Lincoln State School, also known in this period as the Asylum for Feeble-Minded Children, had been established in 1865 to provide care, support, and training for the mentally deficient child. It had its own hospital, shops, and farm. Illinois, Board of World's Fair Commissioners, *Brief History of the Charitable Institutions of . . Illinois*, 113; RG 253.123, Photographic File, Lincoln State School, boxes 1 and 2, Illinois State Archives, Springfield, Illinois.

52. The expenditures of the committee for photographic work included payments to the Chicago photographers J. W. Taylor ($75), Frank H. Hall ($428) and W. F. Short ($1,861). Together with the Brouse & Martin payments of $1,750, the cost of photography for the displays was more like twice the $3,000 amount reported for photographs, but the higher figure may have included related work, such as framing and copying. Illinois Board of World's Fair Commissioners, Records of Proceedings, 1891–1893, Wilson Garrard Collection, Illinois State Historical Library, Springfield.

53. A. C. Hall, Assistant Superintendent, Bureau of Charities and Corrections, to Charles S. Hoyt, Secretary, State Board of Charities, Albany, New York, Sept. 23, 1893, in Correspondence, of the Secretary of the Board of Charities, A1977 38, D5/1, vol. 38, New York State Archives.

54. Betts, "The Tenement-House Exhibit," 589–92. Maren Stange has pointed out the significance of this event, but in fact it was not without important precedents in the use of photographs to educate the public about charitable and penal work, given what was presented at the Exposition and even earlier at the Centennial. Stange, *Symbols of Ideal Life*, 28–46.

55. Potts, "Social Ethics at Harvard," 91–97; F. G. Peabody, "Christianity and the Social Question," in World's Parliament of Religions, *World's Congress of Religions*, 901–9.

56. G. Browne Goode to the Honorable Edwin Willits, Chairman, Board of Management, Government Exhibit, June 30, 1892, in RU 70, box 32, folder 2, SIA. George Brown Goode, "First Draft of a System of Classification for the World's Columbian Exposition," in U.S. National Museum, *Annual Report*, 1891, 711.

57. Molella, "The Museum That Might Have Been," 241–42.

58. "The Washington Convention," *Photographic Times* 20 (Aug. 22, 1890): 411. The Morse camera, donated to the National Photographic Association by its owner in 1872, was subsequently given to the association's former secretary, Albert Moore, at the time of its dissolution in lieu of money it owed him. The Smithsonian purchased it from Moore in 1888. Catalogue files and typescript entitled "History of the Section of Photography of the Smithsonian Institution: Its Establishment and Early Activities," Division of Photographic History, Smithsonian Institution.

Thomas Smillie, who emigrated from Edinburgh in 1848, spent two years in the study of chemistry and medicine at Georgetown College. He gave up this career for health reasons and took up photography. Although he had been employed by the Smithsonian Institution to do photographic work since 1871, he did not hold a full-time position there until 1882. In addition to Smillie's work for the various bureaus of the Smithsonian, he also provided work for a number of government departments, including the Light House Board, the Fish Commission, and the Department of Agriculture. His enlargement work for the London Fisheries Exhibition in 1883 was awarded both gold and silver medals. Haberstich, "Photographs at the Smithsonian Institution"; "Smithsonian Institution: History of the Department of Photography," Smillie Files, Division of Photographic History, Smithsonian Institution.

59. "Scheme for a Historical Photographic Exhibit at Chicago in 1893, Arranged Chronologically," RU 70, box 39, folder 8, SIA.

60. Bronner, "Object Lessons," 224. The Bureau of Ethnology, founded in 1879 by Major John Wesley Powell, who was its director until his death in 1902, continued a line of research begun by Powell during his years of survey work. Powell's goal was to organize the systematic study of aboriginal populations, historical migrations, and contacts

among American Indian tribes. Beyond exploration, observation, and data collection, the ultimate goal of this positivist moral enterprise was a synthesis that would lead to an understanding of universal laws of human development. The linguistic mapping project Powell originated was completed in 1891 and was a key exhibit at the Exposition. Powell shared Otis T. Mason's views on the unilinear evolution of mankind, with progress from savagery to democracy defined by specific stages of technology. For a critique of this ethnographic approach, see Rydell, *All the World's a Fair,* 55–60. For an extensive discussion of the development of professional ethnography, see Hinsley, *Savages and Scientists,* 150–54; and Fagin, "Closed Collections and Open Appeals," 250–55.

61. When the updated facilities for photography were built for the museum in 1881, space was allotted for the bureau's photographic work, which meant that Smillie and Hillers were working in close proximity, although their two collections of negatives were quite separate and distinct. Fleming and Luskey, *North American Indians,* 178.

62. The handwritten list that resulted was grouped into sections numbered Chicago 1 through Chicago 6, with fifty photographs in each section (some of which corresponded to those in the Jackson catalogue), with each entry followed by a descriptive phrase, e.g., "951, Mo-mukh-pi-tcha, 3 male figures." "List of photographs from the [illeg.] belonging to the Bureau of Ethnology," RU 70, box 39, folder 8, SIA.

63. European museums had used the life-group format much earlier. The mannequins used in the Centennial were substitutes for living-people displays, which were considered too expensive to stage at that event. Jacknis, "Franz Boas and Exhibits," 81.

64. Goode, Part 2: "Recent Advances in Museum Method," in U.S. National Museum, *Annual Report,* 1893, 52–55; "Fine Exhibit from the Smithsonian Institution," *Evening Journal Office* [1893; no further information given], RU 70, box 41, folder 12, SIA.

65. Fleming and Luskey, *North American Indians,* 143–44; Hinsley, *Savages and Scientists,* 215–19. Mooney worked on "several groups of life-size figures" from "photographs and costumes obtained" from field trips to the Kiowa reservation in the southeastern part of the Indian Territory in 1891 and 1892. U.S. National Museum, *Annual Report,* 1891, 52. The commercial photograph entitled *Cowboy* in the Smithsonian Institution Archives had a memorandum attached to it noting that it should be sent to the taxidermist Carl Akeley & Company and dated Jan. 31, 1893; RU 70, box 39, SIA.

66. Cushing was regarded as the precocious genius of the bureau, and he spent several years living with the Zuni and gathering extensive field notes, many of which remain unpublished. Hinsley, *Savages and Scientists,* 192–207. Cushing also stood in for a posed photograph showing stone-tool making for the Powhatan Indian figure group, part of W. H. Holmes's display of stone implement making by American Indians (neg. no. 56,322, National Anthropology Archives, Smithsonian Institution).

67. The expedition was the first undertaken by the bureau under Powell's direction. It was led by James Stevenson, and it spent several seasons investigating the extensive material culture of the Zuni pueblos in New Mexico and those along the Rio Grande. In 1881 Stevenson and Hillers concentrated on Zuni Pueblo, where he had also photographed in 1879 as part of Frank Hamilton Cushing's research staff. Fowler, *Western Photographs,* 82–83, 96; Fleming and Luskey, *North American Indians,* 140–41.

68. Trennert, "Selling Indian Education," 211.

69. On December 29, 1890, on the Pine Ridge Reservation at Wounded Knee Creek, a group of 340 Miniconjou Sioux under the leadership of Big Foot, presumed to be heading for a hostile encampment, were surrounded by 500 members of the U.S. Cavalry under General Nelson Miles. When attempts to disarm the Indians were unsuccessful, they were shot, and two-thirds of the group were killed. Fleming and Luskey, *North American Indians,* 48; Hinsley, *Savages and Scientists,* 216–18.

70. The collection of fifty-eight framed paintings was transferred from the Department of Ethnology to the National Museum of American Art in 1985 (accession nos. 164.626–164.683). See the section later in this chapter on the Bureau of the American Republics.

71. W. E. Safford to William Curtis from Lima, Peru, June 22, 1891, in RU 70, box 40, folder 1, SIA.

72. The United States section of the Madrid exposition had several displays with photographs, including those of the Peabody Museum's excavations at Copán in Honduras and the Hemenway Expedition's photographs of the Tusayan Indians of Arizona. The Smithsonian's Bureau of Ethnography displayed some 1,300 photographs of Indians from eighty-five different tribes in frames and albums, some of which were probably in the list cited in note 62. U.S. Congress. "Report of the United States Commissioners to the Columbian Historical Exposition, Madrid, 1892–1893." 52d Cong., 3d sess., 1894–95, H. Ex. Doc. 100.

73. U.S. National Museum, *Annual Report,* 136–37. Under the direction of Dr. Cyrus Adler, the collecting of photographs and materials had begun in preparation for the exhibit on biblical themes for the Ohio Centennial of 1888. Adler held various positions at the Smithsonian from 1888 to 1908. In 1893 he was Assistant Curator of Oriental Antiquities, an offshoot of the Ethnography Division. His personal photograph collection and other photographs he acquired for the museum form part of the Pictorial Records

of the Middle East collection, Photo Lot 97 in the National Anthropological Archives of the Smithsonian Institution. Ziolkowski, "Heavenly Visions and Worldly Intentions," 9–15.

74. RU 70, box 39, Folder Labels folder, SIA; U.S. National Museum, *Annual Report, 1893,* 71–73.

75. A copy of this photograph with the caption "Group of Jews, at Jerusalem, 154,991 (245)" is held in the Smithsonian's National Anthropological Archives, Adler Collection, Photo Lot 97, Israel box, no. 04056800. Vaczek and Buckland, *Travelers in Ancient Lands,* 179; Nir, *The Bible and the Image,* 135–38. Other government-sponsored trips to Palestine included those by the British in 1864 and 1868, the Americans in 1870, and the Germans in 1877. Phillips was a corporal in the Royal Engineers and spent two seasons in the Near East, where he produced 400 photographs for the fund. Only two Jewish subjects were represented in the series. Perez, *Focus East,* 77, 204–5.

76. The Bonfils establishment included a chain of studio outlets run by family members that specialized in photographs of religious and tourist subjects. Félix Bonfils, the first French photographer to settle in Beirut, arrived in 1867 after serving as a soldier in Lebanon. He died in 1885, and the company was carried on by his wife and son. When they were assembling their photographic collections between 1889 and 1891, other institutions, such as the Harvard Semitic Museum, followed a similar pattern of acquiring them from the British Museum and foreign commercial firms such as Bonfils. Nir, *The Bible and the Image,* 85, 101–7; Gavin, "Photography and the Social Sciences," 52–53, 61.

77. Nir, *The Bible and the Image,* 160. A number of photographs showing Egyptian religious sites by G. Lekegian, an Egyptian commercial photographer who had also had a lucrative concession in the "Streets of Cairo" section on the Midway, were included in the publication on the Congress of Religions. See World's Parliament of Religions, *World's Congress of Religions,* 516, 557, 594, 628, 692.

78. RU 70, box 39, Folder Labels folder, SIA; George Merrill to Mr. Earll, Nov. 3, 1892, in RU 70, box 39, folder 8, SIA; U.S. National Museum, *Annual Report, 1893,* 180–85.

79. Individual titles of the photographs by James (nos. 60429–50 and 60549–62) and Johnston (no. 60226–50) appear in the 1892 accessions register for the Department of Geology of the U.S. National Museum. A number of Johnston's prints had originally been commissioned in 1891 for an article in *Demorest's Family Magazine* and appeared subsequently in her publication *Mammoth Cave by Flashlight.*

80. Captain William L. Marshall to Captain John G. D. Knight, Corps of Engineers, Jan. 31, April 1, 1891; and Marshall to Frederick V. Abbot, Captain of Engineers, Sept. 5, 1891, RG 77, boxes 42 and 34, NA. Marshall was in Chicago from early 1891, when he was placed in charge of the Corps of Engineers exhibit. His correspondence with Captain John G. D. Knight in Washington provides a close look at the development of this exhibit, its reliance on photography, and the ways in which Marshall was able to bypass some of the difficulties ensuing from the late allocation of funds for the government exhibits.

81. Captain William L. Marshall to John D. Knight, Corps of Engineers, April 7, 1891, RG 77, box 34, no. 2279, NA.

82. Advertising Circular: "Proposal for photographic transparencies on glass and enlarged bromide positives," RG 77, box 34, no. 2279, NA. Marshall's estimates for the transparencies were from twenty-two to twenty-five dollars each, and it is unclear which Chicago firm actually undertook the work.

83. World's Columbian Exposition, *Official Catalogue,* pt. 16, pp. 54–61. A Lieutenant Jervey was in charge of the installation of the exhibit itself. The catalogue for the government exhibit lists the general subjects covered by the displayed photographic material and a descriptive title for the seventeen albums, along with the number of prints in each. Examples of titles would include the Library of Congress (16 views), the Great Kanawha River Improvement, West Virginia (70 views), the Mississippi River Commission Works (55 views) and Willets Point, Fort Monroe, Old Fortifications (71 views). Eleven of the display albums containing duplicates of photographs used in the exhibit were forwarded to the Corps of Engineers' Engineering Department Library in Washington at the close of the exhibit, but they are apparently not extant. John Thompson has identified an album by Henry Bosse, "Views of the Mississippi River," with cyanotype prints, as part of the Chicago display and possibly one of the duplicate albums on view; Thompson, "Henry Bosse," 11–14. Additional information was supplied by Ron Deiss of the U.S. Army Corps of Engineers, Rock Island, Ill.

84. No trace of this report has been found, but it is clear that Marshall thought that the Government Board would undertake its publication. The death a few months later of Major Clifton Comly, the War Department's representative on the Government Board and chairman of the department's Committee on Photography, may have been a factor in its not being published. For a discussion of the Committee on Photography, see chapter 4. Captain William L. Marshall to Major Clifton Comly, April 16, 1894, RG 77, box 34, no. 2279, NA.

85. Half of the funding for the Bureau of the American Republics in 1892 came from the representative countries and the other half from the United States. For the partici-

pants, see note 89. Curtis stressed the commercial nature of the exhibit and mentioned plans for moving the whole display to New York City for a permanent commercial museum. Library of Congress, Reference Department, *Guide to Special Collections*, 43–44; William E. Curtis, "Second Annual Report of the Bureau of the American Republics," 52d Congress, 2d sess., 1892, Exec. Doc. 84, p. 24. For a detailed description of the bureau's exhibition planning, see Johnson, *History of the World's Columbian Exposition*, 2:358–86.

86. U.S. National Museum, *Annual Report*, 1891, 136. Curtis purchased camera equipment from the Eastman Company, which he hoped would donate it for advertising purposes. The company did not do this, but it did immediately supply the equipment on Curtis's request even though it was concerned about a possible delay in payment due to the government's delay in appropriating funds. William Curtis to Miss F. B. Johnston, Jan. 9, 1891, Frances Benjamin Johnston Papers, reel 3, MDLC.

87. William E. Safford to William E. Curtis, Lima, March 25, 1891, RU 70, box 40, folder 1, SIA.

88. Curtis's 1891 correspondence with Frances Benjamin Johnston covers the ordering of the camera outfits and numerous requests for rolls of film for use by his agents beginning in January 1891. Letters between Johnston and the Eastman Company cover aspects of her handling of these orders, some misunderstandings on quotes given and specific orders for enlargements used in both the bureau and the La Rabida displays. George Eastman to Frances Benjamin Johnston, April 14, 1891, Johnston Papers, reel 3, MDLC. See also the discussion of government photographs in chapter 4.

89. The total number of exhibit items, assumed to be mostly photographs, for each member country is as follows: Mexico, 183; Guatemala, 56; Honduras and British Honduras, 15; Costa Rica, 43; Nicaragua, 24; El Salvador, 29; Colombia, 94; Venezuela, 76; Ecuador, 49; Paraguay, 13; Peru, 103; Bolivia, 76; Chile, 82; Brazil, 93; Argentina, 41; Uruguay, 45; West Indies, 86; and Santo Domingo, 29. For an individual caption list of these items, see Thomas Wilson, "A Collection of Pictures and Other Objects Illustrating the Manners, Customs, and Conditions of the People of the Latin-American Republics" in World's Columbian Exposition, *Report of the Committee on Awards*, 125–47. The Curtis Collection in the Rare Books Division of the Library of Congress includes twenty-two photograph albums, which cover some of the areas represented in the Exposition display and presumably duplicates of displayed material in a smaller format. Volume 21, for example, has selections of Venezuelan material, and volume 22 has photographs from Cuba, Jamaica, and Santo Domingo.

90. Some of Ober's views were also reproduced in Curtis's catalogue of Columbian material in the La Rabida display and were on display there as well. The uneven quality of the work can be seen by comparing two original photographs in Curtis's own collection, one showing the harbor of Santo Domingo and the other the ruins of La Isabela, one of the earliest settlement sites. The former image is reproduced clearly in the catalogue (p. 94), while the view of the Isabela ruins (p. 70) has been heavily worked over for reproduction due to the poor quality of the original image. Ober removed a number of surface artifacts from these sites for the La Rabida display at the Exposition. William Eleroy Curtis Collection, vol. 22, Rare Books Division, Library of Congress.

91. The reconstruction of Columbus's fleet was undertaken under the direction of Lieutenant William Little of the U.S. Navy in Spain. The *Santa María* was usually crowded with spectators, but the other two ships did not admit visitors. A second version of Dumont's photograph showing a smoking tug with the ships in tow five miles outside of Rochester, New York, on Lake Ontario, was considered "unpoetic" and was "very properly" omitted from the artistic journal *Sun and Shade*, although it was reproduced as a frontispiece in the *Photo Times*. "Columbus Caravels, Photogravure, John E. Dumont, Copyright," *Photo Times* 23 (Sept. 15, 1893): frontispiece.

92. William E. Curtis to Roger Welles, Jan. 17, 1893, Roger Welles Collection, Correspondence, 1884–1926, MDLC. Thomas Wilson, Judge, "Collective Exhibit in the Convent of La Rabida, at the World's Columbian Exposition," in World's Columbian Exposition, *Report of the Committee on Awards*, 196–200.

93. Thomas Wilson, Judge, "Collective Exhibit in the Convent of La Rabida, at the World's Columbian Exposition," in World's Columbian Exposition, *Report of the Committee on Awards*, 196; Flinn, *Official Guide*, 41–42.

94. "Pictures for the Fair: Large Contract for the Government Completed by the Eastman Company," *St. Louis and Canadian Photographer* 10 (Sept. 1892): 341.

95. Fowler, *Western Photographs*, 133–34, 146; Fleming and Luskey, *The North American Indians*, 178; U.S. Geological Survey, *Annual Report*, 1890–91, 136–38; 1891–92, 53–54; 1892–93, 47; 1893–94, 77, 200.

96. The Grand Prix was the highest award given in each of the classes, usually to only one exhibitor. The USGS exhibit included Indian photographs as well as landscape views. U.S. Commission to the Paris Exposition, 1889, *Reports*, 1:425.

97. "Notes from the Columbian Exposition, Chicago, 1893," *Scientific American* 69 (Sept. 9, 1893): 163; "No. 60589 (old number 30332) through Professor F. W. Clarke,

Feb. 19, 1896," Accessions Register, Geology Department of Museum of Natural History, Smithsonian Institution.

98. F. W. Clarke to the Honorable Secretary of the Interior, Aug. 10, 1893, RG 48, box 1, no. 386, NA. This letter included a general report on the Interior Department exhibit as a whole, including displays by the Indian Office, the Bureau of Education, and the Patent Office.

99. These included the view of the Grand Canyon from Lava, April 1872 (a photograph of Hillers by James Fennemore, third from right) and the view of Mukuntuweap Valley in Zion Canyon (fourth from the right). These are reproduced in Fowler, *Western Photographs*, pls. 2 and 4.

100. Timothy O'Sullivan also made a very similar view of Canyon de Chelly in 1873 as part of the Wheeler Survey. Goetzmann has noted that this was itself "a duplicate in photography of Richard Kern's drawing of 1849." Kern was the first painter to work in this spectacular part of Arizona. O'Sullivan had more license in his work with the Wheeler Survey, which was less scientific in its purposes. The Hillers photograph of Canyon de Chelly is reproduced in Fowler, *Western Photographs*, pl. 89; see also pp. 96, 106. Goetzmann and Goetzmann, *The West of the Imagination*, 105, 203; Naef and Wood, *Era of Exploration*, 129–31 (O'Sullivan's photograph of Canyon de Chelly, pl. 63).

101. In characterizing the changes after the 1870s, Hales discusses the work of George Barker in relation to the later development of W. H. Jackson's commercial work. Hales, "American Views and the Romance of Modernization."

102. Fowler states that the purpose of Hillers's field trip to Yosemite was presumably to obtain material for the Exposition; see *Western Photographs*, 155–56.

103. California, World's Fair Commissioners, *Final Report*, 168. The Yosemite image was one with a long history, discussed in Goetzmann and Goetzmann, *The West of the Imagination*, 166. For background on Watkins, see Naef and Wood, *Era of Exploration*, 79, 81–86.

104. Photographs by C. C. Curtis of the dismantling of the General Noble sequoia are held in the Special Collections of the California State University Library in Fresno. The Big Tree stump was created from two sets of fourteen-foot staves and two cross sections of the original tree cut fifty feet from ground level. The tree was located in General Grant Park in Tulare County. Following the Exposition the stump was reassembled on the grounds of the Department of Agriculture in Washington, D.C. Later it was moved to the Arlington Experimental Farm in Virginia. Schutt, "World's Fair Tree," 1–2. For a discussion of the contradictory responses elicited by the issue of development in relation to the Big Trees, see Anderson, "Kiss of Enterprise," 249, 268.

Chapter 4. Incorporating Photography

1. Trachtenberg, *Incorporation of America*, 230.

2. Knutson, "White City," 16–18.

3. Hales has characterized the Chicago board as the "controlling elite" in efforts to monopolize the commerce of photography at the Exposition. Hales, *Silver Cities*, 138.

4. Born in 1844, Arnold initially came to Buffalo as a young traveling salesman and was introduced to the camera at this time. Soon he was touring Europe and making architectural photographs which brought him into contact with architects in New York City, whom he supplied with these views. He also published them in 1888 in *Studies in Architecture at Home and Abroad*. *Buffalo Courier Express*, May 9, 1927.

5. Hales has written extensively on the role Arnold played in the creation of the "grand style" in urban photography at the Exposition; see *Silver Cities*, 140–51.

6. Council of Administration, Minutes, April 18, 1893, CHS.

7. Campbell copyrighted most of his own published photographs and employed several photographers, including O. M. Morris & Company, who did a number of views of building construction and sculptural work. The scrapbooks of the firm of McKim, Mead and White, one of the Exposition's architects, include a large collection of Arnold's photographs from the architectural journals. Office Records, Chicago, 1893, Scrapbook, AA712 M195 2, McKim, Mead and White Collection, Avery Library, Columbia University.

8. Some of Johnston's photographs were published along with architectural drawings and portraits of leading figures by other photographers in her article "The Evolution of a Great Exposition," which appeared in *Demorest's Family Magazine* in April 1892. H. C. Demorest to Johnston, July 3, 1891, and M. P. Handy to Johnston, June 27, 1892, Johnston Papers, MDLC. See also note 73.

9. The eight bound scrapbooks each measure about twenty by twenty-six inches. They are composed of pasted typewritten reports by Burnham and his associates and are integrated with plans and photographs by C. D. Arnold and by the other official photographer, Harlow D. Higinbotham. This final report, which originally belonged to Chicago's Field Columbian Museum, became part of the collection of the Burnham Library of the Chicago Art Institute in 1934. Joan E. Draper, in Burnham, *Final Official Report*, 1:x.

10. The two-volume set of reports carried the inscription "Photographic Views of the Grounds, Bldg., etc, of the WCE, Collected and Arranged by George R. Davis, Director General." The albums were presented to the Chicago Historical Society in 1912 by Dr. Otto Schmidt, a member of the society since 1894 and later its president from 1923 to

1932. How the albums came to be in his possession is not known. Vols. 1 and 2, C-1986:449, Prints and Photographs Department, CHS; Board of Directors, Minutes, Dec. 8, 1893, vol. 44, CHS.

11. These albums, with their handwritten indexes, came into the Chicago Public Library's possession in March 1896, and all but two volumes were subsequently removed and cut down to fit storage boxes. Because the library lacks registers for the period, their provenance cannot be verified, but their extensive scope (numbering more than 1,000 individual prints) and careful organization indicate their use for reference and administrative purposes. Volume 1 (68 prints) and volume 11 (51 prints) are chronological views of the construction phase, whereas volume 8 (97 prints) includes views of statuary from the major Exposition buildings, and volume 10 (89 prints) is devoted to views of the Midway. Special Collections, Chicago Public Library.

12. Hales gives a descriptive and thematic reading of the photographs covering the construction views in volumes 1 and 2 and the completed Exposition views in volume 3. He stresses the construction of specific viewpoints, images of workers, and the record strategy of the project, but he makes no connection to the function served by the album or how it relates to other examples of this type of collected format material. Hales, *Constructing the Fair*, 9.

13. Leiter had made his fortune in partnership with Marshall Field after 1865, when they bought out the business belonging to Potter Palmer. Leiter's son Joseph held a substantial collection of platinum prints similar to those in the Van Horn and Davis albums that were donated to the Chicago Historical Society in 1933. The McKim, Mead and White album contains a series of prints that is nearly identical to those in the portfolio/album at the University of Texas, indicating that such work was readily available for a special clientele (Figure 4.3 is the same as number 3 in this album). Twyman, *History of Marshall Field & Co.*, 14, 17, 21, 63; Leiter collection, boxes 1–3, Prints and Photographs Department, CHS; forty-seven prints formerly in vol. 10 of a group of albums (AA/712/M195), McKim, Mead and White Collection, Avery Library, Columbia University.

14. Disputes between G. Moses, whose original offer had been accepted by the Exposition board, and Edward Wilson, in partnership with Irving Adams from the Centennial, resulted in Wilson paying $5,000 for the photographic concession at the Cotton Centennial. Moses was hired to make passbook photographs, but in practice Wilson also took over this work. According to a pseudonymous writer, more than 200 "first class photographers" were expected to be employed, but only 85 were engaged, and those at "ca-

pricious salaries." Roxey [pseud.], "World's Cotton Centennial," *Photographic Eye* 14 (Feb. 1885): 2.

15. George Eastman to John Dickson, Secretary of the Executive Committee, World's Columbian Exposition, April 4, 1891. In a second letter the same day to the director general, Eastman also included a proposal for the construction of a building that would house the work of the photographic concession, comprising "the greatest photographic exhibit that was ever made at any Exposition." Both letters are in the Eastman Kodak Company, Correspondence, bk. 1, George Eastman Collection, GEH.

16. George Eastman to Sam A. Crawford, Secretary, Ways and Means Committee, Oct. 14, 1891, Eastman Kodak Company, Correspondence, bk. 1, George Eastman Collection, GEH.

17. No record exists of the board's response to the Eastman plan, but an unidentified reported offer of $75,000 for a concession on landscape, portrait, and architectural photography was not sufficient to dissuade the Ways and Means Committee from setting up its own business. "Photography at the World's Fair," *American Amateur Photographer* 4 (Sept. 1892): 407.

18. The Committee on Ways and Means made the official appointment of the photographers as follows: Harlow D. Higinbotham "jointly with C. D. Arnold" with "the power of the two photographers to be equal and to be defined by a written contract." Higinbotham was placed in charge of business affairs, and Arnold of the "art department." Board of Directors, Minutes, April 14, 1893, vol. 44, and Council of Administration, Minutes, April 18, 1893, both in CHS. Tom Yanul of Chicago has been researching details of Arnold and Higinbotham's working relationship within the Department of Photography that should clarify the roles of these two photographers in the production of the offical work for the department.

19. The Photographic Department's personnel and expenditures for selected months in 1893 are as follows:

	Staff	Expenditures
February	13	$ 864.32
March	21	1,341.62
July	95	5,305.53
August	168	5,869.00
November	45	2,691.51
December	25	1,650.00

Total expenditures for 1893 were $32,897.13. Compiled from "Comparative Statements of Force Employed and Compensation Paid in Auditor's Office Reports for July 1892–May 1894," Treasury Department, Office of the Chief Clerk, RG 56, NA.

20. Todd had been in the employ of the Department of

Photography since before November 1892 when his salary was increased from sixty to seventy-five dollars a month. Otto G. Scharf's salary rose from seventy-five to a hundred dollars a month at the request of the director of works, Daniel Burnham. Carl Pontus Petrini, a Swedish commercial traveler and photographer, may have also worked in the department under Arnold. A collection of his Exposition prints is held by the Chicago Historical Society. Council of Administration, Minutes, Dec. 6, 1892, CHS; Carl D. Petrini, typescript, C-80:008, Petrini Collection, Prints and Photographs Department, CHS. For Dundas Todd, see also chapter 5.

21. Lantern-slide makers known to be in the employ of the Department of Photography included J. S. Le Bean, whose monthly salary was seventy-five dollars. Council of Administration, Minutes, Dec. 1, 1892, CHS. For information on comparable women photographic employees in Australia in the same period, see Brown, "Photography as Occupation in Late Nineteenth Century Colonial Australia," 11.

22. Gusawist [pseud.], "A Story of the World's Fair," *St. Louis and Canadian Photographer* 12 (Sept. 1894): 426–28.

23. "The World's Fair Official Photographer," *American Amateur Photographer* 5 (April 1893): 164.

24. "Appendix C: World's Columbian Exposition; Report of the Auditor to the President, June 30, 1895," in World's Columbian Exposition, *Report of the President to the Board of Directors,* 340. One should be cautious about the $37,000 figure, which is described as "Photographic receipts, net." It is unclear whether it included the 20 percent of the profits paid out to Arnold and Higinbotham. Similarly, the disbursements figure of $6,528.87 for "Photographic labor and material" may refer to original payments to Arnold and Higinbotham plus the cost of materials but may not include the salaries of employees of the Department of Photography. The cost of constructing the Photography Building was $6,371.27.

25. Council of Administration, Minutes, April 18, 1893, CHS.

26. Editorial, "Photographing at Chicago," *American Amateur Photographer* 5 (June 1893): 264. The editor suggested that employing two or three experts to make good-quality photographs and circulate them throughout the country would induce many more visitors to come to the Exposition, and ultimately this would produce much larger profits. A correspondent who was said to have considerable "knowledge of the state of affairs" of the Photography Department was quoted as saying that report that the lantern slides were by the department was true. "The World's Fair Photographic Department," *American Amateur Photographer* 5 (May 1893): 262.

27. The American Lantern Slide Interchange annually reviewed slide entries. In 1893 it accepted nearly 900 slides for exhibition purposes in sets representing the various submitting photographic societies throughout the country, as well as four international sets. *American Amateur Photographer* 5 (Dec. 1893): 580.

28. The prices listed in the *Official Views of World's Columbian Exposition Photographs* were as following: 8″ × 10″, $0.50; 11″ × 14″, $1.00; 18″ × 22″; $2.00; and 13″ × 42″, $5.00. J. P. B., "The Amateur at the World's Fair," *American Amateur Photographer* 5 (July 1893): 322. The Eastman Company had a contract to provide materials to the department. In addition to the traditional albumen paper, the department used the company's new gelatin chloride "Solio" paper because it was faster to process. Council of Administration, Minutes, July 19, 1893, CHS; George Eastman to Lewis Jones, May 30, 1893, bk. 1, Eastman Kodak Company, Correspondence, George Eastman Collection, GEH.

29. Arnold's equipment endorsements included a statement of his exclusive use of the American Optical Company's apparatus and the firm's panoramic camera, which appeared as an advertisement in the form of a full-page handwritten letter in the *Photographic Times* 23 (Sept. 22, 1893): xxi.

30. In its uncatalogued section, the Prints and Photographs Division of the Library of Congress holds an extensive collection of Arnold photographs submitted for copyright, with individual dates. These can be matched by number with the copyright records held in the Copyright Registration Division of the Library of Congress. The procedures for registering a copyright for a photograph were repeatedly described in the journal literature; see, for example, Ernest Edwards, "The Copyright Act of March 1891," *Photographic Mosaics for 1982,* 130–32; and "Copyright Law of the United States," *American Annual of Photography and Photographic Times Almanac* (1892), 324–26.

31. World's Columbian Exposition, *Official Views of the World's Columbian Exposition;* World's Columbian Exposition, *Portfolio of Views.* Both *Official Views* and *Portfolio of Views* were issued by the Department of Photography, the former under both Arnold and Higinbotham's names in various versions. There were two editions of the photogravures of *Official Views,* one in a large format with fifty plates and a descriptive text copyrighted in September 1893 and the other a more popular version in a 5¼″ × 7½″ size with 115 plates. The *Portfolio of Views* was considerably less expensive because it was printed using the chemitype process, a variant halftone process patented 1893. Nevertheless, it was well produced, with plates in warm brown tones.

32. F. Dundas Todd, "Hand-Camera Guide to the World's Fair," *American Amateur Photographer* 5 (April 1893): 167. For similar views, see in particular *Twilight, Across Wooded Island,* by the New Jersey amateurs T. A. and C. G. Hine, reproduced in the Exposition special of *The Cosmopolitan,* Dec. 1893, p. 169.

33. Archibald Treat, "Cameras at the Fair," *Pacific Coast Photographer* 2 (Dec. 1893): 457. Ultimately, Burnham and Millet's publication *World's Columbian Exposition: The Book of the Builders* was illustrated with drawings rather than photographs. According to Peter Hales, Arnold's negatives were eventually turned over to the Exposition officials following the Executive Committee meeting of January 10, 1894. No other official mention of the disposition of the 15,000 negatives appears, however, which may indicate that this was not carried out. Hales, *Constructing the Fair,* 50 n. 39.

34. "The World's Fair Photographic Privilege," *American Amateur Photographer* 4 (Oct. 1892): 459. Ryder, a well-known professional photographer whose work had been prominent at the Centennial, had put forward Jackson's name in connection with his critique of the monopolistic official practices. J. F. Ryder, "Photography at the World's Fair," *Wilson's Photographic Magazine* (Sept., 1893): 422–23.

35. Hales, "Photography and the World's Columbian Exposition," 257–259.

36. See William Henry Jackson, *The White City (As It Was)* and *Jackson's Famous Pictures of the World's Fair.* Eighteen of the original Jackson albumen prints are held by the Chicago Historical Society.

37. The unattributed Jackson prints included in *Dream City* were titled *Eastern Verandah of the Woman's Building* (p. 217), and *Looking Lakeward from the Statue of Industry* (p. 43, cropped). These were issued in the popular "art folios" format in twenty sets, each with four 17″ × 17″ plates reproduced in halftone and later assembled for binding. Each set cost ten dollars. A number of plates in *Dream City* also appeared in the Historical Publishing Company's very similar pictorial book, *The Magic City,* with a text by J. W. Buel. The Historical Publishing Company was also a St. Louis firm.

38. Ernest Edwards, a British portrait photographer, came to the United States in 1872, bringing with him a form of his patented collotype process, called "heliotype," which used metal plates. In 1885 he founded the New York Photogravure Company for the production of finely printed plates, and in 1888 he established his unusual journal *Sun & Shade.* Initially the journal incorporated a wide range of subject material, including enlarged microscopic plates, record photographs, fine-art reproductions, and architectural views, but later it focused on work by some of the new

"aesthetic" photographers. Welling, *Photography in America,* 277.

39. In 1893 Thomas Harrison published a souvenir collection of his "instantaneous photographs" taken just that August and September that was entitled *A Trip Through the Columbian Exposition with a Camera.* The quality of the halftone reproductions in this work does not do justice to the images in the original prints, a number of which are in the collections of the Chicago Historical Society and the New York Historical Society. Some of his images also appeared, unattributed, in the souvenir publication by Henry E. Flower, *Glimpses of the World's Fair,* also published in 1893.

40. The cost of special photographic orders for reproductions in April 1893 were as follows:

Size (in inches)	First Photograph	Second Photograph
5 × 8	$1.80	$0.30
8 × 10	3.00	0.50
11 × 14	5.00	1.00
18 × 22	10.00	2.00

Source: Council of Administration, Minutes, April 18, 1893, CHS.

41. "The World's Fair Official Photographer," *American Amateur Photographer* 5 (April 1893): 165. There were also various claims that the Department of Photography's treatment of individual newspapers depended on "pull." "The World's Fair Official Photographer and His Monopolistic Concession," *American Amateur Photographer* 5 (May 1893): 218.

42. Photographic journals, especially the *American Amateur Photographer,* picked up on locally reported news, such as the *Chicago Daily Times* article of April 14 titled "Scents of a Scandal—Photographer Arnold and his Nepotic Concession at the Fair." "The World's Fair Official Photographer and His Monopolistic Concession," *American Amateur Photographer* 5 (May 1893): 217.

43. Report by Oscar R. Hundley, May 19, 1893, in the Final Report of World Columbian Commission, 2:153–55, RG 43, NA. After the adoption of the report, the committee was requested to secure from the director general copies of all official records in regard to the photographic concession, but it is unlikely that this was ever undertaken.

44. Council of Administration, Minutes, April 18, 1893, CHS. Aldrich noted that the level of workmanship on official photographs was not reproduction quality, noting he had spent fifty dollars on official pictures, none of which could be used. Letters submitted to Mr. John Sterns, Member, World Columbian Commission, from H. L. Aldrich, July 17, 27, 1893, in Final Report of the World's Columbian Commission, 2:209–10, 212, 214, RG 43, NA.

45. Darrah, *Stereo Views*, 109–10. For a comprehensive discussion of the stereograph in relation to the American cultural scene, see Earle, "The Stereograph in America: Pictorial Antecedents and Cultural Perspective," in Earle, *Points of View*, 9–20.

46. Benjamin West Kilburn took up photography in 1855, and in 1865 he formed a photographic business in Littleton, New Hampshire, in partnership with his brother Edward. Benjamin Kilburn began with his own local views of the White Mountains of New Hampshire and later extended his work to include Mexico, Egypt, and Europe. He made all of his own negatives until 1876, after which he purchased the work of other photographers, eventually accumulating a collection of some 75,000 negatives. Darrah, *Stereographs in America*, 42–47; "Benjamin West Kilburn," *Photographic Times* 23 (May 19, 1893): 257–58.

47. Kilburn's concession was granted on January 14, 1893. James Davis was a typical self-made man, having spent the early part of his life supporting his widowed mother in Kansas while pursing his education. He began work with the B. W. Kilburn Company in 1878 during a reorganization of the company's marketing and promotion programs. After Kilburn's death in 1904, Davis purchased the entire collection, reselling it four years later to the Keystone View Company of Meadville, Pennsylvania. "Kilburn," *Photographic Times*, 23 (May 19, 1893): 257–58; Darrah, *Stereographs in America*, 113; Board of Directors, Minutes, Feb. 10, 1893, CHS.

48. Darrah, *Stereographs in America*, 45. The record books for the negatives of the Kilburn company in the collection of the California Museum of Photography at the University of California–Riverside include a comprehensive list of some 1,350 Exposition photographs with, for example, titles and numbers. These concur with the listings under Kilburn's name in the record file of the Copyright Registration Division in the Library of Congress. The wholesale price for the Kilburn stereographic views was seven dollars a gross, and viewers cost thirty-five dollars a gross. Tom Heseltine notes that the Department of Photography had already made some negatives, probably in 1892. They are mounted differently from the gray mounts used by Kilburn. Kilburn had made some twenty views of the Exposition's buildings in 1891 during a routine trip to Chicago. Heseltine, "Chicago Through the Stereoscope," 15.

49. Originally from Sweden, Louis Melander worked with his brother Silas, who had studied with and assisted the Chicago photographer Alexander Hesler in the mid-1860s. Louis and Silas traveled extensively with their stereo business, which thrived in the 1880s. Phillips, *The West*, xiii.

50. Undated newspaper clipping, scrapbook, William Croffut Papers, Manuscripts Division, Library of Congress.

51. Heseltine, "Chicago Through the Stereoscope," 16. The Exposition crowd is the subject of other Kilburn views as well, such as his stereograph captioned "Great crowd and Liberal Arts Building . . . ," a scene that is more interesting for the instant of movement it captured than for the individuals it depicted. Two different views of the same scene taken in quick sequence appear on the same captioned mount in the collections of the American Antiquarian Society and of Charles Rand Penney, which shows that there was some latitude in the company's production procedures.

52. Advertisement of slide views in *The Columbian Exposition*, n.p.

53. Burnham, *Final Official Report*, 7:61–62.

54. Caroline Barrett White, from Brookline, Massachusetts, was an avid diarist whose journal covers sixty-five years from 1849 to 1914, including her trip to the Exposition from July 6 to 17. Octavo vol. no. 23, Caroline Barrett White Papers, American Antiquarian Society. A dramatic drawing reproduced in the July 22 issue of the *Scientific American* showed the firemen clinging to or falling from the tower, a pictorial invention since the stereographs were all taken from too great a distance to record this part of the event.

55. See Kilburn stereograph no. 8013, captioned "Long may it wave, Columbian Exposition," Charles Penney Collection. A variant view with the same title and number, held by the American Antiquarian Society, shows the flag blowing full and centered in the fountain.

56. Bellamy was on the staff of *The Youth's Companion*, and had proposed as acknowledgment of the Columbian anniversary on October 21 that the flag should be flown over every school in the country and the pledge of allegiance recited. His original handwritten text for the allegiance was: "I pledge allegiance to my Flag and [to] the Republic for which it stands—one Nation indivisible with Liberty and Justice for all." Francis J. Bellamy Collection, Manuscripts Collection, Rush Rhees Library, University of Rochester.

57. Charles Melford Robinson, "The Fair as Spectacle," in Johnson, *A History of the World's Columbian Exposition*, 1:499.

58. For an extensive list of stereo makers of Exposition views, see Heseltine, "Chicago Through the Stereoscope."

59. "Kilburn & Davis vs. Underwood et al.," *Photographic Times* 23 (Sept. 15, 1893): 413. The Underwood firm had gone far since its beginning in 1880. By 1882, the two brothers, Elmer and Ben Underwood, had set up a

distribution business for the territory west of the Mississippi. They represented three leading stereo companies: Bierstadt of Niagara Falls, Jarvis of Washington, D.C., and Littleton Views of New Hampshire. Underwood had distribution offices in Baltimore and Liverpool. Its main office moved to New York in 1891, and it began producing stereos from photographs by staff photographers. A key to the firm's success as a distributor was its saturation of local markets through door-to-door canvassing by young college students. Darrah, *Stereographs in America*, 109–10; "Legality of the World's Fair Stereoscopic Privilege," *American Amateur Photographer* 5 (Sept. 1893): 413.

60. Under Gibson's original concession for portrait work, approved in February 1893 by the Executive Committee, he was required to build his own studio and return to the Chicago Exposition board 30 percent of his gross receipts from passbook portraits and 50 percent from visitor portraits. In April, these charges were waived due to the high volume of his work, and he eventually earned $8,448 without having to return anything to the administration. Board of Directors, Minutes, March 10, 1993, vol. 44, and Executive Council Minutes, April 5, 1893, vol. 35, CHS; (Gibson) No. 7 Concession Agreement, April 3, 1893, in vol. 6, World's Columbian Exposition Concession Agreements, Library Collection, CHS; "World's Columbian Exposition, Department of Collections, May 1, 1893, to February 10, 1894," in World's Columbian Exposition, *Report of the President to the Board*, 484.

61. World's Columbian Exposition, *Report of the President to the Board*, 365. Moses Handy, the director of publicity, was among those whose unidentified passbook photographs were posted for claiming, which indicates that there were some glitches in the system. "Their Dignity Offended, Foreign Commissioners Object to Having Their Photographs on Their World's Fair Passes—Foreigners have their grievances," *New York World*, April 4, 1893; Moses Handy scrapbook, William Clements Library, University of Michigan.

62. S. R. Koehler to R. E. Earll, Oct. 17, 1893, RU 70, box 35, folder 15, SIA.

63. The *Chicago Times* series was issued in twelve parts, with 240 plates printed in halftone along with descriptive captions. The series was published without attribution by the American Engraving Company. Some of Gibson's photographs can be verified through reference to annotations in a similar publication annotated by Frank H. Smith that includes many of the same photographs. Smith, *Pictorial Album and History of the World's Fair and Midway*, Gibson Collection, Prints and Photographs Department, CHS.

64. The Algerian dancer's portrait also appeared in Smith's *Pictorial Album*. For a very useful critique of two approaches to the representation of Middle Eastern women—

the semiotic reading of commercial photographic postcards in Malek Alloula's *The Colonial Harem* and the historical view in Sarah Graham-Brown's *Images of Women: The Portrayal of Women in Photography of the Middle East, 1860–1950*—see Coombes and Edwards, "Site Unseen." For a historical overview of photography in general in this period, see Perez, *Focus East*, 105.

65. *The Dancers of Cairo Street* is also a good example of the loose contemporary standards for crediting photographs. It appeared in books by the photographers Dundas Todd (as *The Dancers of Cairo Street*) and Thomas Harrison (as *Three Stars on the Nile*), as well as unattributed in Buel's *The Magic City*, where it was entitled *Three Dancing Girls from Egypt* and was accompanied by a lengthy and unflattering caption. Todd, "Snapshots"; or, *The World's Fair through a Camera*, 177; Harrison, *A Trip Through the Columbian Exposition with a Camera*, n.p.

66. N. D. Thompson, the St. Louis publisher of *The Dream City*, in responding to the interest shown in the Midway photographs in that publication, purchased two extensive collections for publication following the Exposition. Place & Coover retained copyright on their photographs, but it is not clear who the other photographer was whose collection was also reproduced. See *Oriental and Occidental: Northern and Southern Types of the Midway Plaisance*.

67. Board of Directors, Minutes, July 14, 1893, vol. 44, CHS.

68. The semicommercial nature of the enterprise, which netted some $87,000 for its owners, was an example of the merging at the Exposition of profitable business exploitation and educational display. *The Cliff Dwellers*; World's Columbian Exposition, *Report of the President to the Board*, 483.

69. "The World's Fair Photographic Department," *American Amateur Photographer* 5 (May 1893): 262. The Australian journalist A. G. Stephens recounted in detail the way he circumvented the permit fee by checking his camera in a parcel office before leaving each day. His press pass had been lost in the bureaucracy. A. G. Stephens, "An Australian in the States: Yankee Notions," *Truth*, Aug. 27, 1893, in Moses Handy Scrapbook, William Clements Library, University of Michigan.

70. H. L. Harris to Mr. Seager, private secretary to the Secretary of War, Oct. 12, 1894, RG 94, box 281, no. 24585, NA.

71. References to Smillie's photographic students are in notes for the Smithsonian's annual reports from 1882 to 1897; RU 158, box 21, SIA.

72. After graduating from high school, Johnston had studied art in Paris at the Académie Julian in 1883 and was associated with the Washington Art Student League, later

part of the Corcoran Gallery. Following her training with Smillie, Johnston began supplying articles and photographs to a number of illustrated magazines and newspapers. Before the construction of her own professional studio in 1894, she developed her photographic plates in her bathroom and printed them in her bedroom window. Anne Peterson, "Introduction" in Johnston, *Women of Class and Station,* 9–15.

73. Johnston, "The Evolution of a Great Exposition," *Demorest's Family Magazine* 28 (April 1892): 319–28. Johnston had been unable to secure a sitting by Mrs. Potter Palmer, so the article included the frequently reproduced portrait of her by the Chicago photographer M. J. Steffens. The letters were mostly about exchanging prints, a copy of Johnston's recent article for *Demorest's* on coal miners, portraits that Johnston had made of Arnold, and lantern slides of the Exposition that Arnold sent her. Moses Handy to Johnston, Jan. 22, 1891, Johnston Papers, reel 3, MDLC.

74. Director General George R. Davis, to Johnston, Sept. 21, 1893, Johnston Papers, reel 4, MDLC. Authorization letter to Grabill from Director General, Oct. 12, 1893, in HUG 1717.2.13, box 34, folder: World's Columbian Exposition Assets, Harvard University Archives, Pusey Library.

75. Henry L. Harris to Johnston, Jan. 22, 1894, Johnston Papers, reel 4, MDLC. Harris describes working with Johnston on two occasions in the Alaska Gallery, where problems of light and reflection prevented the making of good negatives.

76. "Catalogue of Prints from 6½" x 8½" negatives taken under the direction of the Committee on Photographing U.S. Government Exhibits at the World's Columbian Exposition. (No. 1–76)," RG 94, box 281, no. 24585, NA. Henry L. Harris to Frances Benjamin Johnston, Jan. 31, 1894, Johnston Papers, reel 4, MDLC. In this letter Harris presented a summary of the completed negatives and the proposed printing to be done and asked for estimates from Johnston and Smillie on the cost for such work.

77. "Committee on Photography," Sept. 4, 1893, RU 70, box 32, folder 2, SIA. Costs were to be divided among the departments according to the number of negatives and prints made for each. The summary prepared in early 1894 indicated that the Smithsonian had spent $248, the Treasury Department $84, and the Navy Department $94, with a total expenditure for the negatives of $645. No entry was made for the War Department itself in this summary. [Clifton] Comly to Edwin Willits, Chairman, [Government] Board of Management, April 12, 1894, RU 70, box 36, folder 15, SIA.

78. The Photographic History Division of the Smithsonian holds six of the 20" x 24" prints with a handwritten inscription of Smillie's name. The division also holds sev-

eral large-plate negatives of the Exposition in its uncataloged material, which were unavailable at the time of this research but which may relate to these Exposition photographs. Four additional 20" x 24" albumen prints of views taken from the Government Building and showing the Government Plaza, the *Illinois,* and the Coast Guard sections of the Exposition carry no identifying authorship and are in RU 26, U.S. Coast Guard (LH), Still Pictures Branch, NA.

79. Connecticut, Board of Lady Managers, *History of the Work of Connecticut Women.* The plates in this publication were *The Court of Honor* (no. 12316), *The Mechanic Arts, The Administration Building, The Lagoon* (no. 2314), *Door of the Transportation Building* (no. 12317) (see Fig. 4.25), and *Fine Arts Building* (no. 12928). Note: the numbers in parentheses refer to identical cyanotype prints held in the Smithsonian Institution archives from the Government Board's Committee on Photography collection; RU 70, box 64, SIA.

80. F. Dundas Todd, "Hand-Camera Guide to the World's Fair," *American Amateur Photographer* 5 (April 1893): 166. Photographs of Transportation Building: no. 12328, also no. 12330, and no. 12324. The preceding numbers, written on the negative plate, do not correspond to the original series system used by the photographers for the committee work. They were added later when the material was brought into the collection of the U.S. National Museum. RU 70, box 64, folder 2, SIA.

81. Clifton Comly, Representative, War Department, to Assistant General, U.S. Army, Oct. 23, 1893, RG 94, box 281, no. 24585, NA.

82. The correspondence between Harris and Johnston confirms that Johnston was placed in charge of printing procedures, especially for the large 20" x 24" plates and probably for the other platinum work in the 11" x 14" and 8" x 10" sizes. Her ability to use this paper was acknowledged by Harris, who concentrated on aristotype prints. See Henry L. Harris to Frances Benjamin Johnston, Jan. 13, 1894, Johnston Papers, reel 4, MDLC.

83. Harris to the secretary of war, Oct. 5, 1894, RG 94, box 281, no. 24585, NA. Accompanying the War Department report was a catalogue of the various photographs independent of those in the report. With Comly's death in April 1894, Harris took over the job of putting together the War Department report as well as supervising the photographic work for the Photographic Committee.

84. The collection of eight government albums in the Library of Congress is as follows: the Treasury Department album transferred in 1910, views of government Exposition displays, lots 8353, 7097, 8354; views of Smithsonian Exposition displays, lot 8355; general Exposition views, lots 7098; War Department albums transferred in 1914, general Exposition views, lots 6495, 7233, 6641a, 6641b. The original numbering system used on the prints in these

albums is uniform, with the same number used for identical views in different sizes. The system is also consistent with that used for two sets of photographs showing the army display now held in the National Archives; RG 165, EC 2724–2759 (broken album) and EC 2800–2855. A later set of prints without original series numbers, presumably made from the original set of negatives, is also held in the National Archives; RG 111-RB, boxes 22–24.

85. For photographs, see RG 111-RB, box 23, nos. 4010 and 4019, Still Pictures Branch, NA.

86. The other figure was of Sergeant Brainard, who kept the surviving group together until their eventual rescue. Goetzmann, *New Lands*, 441–44.

87. The Libby Prison Museum had opened in Chicago in 1889 after being removed from its original site in Richmond in 1888. Artifacts and original photographs of the war and events associated with the prison were on display, including photographs by Frederick Gutekunst. Libby Prison War Museum Association, *Libby Prison War Museum*; Cameron, *History of the World's Columbian Exposition*, 780–87.

88. Henry L. Harris to Frances Benjamin Johnston, Jan. 4, 1894, Johnston Papers, reel 4, MDLC.

89. RG 94, box 281, no. 24585, NA; Henry L. Harris to Frances Benjamin Johnston, Jan. 31, 1894, Johnston Papers, reel 4, MDLC. The "List of Prints from 20″ × 24″ negatives forwarded with report of Representative of War Department to the Secretary of War" records the titles of 33 of the 20″ × 24″ negatives and indicates that most were general views of the kind that would have hung well in government offices.

90. Harris reported an incident concerning a "government photographer" who was advertising in the *Washington Star* about the availability of photographs of the Exposition. It was unclear who had placed the advertisement, but it increased Harris's caution in allowing use of the material, and he advised Johnston of this policy again in January. Harris to Frances Benjamin Johnston, Dec. 14, 1893, Jan. 27, 1894, Johnston Papers, reel 4, MDLC.

91. Bolton & Company (later the Autotype Company) to H. L. Harris, Nov. 1, 1893; and F. P. Thorp to Lieutenant Harris, Aug. 25, 1894, both in RU 70, box 36, folder 15, SIA. F. P. Thorp purchased the mortgage and business of the Bolton company from S. E. Norton. In March 1894 the Lee and Laird Publishing Company of Chicago stated that it had bought some government views "in open market" and, since they were not copyrighted, had proceeded to use them. Major Comly brought this to the attention of the Committee of Photography. Harris to Frances Benjamin Johnston, March 1, 1894, Johnston Papers, reel 4, MDLC; Major Clifton Comly to General A. D. Hazen and Professor G. Brown Goode, Members of the Committee on Photography, March 12, 1894, RU 70, box 36, folder 15, SIA.

92. The disposition of the rest of the negatives following the completion of the reports is unclear, but Harris said: "The negatives of the photographs forwarded to the Secretary were paid for from the allotment of the War Department Exhibit and in that light may be regarded as the property of the War Department, though it has been the understanding that those not now in store at the National Museum in Washington would eventually be sent there for safe keeping after all prints desired from them have been made." Harris to John Seager, private secretary to the Secretary of War, Oct. 12, 1894, RG 94, box 281, no. 24585, NA.

93. The numbers that appear on the cyanotype prints in the Smithsonian Archives group are still used by the Printing and Photographic Services. Cyanotype contact prints were generally working prints for reference purposes rather than display. The views showing the ethnology displays at the Exposition in the National Anthropology Archives were also cyanotype contact prints.

Chapter 5. Making Alternative Images

1. M. Y. Beach, "A Lazy Amateur's Musings," *American Amateur Photographer* 5 (Sept. 1893): 419.

2. For a discussion of this process in American society as a whole, see the introduction to Wrightman and Lears, *Culture of Consumption*, xii.

3. Catharine Weed [Barnes] Ward, "Amateur Photography: Read at the World's Congress of Photographers, August 2, 1892," *Amateur Photographer* 5 (Aug. 1893): 360. Barnes reiterated her position on the role of amateurs in several speeches and articles reprinted in overseas journals, and in 1892 she had addressed the British Convention of Photographers on the state of American amateur photography. Catharine Weed Barnes, "But An Amateur," *Photographic Mosaics for 1891*, 204. See also Catharine Weed Barnes, "Amateur Photography in America: Reprinted from *The Photo Beacon*," *Australian Photographic Journal* 1 (Nov. 1892): 11–13.

4. The sources that employed these terms are too numerous to cite, but a representative sample is provided. The popularity of the term *Kodaker* can be seen in its use by Gilbert and Sullivan in their new opera *Utopia, Limited* in which a chorus of dancers holds Kodak cameras for one of their scenes. "The World's Fair Official Photographer," *American Amateur Photographer* 5 (April 1893): 165; "The Kodak in Opera," *Photo Beacon* 6 (Dec. 1893): 425–26 (reprinted from the Rochester *Democrat and Chronicle*).

5. "Club Types, by the Man About Town," reprinted from the *Amateur Photographer* in *Photo Beacon* 5 (April 1893): 166–67.

6. The formula approach to artistic photography included methods for organizing the central motif, the placement of the horizon line, the position of the viewing angle, the composition of figures, and the use of light and shade. Simple guidelines were distilled from more lengthy texts like H. P. Robinson's *Pictorial Effect in Photography,* originally published in 1869 and in its fourth printing by 1893. See Brown, "Versions of Reality," 1:70–73.

7. Horace Herbert Markley, "Amateur Photography at the World's Fair," *Cosmopolitan* 16 (Dec. 1893): 169. For economic reasons, amateur photography was still restricted to those able to afford leisure activities and participate in the emerging world of consumerism. This was certainly not an option for the average working-class family with an income of $500 a year, as noted at the Exposition in the display of the New York State model worker's home. Katherine Bement Davis, "Report on the Exhibit of the New York State Workingman's Model House," in New York, Board of General Managers, *Report,* 396, 406–7.

8. C. D. Irwin, quoted in "Press Comments on the World's Fair Privilege," *American Amateur Photographer* 5 (July 1893): 329. Irwin stressed that the effect of a liberal photographic policy would be to produce free advertising for the event by both official and amateur work.

9. Interested parties were asked to send in their names, and a form letter was published to encourage amateurs who did not belong to societies to participate by writing directly to the Ways and Means Committee of the Exposition board. Editorial, "Photography at the World's Fair," *Photo-American* 3 (July, Aug. 1892): 266, 295–96; "The World's Fair Photographic Privilege Petitions," *American Amateur Photographer* 4 (Sept. 1892): 408–9; F. C. Beach, "The World's Fair Photographic Privilege," *American Amateur Photographer* 4 (Aug. 1892): 366–67.

10. The response by the Ways and Means Committee of the Chicago Board to Sir Henry Trueman Wood, British Commissioner to the Fair, was reproduced along with a letter by Albert Levy, a leading French photographer, protesting the imposition of such regulations. "Photographing at the Chicago Exhibition," *American Amateur Photographer* 5 (March 1893): 135; see also A. N., "The Possibilities of the World's Fair," *Photo Beacon* 5 (Feb., 1893): 47–49.

11. J. P. B., "Correspondence: The Amateur at the World's Fair," *American Amateur Photographer* 5 (July 1893): 322. "Admittance of the Camera to the World's Fair Grounds," *American Amateur Photographer* 4 (Nov. 1892): 501–2.

12. The board's reply to F. C. Beach in response to his November 1892 query was reproduced the following March. Beach made a point of reprinting official correspondence, articles from Chicago newspapers, and the opinions of his readers on this issue throughout 1892 and 1893.

"World's Fair Photographic Privilege," *American Amateur Photographer* 5 (March 1893): 120.

13. While the amateurs considered the reduction in the permit fee a step in the right direction, no changes were made with respect to restrictions on camera size or the use of tripods. "Photography at the World's Fair," *Photo Beacon* 5 (Aug. 1893): 262.

14. F. Hopkinson Smith, "A White Umbrella at the Fair," *Cosmopolitan* 16 (Dec. 23, 1893): 154.

15. For the 1889 Paris event, the admission fee for a camera for one day was twenty francs (four dollars), or 300 francs (sixty dollars) for a season pass. "An Old Amateur," "Chicago Press Comments on the Photographic Privilege," *American Amateur Photographer* 5 (June 1893): 277–78 (reprinted from the *Chicago Post*).

16. Fred Felix, "A Camera in the World's Fair Grounds," *American Amateur Photographer* 4 (Sept. 1892): 409–11.

17. F. Hopkinson Smith, "A White Umbrella at the Fair," *Cosmopolitan* 16 (Dec. 23, 1893): 150–52. Smith encountered further difficulties in attempting to make drawings in the art gallery until he was able to persuade the security guards of his semi-official status.

18. "Dark-Room Facilities at the World's Fair," *American Amateur Photographer* 5 (March 1893): 121.

19. Eastman to Alva Strong, May 16, 1893, Eastman Kodak Company, Correspondence, bk. 1, George Eastman Collection, GEH.

20. For a description of the process of renting a camera, see Jenks, *The Century World's Fair Book for Boys and Girls,* 86.

21. By 1893 there were eight different Kodak models, each of which provided prints of slightly different sizes and/or additional film capacity. The No. 2 Kodak, with its circular image, retailed for $32.50 and, when loaded with 100-exposure film, weighed two pounds, whereas the No. 3 Kodak weighed four pounds when loaded and retailed for $40.00. The No. 4 Folding Kodak, was a new, more compact construction that cost $50.00, and there were Junior versions of both the No. 3 and No. 4, with less capacity but greater portability. The No. 5, with its 5″ × 7″ negatives, was not permitted at the Exposition. *The Kodak Camera* (trade catalogue; Rochester, N.Y.: Eastman Company, 1890), 14–23.

22. Advertisement for the "Kolumbian Kodak," Corporate Business Archives, Eastman Kodak Company, Rochester, N.Y. The Eastman advertisement continued: "How to get the most pictures for the smallest outlay of cash and trouble is a question that will confront every amateur who attends. The Kodak solves the problem. Our new Columbian spools of film for use in the Nos. 2, 3, and 4 Kodaks contain 200 exposures and weigh but a few ounces. Equipped with a Kodak and special spool the photographer

can take 200 pictures without re-loading—a decided advantage where $2.00 a day must be paid for the privilege." Photo Advertisement File, Corporate Business Archives, Eastman Kodak Company, Rochester, N.Y.

23. "World's Fair Jottings," *Photo Beacon* 5 (March 1893): 104.

24. Johnston had apparently approached Eastman in December 1890 with an idea for a book that would advertise the Kodak camera, but he was more interested in articles, especially an article on women using Kodaks. Johnston interviewed several prominent women for an article she finished in August 1891 and for which she received $200. George Eastman to Frances Benjamin Johnston, Dec. 17, 1890, Aug. 6, 13, 1891, Johnston Papers, reel 3, Manuscript Division, Library of Congress.

25. Catherine Weed [Barnes] Ward, "Amateur Photography: Read at the World's Congress of Photographers, August 2, 1892," *American Amateur Photographer* 5 (Aug. 1893): 363; *The Vanishing City*, n.p.

26. *Off for the World's Fair with a Trokonet*, 5–19. The Photo Materials Company was formed in 1892 by former employees of the Eastman Company, including Henry Reichenbach, a research chemist and manager who had been in charge of the Kodak Park Works; S. Carl Passavant, a chemist and superintendent; and Gustave D. Milburn, the supervisor of traveling salesmen and demonstrators. Jenkins, *Images and Enterprise*, 90.

27. Two Dollars a Day [pseud.], "Photographic Apparatus and Material at the World's Fair," *Photo Beacon* 5 (Aug. 1893): 284. This generous review of the company's display described the new No. 1 Trokonet on display as "a light, compact, serviceable camera, simple in its movements," a "bagatelle" producing a 3½" square image with a fixed-focus lens. Other larger versions were proposed but were not available at the Exposition. In fact, production of this camera lasted only a year, after which the firm concentrated on its "Kloro" gelatin chloride paper. The company was purchased by Eastman in 1898. Jenkins, *Images and Enterprise*, 168.

28. "Free Dark Rooms at the Fair," *Photo-American* 4 (Aug. 1893): 299.

29. "Columbian Visitors' Association Dark-Room," *American Amateur Photographer* 5 (March 1893): 121; Julius Wilcox, "Reminiscences of World's Fair Photography," *American Amateur Photographer* 6 (Oct. 1894): 462.

30. F. C. Beach, "Editorial Comment," *American Amateur Photographer* 5 (May 1893): 214.

31. "Photography at the World's Fair," *American Amateur Photographer* 5 (Sept. 1893): 370. See also "Correspondence: The World's Fair License System," *American Amateur Photographer* 5 (Feb. 1893): 77; Horace Herbert Markley, "Ama-

teur Photography at the World's Fair," *Cosmopolitan* 16 (Dec. 1893): 173.

32. "Photography at the World's Fair: How to Manage It," *Wilson's Photographic Magazine* 30 (April 1893): 158–59.

33. Markley, "Amateur Photography," 168.

34. W. A. Morse, "Visiting the World's Fair with the Camera," *American Amateur Photographer* 5 (June 1893): 266.

35. F. Dundas Todd, "Hand-Camera Guide to the World's Fair," *American Amateur Photographer* 5 (April 1893): 166–67.

36. Todd had also included a photograph taken from the same perspective in his publication "*Snapshots*"; or, *The World's Fair Through a Camera*.

37. Archibald Treat, "Cameras at the Fair," *Pacific Coast Photographer* 12 (Dec. 1893): 457.

38. Harold Serrell, "In Sunlight and Darkness; or How I Exposed and Developed My Plates of the World's Fair," *Anthony's Photographic Bulletin* 25 (Jan. 1894): 11. In this article Serrell describes the camera he adapted to meet the 4" × 5" regulation and the development treatment required to compensate for the overexposed negatives he had taken.

39. Louis Clarence Bennett, "Photographing at the World's Fair," *Photographic Times* 23 (Aug. 1893): 449. Bennett had developed more than 1,000 films, 800 of which were entirely useless. The Triad camera (which until 1891 had been called the Mascot) was produced by the American Optical Company and distributed by the Scoville and Adams Company. It was a small detective camera and could use roll or sheet film.

40. This was taken from an advertising testimonial by G. S. Yauger of Omaha on May 3, 1893, for the Eastman Company. It was based on his experiences while on an excursion to the Fair. Photo Advertisement File, Corporate Business Archives, Eastman Kodak Company, Rochester, N.Y.

41. Markley, "Amateur Photography," 173. Julius Wilcox noted that by October he had encountered many disadvantages in photographing buildings due to the sun being so far south that the northern faces were difficult to photograph. By October, for example, the Transportation Building could only be photographed in the early morning. Julius Wilcox, "Reminiscences of World's Fair Photography," *American Amateur Photographer* 6 (Oct. 1894): 463.

42. George Eastman to Alva Strong, May 15, 1893, in Eastman Kodak Company Correspondence, bk. 1, Eastman Archives, GEH. According to Eastman's letter, he took a No. 4 Kodak camera and "made 112 exposures, nearly all of which were good," while Walter Hubble "took a #2 with him and made 186 exposures with only 13 failures." The

168 No. 2 Kodak images in the Lyndon Welles Collection must have been those taken by Hubble, but Eastman's 4″ × 5″ photographs have not been located.

43. Sidney Colgate to George Eastman, May 19, 1893, George Eastman Personal Letters, box 4, George Eastman Collection, GEH. It is unclear whether the set of copy prints Eastman sent to Seamon and Colgate as a souvenir of the trip were made by Hubble or Eastman himself.

44. Charles Hine succeeded his father, Charles Cole Hine, as editor of insurance journals and head of the Underwriters & Credit Bureau. With his brother Thomas, Hine co-produced a number of photographs published in the special December 1893 Exposition issue of the *Cosmopolitan* (one of which was reproduced in the *Photographic Times* 23 [Nov. 10, 1893]: 637). Charles Gilbert Hine Papers, Staten Island Historical Society.

45. One of Bartlett's photographs was reproduced in the *American Amateur* 5 (Dec. 1893): 551. The Buffalo Camera Club made no distinction between amateurs and professionals in its constitution. By 1892 the club had its own permanent premises and was "identified with the progress of art-culture" in the city. Bannon, *The Photo-Pictorialists of Buffalo,* 18, 87–88, 104–7. An illuminated night view by W. S. Truescott of the Rockford Camera Club in Illinois was taken on an Excelsior Dry Plate with an exposure of only four seconds, compared to Bartlett and Hines's three-minute exposure, but the effect was not very convincing. "Our Illustrations," *Photo-American* 4 (July 1893): 285, 300. See also "Night Photographs of the World's Fair," *American Amateur Photographer* 5 (Dec. 1893): 574.

46. The album that included this photograph was made as a lined notebook with slits for mounting original cyanotype prints covering a wide range of subjects throughout the Exposition. One of the prints carries a page number of 69, indicating that it was part of an extensive collection in its original form, though only eight have been found in the subject files of the Chicago Historical Society. Cyanotype prints, from a dispersed album, gift of Rutgers University, anonymous photographer, Vertical File, Prints and Photographs Department, CHS.

47. The Lee & Laird Company also produced another souvenir publication, *The Vanishing City,* all of the views for which were taken with No. 4 Kodak, and several of which were used in *Glimpses of the World's Fair,* although without the lengthy captions. Lee & Laird's more elaborate and larger-format portfolio, *Beautiful Scenes of the White City,* followed the more conventional formula for pictorial albums, reproducing official and commercial views.

48. The Ferris wheel's perfect pinion wheel was 250 feet in diameter and was mounted on a single axle 140 feet above the ground on two towers. It was driven by a mechanized sprocket-wheel-and-chain device and held thirty-six well-appointed cars with forty steel seats each. George Ferris, the young engineer who had designed the ride, had applied his experience in constructing steel bridges to the project and was only granted the concession in December 1892. A tribute to American engineering, the Ferris wheel was constructed from steel parts made in Detroit and shipped to Chicago for assembly, which was completed in five months. The ride opened to the public on June 21. Ferris died of tuberculosis just two years after the closing of Fair. Carl Snyder, "Engineer Ferris and His Wheel," *Review of Reviews* 6 (Sept. 1893): 269–76.

49. Sandweiss notes that for those interested in displays of the cultural life of the various nations, the Midway was also a more popular area than the relatively staid and formal foreign government buildings. Sandweiss, "Around the World in a Day," 111. At the 1889 Paris exposition the colonial city exhibit, complete with 182 Asians and Africans in a simulated native village, turned out to be one of the main attractions for the event's 30 million visitors. As James Gilbert has pointed out, the Chicago Midway—which under its original director, F. W. Putnam, was to be a "Street of All Nations"—became a true commercial enterprise under the guidance of the entrepreneur and impresario Sol Bloom. Gilbert, *Perfect Cities,* 43, 87.

50. A second model working-class home was included as part of the New York State exhibit, with statistics on living on an annual budget of $500 for housing, clothing, and food. Davis, "Report on the Exhibit of the New York State Workingman's Model House," in New York, Board of General Managers, *Report,* 395–411, 414–25.

51. "The Aztec Building," *Chicago Times Portfolio,* pt. 9, p. 403. For a views of the Aztec village and the Philadelphia workingman's house, see prints 293,230.1900 and 293,230.1877 in the Photographic History Division, National Museum of American History, Smithsonian Institution.

52. Snider, *World's Fair Studies,* 300.

53. Mrs. Mark Stevens, *Six Months at the World's Fair,* 96–99, 109. The Moorish Palace, which earned $450,000, included a number of other concessions as well, such as the Panopticon, a collection of lifelike wax figures from history and literature, including Shakespeare and Inspector Byrnes, the author of *Professional Criminals in America.* The Panorama of the Bernese Alps, owned by Benjamin Henneberg, grossed $64,232—about the same as the Volcano of Kilauea, which had a lecturer on hand to explain the points of interest in the panorama. Flinn, *Official Guide to the Midway Plaisance,* 26–27, 34–35; World's Columbian Exposition, *Report of the President to the Board of Directors,* 482–83.

54. The Electric Scenic Theater was owned by Arthur Schwartz and grossed $22,897. Flinn, *Official Guide*, 9–10; World's Columbian Exposition, *Report of the President to the Board of Directors*, 485.

55. Stanford University, Department of Art, *Eadweard Muybridge*, 24–25, 30–33, 71–74, 95–96. Anita Mozeley has called the Zoopraxographic Hall the first motion-picture theater and the performances there the first commercially presented motion-picture shows, but this interpretation does not acknowledge that Muybridge's device used disks rather than continuous strips of film. Mozeley, "Introduction to the Dover Edition" in Muybridge, *Muybridge's Complete Human and Animal Locomotion*, xxxvi.

56. Muybridge applied for his concession in October 1892 and gained permission to erect a building 50 x 80 feet, to give lectures on the science of animal locomotion, and to sell photographs and "Zoopraxographic Fans." He was to pay one-third of the gross income from the exhibit to the Exposition and to make a $1,000 deposit to assure the contract. World's Columbian Exposition Concession Agreements, vol. 3, no. 8, pp. 1–5, Library Collection, CHS.

57. Edison applied for a concession for a display of 150 kinetoscopes, and it was granted by February 1893. Gordon Hendricks presents evidence from two accounts describing a machine similar to the kinetoscope and concludes that a kinetoscope was at the Exposition, but Charles Musser is more skeptical. Mrs. Mark Stevens, in her published recollections of the Exposition, described the Edison display, specifically noting that the "'kinetograph' at the time of the Fair was not perfected." Stevens mistakenly used the term *kinetograph* instead of *kinetoscope*. A kinetograph was an instrument for talking into a phonograph and being photographed at the same time. This instrument was present, according to a *Scientific American* report of Oct. 31, 1893 (p. 262). Hendricks, *The Kinetoscope*, 32–45, 146; World's Columbian Exposition Concession Agreements, vol. 4, p. 672; Musser, *The Emergence of Cinema*, 72, 504; Millard, *Edison and the Business of Innovation*, 144–48; Stevens, *Six Months at the World's Fair*, 231.

58. The bulk of the publication consists of testimonials regarding *Animal Locomotion*, Muybridge's 1887 book on his work at the University of Pennsylvania—clearly an effort to boost its sales. Appendix A in *Descriptive Zoopraxography* presents an outline of two illustrated lectures, which included photographs of a leaping horse, a kicking mule, and flying birds shown in relation to conventional artistic representations.

59. Flinn, *Official Guide*, 20. The Panorama of Pompeii concession belonged to G. Pandofelli. World's Columbian Exposition, *Report of the President to the Board of Directors*, 483, 488.

60. Mitchell, "The World as Exhibition," 226.

61. Snider, *World' Fairs Studies*, 311.

62. Ragan's album, with extensive captions by Emma C. Bush, was sold by subscription. His introduction claims: "The SUN, using the infallible camera as his pen, is the real author of this book. . . . He cannot be bribed to flattery, or goaded to unfairness. Whether his theme be wild sublime or quiet loveliness, whether he tell of man's work or God's wonders, he speaks the truth, nothing but the truth."

63. The view entitled *Arabic Wedding Procession, Cairo Street, Midway Plaisance*, was a standard tourist commercial view made in Cairo by the well-known commercial photographic firm of Zangaki, which was located in Port Said and was active in the 1870s and 1880s. An original of the same photograph is held in the Cyrus Adler Collection of the Smithsonian's National Anthropological Archives. Ragan, *Art Photographs of the World*, 61, 69, 59; Museum voor Volkenkunde, *Beelden van de Orient*, 89, 91.

64. For a colorful description of the activities on the street, see Shepp and Shepp, *Shepp's World's Fair Photographed*, 508.

65. *The Century World's Fair Book for Boys and Girls* recounts the fictional experiences of two boys from New York City, Philip Rodman and his friend Harry, who with their tutor, Mr. Douglass, spend a week at the Exposition. While Philip rents a camera to take photographs, his friend makes sketches, and both formats provide the illustrations for the book.

66. Jenks, *Century World's Fair Book*, 64, 233–36.

67. Snider, *World's Fair Studies*, 315–16, 318–19. Snider described the camel ride: "Two young ladies, companions, conclude to take a ride together; they mount the camel's back; through some defect in the saddle or some negligence of the driver they topple over, heels upward, fortunately without injury. . . . One of the young ladies refuses very naturally to take that sort of a trip the second time, being both ashamed and scared by her short trial. But the second maiden, on the invitation of the driver, swings herself again on that camel hump, with an air of resolution which makes every heart in the crowd thrill; unabashed by one small reverse she takes her ride alone, and as she sails off, the multitude breaks out into loud huzzas and clappings of hands at the pluck of the little heroine" (318–19).

68. The advances in understanding the languages and literatures of Egypt, improved archaeological techniques developed by Sir Flinders Petrie, and the popular writings of Amelia Edwards contributed significantly to a wide audience for things Egyptian in the late nineteenth century. See Wortham, *The Genesis of British Egyptology*, 92–112.

69. The Temple of Luxor exhibit, initiated by Demetrius Mosconas and A. E. Funk, was begun in 1891 and in May 1892 became part of the larger concession of Cairo Street

owned by George Pangalo. Admission to the temple cost twenty-five cents. The Tombs of the Kings, with a ten-cent admission charge, included replicas of the mummies of Sethy I and Thutmose III uncovered in the early 1880's. The Thomas Cook Company's travel information detailed a twenty-day steamship itinerary from Cairo to the First Cataract. *A Complete 'Guide' to the Egyptological Exhibit,* 9–11; Fagin, *The Rape of the Nile,* 288–95.

70. *The World's Fair at Chicago,* 22–24, 47. In their workshops outside Cairo, Cook's artists had spent two years in building the temple display. Cook also made copies of the Egyptian replicas available to institutions and private individuals. An illustration of the Cook's display in the Transportation Building can be found in Truman, *History of the World's Fair,* 126.

71. By the 1880s the voyage to the East had become for Europeans a "bourgeois rite of passage," and tourists in trips arranged by Cook were often criticized for not being as "serious" as they should have been. Perez, *Focus East,* 45–50.

72. G. Lekegian was probably Armenian and had established a studio in Cairo in 1887. Later he relocated to a site opposite the American Mission near the famous tourist center around the Shepheard's Hotel. In addition to producing his seventy-five cent photograph albums, he provided a number of photographs of Egyptian religious sites as illustrations for World's Parliament of Religions, *The World's Congress of Religions.* Museum voor Volkenkunde, *Beelden van de Orient,* 89.

73. Jenks, *The Century World's Fair Book,* 67, 68. A number of the larger pictorial publications included the popular "baby." See, for example, *The Photographic World's Fair and Midway Plaisance,* 211, 217, and Shepp, *Shepp's World's Fair Photographed,* 510.

74. Koerner, an amateur, had asked to photograph two Turkish sedan carriers for fifteen cents. They demanded fifty cents, and a bargain was struck at twenty-five cents, which Koerner concluded was very lucky, considering the circumstances. On Cairo Street he paid ten cents in a similar deal, although he was originally asked for a dollar. Carl C. Koerner, Jr., "Snap Shooting at the Great Fair: Interesting Experiences of an Amateur with a Hand-Camera at the World's Columbian Exposition," *American Amateur Photographer* 5 (July 1893): 297–98.

75. Charles Melford Robinson, "The Fair as Spectacle," in Johnson, *A History of the World's Columbian Exposition,* 1:493.

76. Koerner, "Snap Shooting at the Great Fair," 296.

77. Horace P. Chandler, "Photography at the World's Fair," *Photographic Times* 23 (Dec. 15, 1893): 739. Chandler was the editor of the *Photographic Times.*

78. Eckley Coxe, Jr., "Photography at the World's Fair,"

Photographic Times 23 (Sept. 1893): 545. Coxe wrote: "Just as I had carefully focused on a man whose only garment was the American flag, then he happened to look up at what I was doing, so he very excitedly waved and motioned to me to take my machine out of the village, which of course I did."

79. Koerner, "Snap Shooting at the Great Fair," 296.

80. Curtis Hinsley, "The World as Marketplace: Commodification of the Exotic at the World's Columbian Exposition," in Karp and Lavine, *Exhibiting Cultures,* 361.

81. Koerner, "Snap Shooting at the Great Fair," 300. The religious taboo against representation had a long tradition in non-Western societies, which is one reason photography in such societies was developed by Europeans from outside rather than from within local communities. Anthropologists also noted the dread that primitive people had of having "their features put on paper, and thus being submitted spiritually to the power of any possessing the picture." Perez, *Focus East,* 74; Sualso "Photographing Savages," *Popular Science Monthly* 43 (Aug. 1893): 570.

82. M. G. Van Rensselaer, "At the Fair," *Century Magazine* 46 (May 1893): 12–13. Marina Griswold Van Rensselaer was a journalist and New York historian.

83. For a thorough discussion of the role of the flâneur and the flâneuse, see Wolff, "The Invisible Flâneuse," 39.

Chapter 6. Conclusion

1. For a thorough discussion of the mechanisms of the Fine Arts Department and its displays, see Carolyn Carr, "Prejudice and Pride: Presenting American Art at the 1893 Chicago World's Columbian Exposition," in *Revisiting the White City,* 74–75, 84–99.

2. "Public Press Points Pushed in Photography," *Wilson's Photographic Magazine* 30 (June 1893): 270–71.

3. "A Nervous Man's Impressions of the Fair," halftone reproduction of wash drawing by Wechsler, *Life* 22, no. 561, p. 203.

4. "Abraham Bogardus, "Summer-y," *St. Louis and Canadian Photographer* 11 (August 1893): 329.

GLOSSARY

Albertype. See Collotype print.

Albumen print. A silver-based photographic image made on paper with an emulsion surface composed of egg white and sensitized in a silver nitrate bath. The negative is printed out directly on the paper with exposure to sunlight and then washed and toned. Introduced in the 1850s, it was the main commercially produced printing paper used through the 1880s.

Ambrotype. A collodion glass negative whitened or bleached with a solution of mercuric chloride. When a black backing is placed behind the glass, the image appears as a positive. A similar process is used for making a tintype except that the surface is blackened tin rather than glass.

Aristotype print. A silver-based photographic image made on paper coated with an emulsion of silver chloride in collodion. The process was introduced in Germany in the late 1860s, with commercial development in the 1880s. In the United States the term *aristotype* also had a generic meaning, referring to both collodion and gelatin chloride papers, which shared several features, including their printing out procedures.

Artotype print. See Collotype print.

Bromide print. A silver-based photographic image made on paper with a gelatin emulsion containing silver bromide, a very active light-sensitive agent. Only a brief exposure with the negative was necessary before developing out the paper in chemicals. The process was introduced in the 1870s, and because it was suitable for enlargements, large glass transparencies, and commercial production, it was beginning to replace albumen prints for commercial purposes by the 1890s.

Carbon print. A colored gelatin photographic image made on paper coated with gelatin sensitized with bichromated potassium. Exposing the paper under a negative and removing excess gelatin produces a hardened image with a permanency not found in silver-based photographs. The pigmented image is also used in photomechanical reproduction as a printing surface for photolithography on metal plates or stone.

Collotype print. A photomechanically reproduced image in ink from a printing plate of metal or glass coated with a bichromated (light-sensitive) gelatin exposed beneath a negative and washed to remove the excess gelatin. The dried surface is inked and printed in the usual lithographic manner. Various trade names (with some variation in processing) include the original albertype (Josef Albert, Austria), artotype (Edward Bierstadt, New York), and heliotype (Ernest Edwards, New York).

Cyanotype print. A photographic image created by iron salts on a paper coated with a mixture of ammonium citrate of iron and potassium ferris cyanide. When exposed beneath a negative, the resulting image is produced in Prussian blue. Introduced in the 1840s, in its applied form it was used for reproducing maps, and because it was easy to work with, it found a certain renewed favor among amateurs in the 1890s.

Daguerreotype. A photographic image on a silvered copper plate sensitized with fumes from iodine crystals and exposed and developed with fumes from hot mercury. After fixing and toning, it is sealed within an airtight frame to prevent deterioration of the surface. Introduced in France and the United States in 1839, by the 1890s it was an historical rather than a current photographic process.

Gelatin chloride print. A silver-based photographic image made on paper coated with an emulsion of silver chloride in gelatin. Like albumen paper, it relied on a printing out process that allowed for eye control in determining when the print was properly exposed, but it was much easier to use than the older process. Many photographic manufacturers introduced their own brands in the 1890s.

Gelatin dryplate. A light-sensitive photographic plate with an emulsion generally coated by machine onto a glass plate, which could be stored for later use. The manufacture of these plates began in the late 1870s, and by the 1890s they had replaced the cumbersome wet collodion process, which required immediate use after chemical sensitizing.

Halftone engraving. A photomechanically reproduced image in ink from a relief plate carrying dots of different sizes. A zinc or other metal plate prepared with a light-sensitive coating is exposed to a negative under a fine screen that breaks the photographic image into dots. After washing the plate to remove residues, it is etched to form a relief of the photographic image for printing with type. First suggested in 1850, it was not developed commercially until the 1880s. In the 1890s it contributed significantly to the expansion of the illustrated press.

Isochromatic plate. *See* Orthochromatic plate.

Orthochromatic plate. A light-sensitive photographic plate with an emulsion treated to render in black and white tones parts of the visible color spectrum when used with compensating light filters. Prior to the early 1880s, natural color (especially in the green tones) was distorted in photographs due to the lack of a sensitive emulsion in making photographic negatives. The term *isochromatic plate* was a synonymous term used in this period.

Phenakistoscope. A hand-held spindle instrument for holding two disks, one with perforated slots and the other with a series of pictures or photographic images of successive movements. When the disks are moved rapidly at the same speed, the eye blends the images, forming a continuous image of motion due to the principal of persistent vision.

Photogravure. A photomechanically reproduced image from an intaglio plate. The plate is grained with a bitumen dust and then a carbon (gelatin relief) image is adhered to the surface, which selectively controls the etching of the plate, creating an image in the pitted surface. The image is then printed in the usual way. Because of its high-quality results for photographic reproduction, the photogravure was favored by art-conscious photographers, especially during the 1890s.

Photolithography. A photomechanically reproduced image from a planar surface, such as stone or metal. After the surface is treated directly with bichromated gelatin to make a photographic image, or after it receives a transfer gelatin image, it is inked and printed. The attraction of greasy ink to gelatin and its repulsion by water is the basic principle of planographic printing. *See also* Collotype print.

Platinum print. A photographic image created with light-sensitive iron salts (ferric oxalate), which are reduced to their ferrous state by exposure and the platinum to its metalic state in developing. Introduced commercially in 1880, the extensive range of finely graduated tones, especially in the middle range, embedded in the matte surface of the paper was a unique and highly valued feature of this paper. The quality of the prints could not be matched by other emulsion-based papers.

Solio print. *See* Gelatin chloride print.

Stereograph. A double photographic image paired in such a way that, when viewed through a stereoscope, the observer sees a single image in three dimensions. The two photographs are made in a special double-lens camera or two single-lens cameras, which makes the two images about three inches apart, thereby replicating the binocular vision of the viewer. The holder for viewing these images is called a stereopticon or stereoscope.

Tintype. *See* Ambrotype.

Transparency. A photographic image on a glass support intended for viewing by transmitted light, such as in a window setting, or with a projected light source, like a lantern slide. For the photographic process used, see *Bromide print.*

Woodbury print. A photomechanically reproduced image in relief printed in ink (pigmented gelatin). A hardened bichromated image produced like a carbon print is pressed against a lead sheet, creating an intaglio mold, which is filled with special ink and printed. Originally patented in Britain in 1868, it was a high-quality method of reproduction used mainly for book illustrations in the 1870s.

For a more detailed description of these processes, see the following sources:

Barger, Susan M., comp. *Bibliography of Photographic Processes in Use Before 1880: Their Materials, Processing and Conservation.* Rochester, N.Y.: Graphic Arts Research Center, Rochester Institute of Technology, 1980.

Bridson, Gavin D. R., and Geoffrey Wakeman. *Printmaking & Picture Printing: A Bibliographic Guide to Artistic and Industrial Techniques in Britain, 1750–1900.* Williamsburg, Va.: Bookpress, 1984.

Crawford, William. *The Keepers of Light: A History and Working Guide to Early Photographic Processes.* New York: Morgan & Morgan, 1979.

Jones, Bernard E., ed. *The Encyclopedia of Early Photography.* 1911. Reprint. New York: Arno Press, 1974.

Nadeau, Luis. *Encyclopedia of Printing, Photographic and Photomechanical Processes: A Comprehensive Reference to Reproduction Technologies, Containing Valuable Information on Over 5,000 Processes.* 2 vols. Fredericton, N.B., Canada: Luis Nadeau, 1989–90.

Reilly, James. *Care and Identification of 19th Century Photographic Prints.* Rochester: Eastman Kodak Company, 1986.

BIBLIOGRAPHY

Manuscripts

American Antiquarian Society, Worcester, Massachusetts
  Caroline Barnett White Papers.
  Stereographic collection.

Art Institute of Chicago. Ryerson and Burnham Library
  C. D. Arnold. World's Columbian Exposition Albums
  Daniel Burnham. "Final Official Report of the Director
  of Works of the World's Columbian Exposition."

Boston Public Library
  Print Department
    Carlo Naya photographs.
  Rare Books and Manuscripts Department
    Freer Collection of World's Fairs of North America.
    Private photographic albums.

Brey, William. Private Collection.
  John Carbutt Collection.

Buffalo and Erie County Historical Society
  C. D. Arnold biographical files.

Charles Rand Penney. Private collection
  World's Columbian Exposition Collection. Publications,
  stereographs, lantern slides, artifacts, and albums.

Chicago Historical Society
  Archives and Manuscripts Department
    World's Columbian Exposition Collection.
      Board of Directors Minutes. Vol. 44. July 8, 1892–
      June 16, 1906.
      Council of Administration, Minutes. Vols. 48–49.
      May 19–August 25, 1893.
      Executive Committee Minutes. Vols. 35, 36. Au-
      gust 17, 1892–November 26, 1895.

Library Collection
  Miscellaneous pamphlet files.
  World's Columbian Exposition Concession Agree-
    ments. Vols. 1–6.
  World's Columbian Exposition publications.

Prints and Photographs Department
  C. D. Arnold Collection.
  World's Columbian Exposition, Construction Views,
    Albums A and B.
  Loban Deardoff Collection.
  J. J. Gibson Collection.
  Joseph E. Hartman Collection.
  W. H. Jackson Collection.
  Joseph Leiter Collection.
  Carl Petrus Petrini Collection.
  Joseph Ryerson (album G).
  Stereographs, lantern slides, prints, vertical and hori-
    zontal files.

Chicago Public Library. Special Collections
  World's Columbian Exposition. Albums 1–13. Lantern
    slides.

Children's Aid Society, New York
  Pamphlets, circulars, and photographic files.

Cincinnati Historical Society
  Photographic Collection
    James M. Landy Collection

Columbia University. Avery Library
  McKim, Mead and White Collection. Scrapbooks, al-
    bums, and photographs.

Eastman Kodak Company, Rochester, New York. Corpo-

rate Archives
Advertisement files.
George Eastman business correspondence.
Ethical Culture Fieldston Schools, New York. School Archives
Manuscript of handbook for World's Fair.
Photographic collection.
Field Museum of Natural History
Anthropology Collection
Alfred P. Maudslay photographs.
Museum Archives
Accession books.
Annual reports.
Photographic Section
C. D. Arnold lantern slides.
Free Library of Philadelphia. Business, Science and Industry Department
1876 Centennial International Exposition Collection.
Harvard University
Harvard University Archives. Pusey Library
F. W. Putnam correspondence.
Psychology Department Exposition display photographs. HU-SF series.
Peabody Museum of Archaeology and Ethnology. Photographic Archives
Exposition photographs of Anthropology Department 93-1. Area 20: Central American, archaeological, boxes 44, 45: Labná and Copán.
Historical Society of Pennsylvania, Philadelphia
Centennial Collection. Photographs and stereographic views.
John Sartain Papers.
Illinois State Archives, Springfield
Illinois Warrant Ledger. WCE 1891–95. RG 105.25.
Photographic File. 1880–1941. Lincoln State School. RG 254.123.
Illinois Historical Library, Springfield
Wilson C. Garrard Papers.
Illinois Board of World's Fair Commissioners. Minute books and ledgers.
George Eastman House, International Museum of Photography and Film
George Eastman Collection.
George Eastman Correspondence. November 15, 1890–February 21, 1895.
George Eastman Personal Correspondence. December 24, 1890–June 2, 1898.
Information Technology
GEH Interactive Catalogue, Biographical File, and Exhibition History File

Library Collection
Photographic publications and journals.
Print Collection
George B. Dryden Collection. 81:2167, 89:1507.
Lantern slides by William Rau, C. D. Arnold, and Samuel Castner.
Albert Lathrop Collection, 81:2864.
Lyndon Wells Collection. 81:1684.
Technology Collection
Trade Manuals and Pamphlets File.
Library Company of Philadelphia
Library
Centennial scrapbooks.
Prints and Photographs Collection
Centennial photographs, albums, and stereographs.
Library of Congress
Manuscripts Division
Duke of Veragua Collection. Christopher Columbus Inventory.
William Crofutt Papers.
Frances Benjamin Johnston Papers. Microfilm.
Roger Welles Papers.
Rare Book Collection
William E. Curtis Collection. Notebooks, vol. 22: "Views of Cuba [and] Jamaica."
Prints and Photographs Division
General stereographs. Lot 11036.
McGrew stereographs. Lot 11538.
Souvenir Publishing Company. Lot 3310.
Algeier Company. Lot 2867, also T500.C1A4
Exposition opening and construction. Lots 10559, 6698.
Catholic schools exhibit. Lot 6874.
Government albums. Lots 7097, 8353–8355, 6641, 6495, 7098, 7233.
A. W. Pentland album. Lot 10984.
Broken album. Lot 4291.
Frances Benjamin Johnston photographs. Lot 11743.
Uncatalogued Exposition collection.
W. H. Jackson panorama print.
Copyright Registration Division
Copyright listings for various photographers and photographic companies.
National Archives
Record Documents
Records of International Conferences, Commissions, and Expositions. RG 43.
Records of the Department of the Treasury. RG 56.
Records of the Bureau of Indian Affairs. RG 75.
Records of the Office of the Chief of Engineers. RG 77.
Records of the Adjutant General's Office. RG 94.

Records of the War Department General and Special Staffs. RG 165.

Still Pictures Branch

Records of the U.S. Coast Guard. RG 26.

Records of the Office of the Secretary of the Interior. RG 48.

Records of the Geological Survey. RG 57.

Records of the Office of the Chief of Engineers. RG 77.

Records of the Office of the Chief Signal Officer. RG 111.

Records of the Public Buildings Service. RG 121.

National Gallery of Canada, Ottawa

Alphonse Bertillon Album. PSC80:286:1–34

New York Historical Society

Manuscripts Collection

American Institute of the City of New York Records.

Prints and Photographs

World's Columbian Exposition stereographs and photographs.

New York State Archives, Albany

New York State Department of Public Instruction. Series A0300. Exhibits of Public School Students' Work. Vol. 2: Van Norman Institute, New York City.

State Board of Charities. Correspondence of the Secretary. A197738.

New York University Archives. Elmer Holmes Bobst Library

Chancellor Henry M. MacCracken Papers.

John and Henry Draper Collection.

New York University Exhibit at the Chicago World's Fair. LD16.

Ohio Historical Society.

James M. Elliot Family Photographic Collection.

Rochester Museum and Science Center. Library Collection

Photographs, pamphlets, and publications on the World's Columbian Exposition.

Smithsonian Institution

Archives

Offices and Special Projects Exposition Records of the Smithsonian Institution of the United States. RU 70.

Audio-Visual and Information Files. Photographic Collection. RU 95.

United States National Museum. Curator's Annual Reports, 1881–1964. RU 158.

National Museum of American Art

William E. Safford Collection. 164,626-83.

National Museum of American History

Division of Mathematics

Clark University Photographs exhibited at the World's Columbian Exposition. PY-74-05-01-42. Psychology Reference File.

Division of Photographic History

John W. Draper Collection.

Frances B. Johnston Collection.

Thomas Smillie Collection.

World's Columbian Exposition. In Topical Photographic Collection.

National Museum of Natural History

Department of Geology

Accessions Register.

National Anthropological Archives

Photographs of Anthropology Exhibitions. Photographic Lot 4.

Composite photographs of skulls by the U.S. Army Medical Museum. Photographic Lot 6a.

Bureau of American Ethnology. U.S. National Museum. Photographs of American Indians and other subjects. Photographic Lot 24.

Division of Ethnology collection (USNM collection). Albums 6–8. Pictorial Records of the Middle East. Photographic Lot 97.

Staten Island Historical Society

Charles Gilbert Hine Collection. Descriptive listing.

University of California, Riverside. California Museum of Photography

B. W. Kilburn Stereographic Company. Negative register books.

University of Kansas. Spencer Museum of Art

Correspondence relating to Dorothy Draper daguerreotype.

University of Michigan. William L. Clements Library

Moses Handy Papers. Boxes 26, 36, 44. World's Columbian Exposition scrapbooks.

University of Rochester. Rush Rhees Library. Manuscripts Collection

May Bragdon Papers.

Francis J. Bellamy Collection.

University of Texas at Austin. Harry Ransom Humanities Research Center.

Photography Collection

Presentation Album, Lord Kurzon of Kedleston.

Photographic Journals.

Published Sources

JOURNALS AND SERIALS CONSULTED

The American Amateur Photographer. 1892–93.

American Annual and Photographic Times Almanac. 1890–93.

The American Journal of Photography. 1892–94.
Anthony's Photographic Bulletin. 1879–80, 1893.
The Cosmopolitan. 1893–94.
Humphrey's Journal. 1867.
Journal of the Society of Amateur Photographers. 1893–94.
The Pacific Coast Photographer. 1893.
The Philadelphia Photographer. 1868, 1873–74, 1876–77.
The Photo-American. 1892–93.
The Photo Beacon. 1893.
The Photographic Eye. 1885, 1893. (Continues *The Eye*).
The Photographic Times. 1876, 1893.
The Practical Photographer. 1893.
Scientific American. 1893.
St. Louis and Canadian Photographer. 1891–93.
St. Louis Practical Photographer. 1876.
Wilson's Photographic Magazine. 1891–93.
The World's Columbian Exposition Illustrated. 1891–92.

Essays and Books Consulted

Adams, W. I. Lincoln. "Photography in the Colors of Nature." *Frank Leslie's Monthly* 36 (August 1893): 249–51.

Alloula, Malek. *The Colonial Harem.* Trans. Myrna Godzich. Minneapolis: University of Minnesota Press, 1986.

Ambler, Louise Todd, Martha Banta, and Eugenia Parry Janis, eds. *The Invention of Photography and Its Impact on Learning: Photographs from Harvard University and Radcliffe College and from the Collection of Harrison D. Horblit.* Cambridge, Mass.: Harvard University Library, 1989.

American Institute of the City of New York. *Catalogue of the 40th Exhibition.* New York: The Institute, 1871.

American Statistical Association. *Papers on Anthropometry.* Boston, 1894.

Anderson, Nancy C. "The Kiss of Enterprise." In *The West as America: Reinterpreting Images of the Frontier, 1820–1920,* ed. William H. Truettner, 237–81. Washington, D.C.: Smithsonian Institution Press, 1991.

Arts Council of Great Britain. *Pictorial Photography in Britain, 1900–1920.* Ed. John Taylor. London: Arts Council of Great Britain, 1978.

Association du Musée des Photographies Documentaires. *Bulletin de l'Association des Photographies Documentaires,* no. 1 (Jan. 1896): 1–38. Proceedings, articles of association, catalogue classification.

Badger, R. Reid. *The Great American Fair: The World's Columbian Exposition and American Culture.* Chicago: Nelson Hall, 1979.

Bannon, Anthony. *The Photo-Pictorialists of Buffalo.* Buffalo, N.Y.: Media Study/Buffalo, 1982.

Banta, Mellisa, and Curtis M. Hinsley, with Joan Kathryn O'Donnel. *From Site to Sight: Anthropology, Photography and the Power of Imagery.* Cambridge, Mass.: Peabody Museum Press, distributed by Harvard University, 1986.

Barger, Susan M., comp. *Bibliography of Photographic Processes in Use Before 1880: Their Materials, Processing and Conservation.* Rochester, N.Y.: Graphic Arts Research Center, Rochester Institute of Technology, 1980.

Beard, Rick, ed. *On Being Homeless: Historical Perspectives; Essays Published to Accompany the Exhibition . . . 24 November 1987 Through 27 March 1988.* New York: Museum of the City of New York, 1987.

Benedict, Burton. *The Anthropology of World's Fairs: San Francisco's Panama International Exposition of 1915.* Berkeley: Scolar Press, 1983.

Bertillon, Alphonse. *Signeletic Instructions, Including the Theory and Practice of Anthropometrical Identification.* Chicago: Werner Co., 1896.

Betts, Lillian. "The Tenement-House Exhibit." *Outlook,* March 10, 1900, 589–92.

Billings, J. S., and Washington Matthews. "On Composite Photography as Applied to Craniology, and on Measuring the Cubic Capacity of Skulls." *Thirteenth Memoir, National Academy of Sciences,* 3 (1886): 105–19.

Boas, Franz, "Remarks on the Theory of Anthropometry." In *Papers on Anthropometry,* 16–32. Boston: American Statistical Association, 1894.

Brey, William. *John Carbutt: On the Frontiers of Photography.* Cherry Hill, N.J.: Willowdale Press, 1984.

———. "On the Rails with William Rau." *Photographica* 17 (September 1988): 3–5.

———. "William Rau's Photographic Experiences in the East." *Stereo World* 2 (May/June 1984): 4–11.

Brey, William, and Marie Brey. *Philadelphia Photographers, 1840–1900.* Cherry Hill, N.J.: Willowdale Press, 1992.

Briant, Roland. "Mounting and Framing." *Journal of the Camera Club* (London) 7 (December 1893): 215–20.

Bridson, Gavin D. R., and Geoffrey Wakeman. *Printmaking & Picture Printing: A Bibliographic Guide to Artistic and Industrial Techniques in Britain, 1750–1900.* Williamsburg, Va.: Bookpress, 1984.

Bronner, Simon J. "Object Lessons: The Work of Ethnological Museums and Collections." In *Consuming Visions,* 217–54.

Bronner, Simon J., ed. *Consuming Visions: Accumulation and Display of Goods in America, 1880–1920.* New York: Norton, 1989.

Brown, Julie K. "Photography as Occupation in Late Nineteenth Century Colonial Australia." *Photoresearcher*, no. 3 (December 1991): 6–19.

———. "Versions of Reality: The Production and Function of Photographs in Colonial Queensland, 1880–1900." Ph.D. diss., University of Queensland, Australia, 1984.

Buel, J. W. *The Magic City: A Massive Portfolio of Original Photographic Views of the Great World's Fair*. 1894. Reprint. New York: Arno Press, 1894.

Buerger, Janet E. "Art Photography in Dresden, 1899–1900: An Eye on the German Avant-Garde at the Turn of the Century." *Image* 27 (June 1984):1–24.

———. *The Last Decade: The Emergence of Art Photography in the 1890s*. Rochester, N.Y.: International Museum of Photography at the George Eastman House, 1984.

———. "Naya's Italy." *Image* 26 (March 1983): 1–18.

Bunnell, Peter C., ed. *A Photographic Vision: Pictorial Photography, 1889–1923*. Salt Lake City: Peregrine Smith, 1980.

Burnham, Daniel. *The Final Official Report of the Director of Works of the World's Columbian Exposition*. New York: Garland Publishing, 1989.

Burnham, Daniel, and Francis D. Millet. *World's Columbian Exposition: The Book of the Builders*. Springfield, Ohio: Columbia Memorial Publication Society, 1894.

California. World's Fair Commission. *Final Report of the California World's Fair Commission, Including a Description of All Exhibits from the State of California*. Sacramento, 1894.

Cameron, William Evelyn, ed. *History of the World's Columbian Exposition*. Chicago: Columbian History Co., 1893.

Campbell, Helen. *Darkness and Daylight; or, Lights and Shadows of New York Life; A Woman's Story of Gospel, Temperance and Rescue Work*. Hartford, Conn.: A. D. Worthington & Co., 1893.

Campbell, John A., ed. *A Biographical History with Portraits of Prominent Men of the Great West*. Chicago: Western Biographical and Engraving Co., 1902.

Carr, Carolyn. "Prejudice and Pride: Presenting American Art at the 1893 Chicago World's Columbian Exposition." In *Revisiting the White City: American Art at the 1893 World's Fair*, 63–123. Washington, D.C.: National Museum of American Art and National Portrait Gallery, Smithsonian Institution, 1993.

Carson, Marian S. "The Eclipse and Rediscovery of Robert Cornelius." In *Robert Cornelius: Portraits from the Dawn of Photography, 1839–1889*, ed. William Stapp, 13–24. Washington, D.C.: Published for the National Portrait Gallery by the Smithsonian Institution Press, 1983.

Cassell, Frank. "Welcoming the World: Illinois' Role in the World's Columbian Exposition." *Illinois Historical Journal* 72 (Spring 1986): 230–44.

Catalogue of Kodaks. Rochester: Eastman Kodak Co., 1892.

The Catholic Educational Exhibit at the World's Columbian Exposition, Chicago, 1893. Chicago: J. S. Hyland and Co., 1896.

"C. D. Arnold of Pan-American Art Fame Dies." *Buffalo Courier Express*, May 9, 1927, p. 1.

Chicago and the World's Fair: Photogravures. Chicago: A. Wittemann, 1893.

The Chicago Times Portfolio of the Midway Types. Chicago: American Engraving Company, 1893.

Children's Aid Society, New York. *The Children's Aid Society of New York: Its Emigration or Placing Out System and Its Results*. New York, 1910.

The Cliff Dwellers. Chicago: H. Jay Smith Exploring Co., World's Columbian Exposition, 1893.

Club der Amateur-Photographen. *Catalog der internationalen Ausstellung künstlerischer Photographien*. Vienna: Club der Amateur-Photographen, 1891.

Coe, Brian. *Colour Photography: The First Hundred Years, 1840–1940*. London: Ash & Grant, 1978.

———. "George Davison: Impressionist and Anarchist." In *British Photography in the Nineteenth Century: The Fine Art Tradition*, ed. Mike Weaver, 215–27. Cambridge: Cambridge University Press, 1988.

The Columbian Exposition: A Visit to the World's Fair, Chicago. McAllister's Series of "Lantern Lectures." New York: T. H. McAllister, 1893.

Commonwealth in Focus: 130 Years of Photographic History. Sydney: International Cultural Corporation, 1982.

Commonwealth Institute. United Kingdom Section. *Catalogue of the Special Exhibition of Photography, Imperial Institute of the United Kindom, the Colonies, and India*. London: Waterlow and Sons, 1895.

A Complete 'Guide' to the Egyptological Exhibit in the Cairo Street Concession at the World's Columbian Exposition. Chicago: Thayer & Jackson Stationery Co., 1893.

Connecticut. Board of Lady Managers. *History of the Work of Connecticut Women at the World's Columbian Exposition, Chicago, 1893*. By Kate Bannon Knight, President of the Board of Lady Managers. Hartford, 1898.

Coombes, Annie E. "Museums and the Formation of National Cultural Identities." *Oxford Art Journal* 11, no. 2 (1988): 57–68.

Coombes, Annie E., and Steve Edwards. "Site Unseen: Photography in the Colonial Empire; Images of Subconscious Eroticism." *Art History* 12 (December 1989): 510–16.

The Cosmopolitan: World's Fair Number. (December 1893).

Crawford, William. *The Keepers of Light: A History and Working Guide to Early Photographic Processes*. New York: Morgan & Morgan, 1979.

Curtis, William Eleroy. *The Relics of Columbus: An Illustrated Description of the Historical Collection in the Monastery of La Rabida*. Washington, D.C.: William H. Lowermilk Co. 1893.

———. *Second Annual Report of the Bureau of the American Republics*. 52d Cong., 2d sess. Sen. Ex. doc. 84 (1892), 1–25.

Daniel, Pete, and Raymond Smock. *A Talent for Detail: The Photographs of Miss Frances Benjamin Johnston, 1889–1910*. New York: Harmony Books, 1974.

Darrah, William Culp. *Stereo Views: A History of Stereographs in America and Their Collection*. Gettysburg, Pa.: Printed by the Times and News Publishing Co., 1964.

Davis, Katharine Bement. "Report of the Exhibit of the New York State Workingman's Model Home." In New York Board of General Managers, *Report*, 364–443. Albany, 1894.

Davis, Keith F. *Désiré Charnay, Expeditionary Photographer*. Albuquerque: University of New Mexico Press, 1981.

Davison, George. "Impressionism in Photography (1891)." In *A Photographic Vision: Pictorial Photography, 1889–1923*, ed. Peter Bunnell, 12–20. Salt Lake City: Peregrine Smith, 1980.

Detroit Publishing Company. *List of Photographs: American Scenes and Architecture, Section I of Catalogue "P" (W. H. Jackson Catalogue)*. Detroit Publishing Co., 1898.

Downey, Dennis B. "Tradition and Acceptance: American Catholics and the Columbian Exposition." *Mid-America* 63, no. 2 (1981): 79–92.

The Dream City: A Portfolio of Photographic Views of the World's Columbian Exposition. St. Louis: N. D. Thompson Co., 1893.

Dredge, James. *Chicago and Her Exposition of 1893: A Stereopticon Lecture Recently Delivered Before the London Polytechnic Institute*. Chicago: H. V. Holmes, 1892.

Earle, Edward W., ed. *Points of View: The Stereograph in America; A Cultural History*. Rochester, N.Y.: Visual Studies Workshop, 1979.

Eder, Josef Maria. *A History of Photography*. Trans. Edward Epstean. 1945. Reprint. New York: Dover Press, 1978.

Edwards, Elizabeth, ed. *Anthropology and Photography, 1860–1920*. New Haven: Yale University Press in association with the Royal Institute of Anthropology, London, 1992.

Emerson, P. H. *Naturalistic Photography for Students of the Art*. 1889. Reprint. New York: Arno Press, 1973.

Enyeart, James. "Reviving a Daguerreotype." *Photographic Journal* 109 (September 1970): 338–44.

Eskind, Andrew, and Greg Drake. *Index to American Photographic Collections*. 2d ed. Boston: G. K. Hall, 1990.

Exposition d'Art Photographique. *Première Exposition d'Art Photographique, Paris, 1894*. Paris: Photo-Club de Paris, 1894.

Fagin, Brian. *The Rape of the Nile: Tomb Robbers, Tourists and Archeologists in Egypt*. New York: Scribners, 1975.

Fagin, Nancy L. "Closed Collections and Open Appeals: The Two Anthropology Exhibits at the Chicago World's Columbian Exposition of 1893." *Curator* 27, no. 4 (1984): 249–64.

Ferguson, Eugene S. "Technical Museums and International Exhibitions." *Technology and Culture* 6 (Fall 1965): 30–46.

Fleming, Paula Richardson, and Judith Luskey. *The North American Indians in Early Photographs*. New York: Harper & Row, 1986.

Flinn, John J., comp. *Official Guide to the Midway Plaisance*. Chicago: Columbian Guide Co., 1893.

———. *Official Guide to the World's Columbian Exposition*. Chicago: Columbian Guide Co., 1893.

Foner, Eric. *Reconstruction: America's Unfinished Revolution, 1863–1877*. New York: Harper & Row, 1988.

Fowler, C. J. "The Photographic Survey." *Photogram* 7 (May 1900): 130–35.

Fowler, Don D. *The Western Photographs of John K. Hillers: "Myself in the Water."* Washington, D.C.: Smithsonian Institution Press, 1989.

Fox, Richard Wrightman, and T. J. Jackson Lears, eds. *The Culture of Consumption: Critical Essays in American History, 1880–1980*. New York: Pantheon Books, 1983.

Gavin, Carney. "Photography and the Social Sciences: In Light from Ancient Lands." In *The Invention of Photography*, ed. Louise Todd Ambler, Martha Banta, and Eugenia Parry Janis, 48–61. Cambridge, Mass.: Harvard University Library, 1989.

Geertz, Clifford. "Art as a Cultural System." *Modern Language Notes* 91 (December 1976): 1473–99.

Gilbert, George. "Draper? First to Photograph the Human Face." *Photographica* 19 (January 1990): 5–9.

Gilbert, James. *Perfect Cities: Chicago's Utopias of 1893*. Chicago: University of Chicago Press, 1991.

Glimpses of the World's Fair: An Interesting Collection of Instantaneous Views, . . . from Recent Photographs by Henry E. Fowler. Philadelphia: Henry E. Fowler, 1893.

Glimpses of the World's Fair: A Selection of Gems of the White City Seen Through a Camera. Chicago: Laird & Lee, 1893.

Goetzmann, William H. *New Lands, New Men: America and the Second Great Age of Discovery.* New York: Viking, 1986.

Goetzmann, William H., and William N. Goetzmann. *The West of the Imagination.* New York: Norton, 1986.

Goode, George Brown. "First Draft of a System of Classification for the World's Columbian Exposition." In *Annual Report of the United States National Museum, year ending June 30, 1891,* 649–60. Washington, D.C.: Government Printing Office, 1892.

———. "Recent Advances in Museum Method." In *Annual Report of the United States National Museum, Year Ending June 30, 1893,* 21–58. Washington, D.C.: Government Printing Office, 1895.

Gover, C. Jane. *The Positive Image: Women Photographers in Turn of the Century America.* Albany: State University of New York Press, 1988.

Graham-Brown, Sarah. *Images of Women: The Portrayal of Women in Photography of the Middle East, 1860–1950.* London: Quartet, 1988.

Graver, Nicholas. "Photographie Medicale: Albert Londé's 1893 book, first in the field." *Journal of the Biological Photographic Association* 42 (1974): 95–102.

Gray, George L. *Souvenir, World's Fair, May 1st to Nov. 1st: Shakespeare Boiled Down,* Chicago: New Home Sewing Machine Co., 1893.

Great Britain. Executive Commission, Philadelphia Exhibition. *The Official Catalogue of the British Section, Philadelphia International Exhibition.* London: Published for Her Majesty's Stationery Office by Eyre & Spottiswoode, 1876.

Green, David. "Veins of Resemblance: Photography and Eugenics." *Oxford Art Journal* 7, no. 2 (1985): 3–16.

Greenhalgh, Paul. *Ephemeral Vistas: The Expositions Universelles, Great Exhibitions, and World's Fairs, 1851–1939.* Manchester: Manchester University Press, 1988.

Greenough, Sarah. "Of Charming Glens, Graceful Glades, and Frowning Cliffs: The Economic Incentives, Social Inducements and Aesthetic Issues of American Pictorial Photography, 1880–1902." In *Photography in Nineteenth Century America,* ed. Martha A. Sandweiss, 261–66. New York: Amon Carter Museum and Henry Abrams, 1991.

Griffin, Michael. "Amateur Photography and Pictorial Aesthetics: Influences of Organization and Industry on Cultural Production." Ph.D. diss., University of Pennsylvania, 1987.

Haberstich, David. "Photographs at the Smithsonian Institution: A History." *Picturescope* 32 (Summer 1985): 5–8.

Hales, Peter Bacon. "American Views and the Romance of Modernism." In *Photography in Nineteenth Century America,* ed. Martha A. Sandweiss, 204–57. Fort Worth: Amon Carter Museum and Harry N. Abrams, Inc., 1991.

———. *Constructing the Fair: Platinum Photographs by C. D. Arnold of the World's Columbian Exposition.* Chicago: Art Institute of Chicago, 1993.

———. "Photography and the World's Columbian Exposition: A Case Study." *Journal of Urban History* 15 (May 1989): 247–73.

———. *Silver Cities: The Photography of American Urbanization, 1839–1915.* Philadelphia: Temple University Press, 1984.

———. *William Henry Jackson and the Transformation of the American Landscape.* Philadelphia: Temple University Press, 1988.

Hankey, J. L. "The Frank M. Sutcliffe Memorial Lecture." *Photographic Journal* 82 (August 1942): 280–94.

Haraway, Donna. "Teddy Bear Patriarchy: Taxidermy in the Garden of Eden; New York City, 1908–1936." *Social Text* 4 (Winter 1985): 20–64.

Harker, Margaret. *The Linked Ring: The Secession Movement in Photography in Britain.* London: Heinemann, 1979.

Harrison, Jerome W. *A History of Photography Written as a Practical Guide and an Introduction to Its Latest Developments.* New York: Scoville Manufacturing Co., 1887.

Harrison, Thomas. *A Trip Through the Columbian Exposition with a Camera: A Selection of Instantaneous Photographs of the Principal Buildings and General Views; From Negatives Made in August and September 1893 by Thos. Harrison, Photographer.* Chicago: Globe Lithographing and Printing Co., 1893.

Hendricks, Gordon. *The Kinetoscope: America's First Commercially Successful Motion Picture Exhibitor.* New York: Beginning of the American Film, 1966.

Heseltine, Tom. "Chicago Through the Stereoscope: The World's Columbian Exposition." *Stereo World* 3 (September/October 1976): 12–19.

Hiley, Michael. *Frank Meadow Sutcliffe: Photographer of Whitby.* London: Gordon Fraser, 1974.

Hinsley, Curtis M. "From Shell-Heaps to Stelae: Early Anthropology at the Peabody Museum." In *Objects and Others: Essays on Museums and Material Culture,* ed. George W. Stocking, Jr., 49–74. Madison: University of Wisconsin Press, 1985.

————. *Savages and Scientists: The Smithsonian Institution and the Development of American Anthropology, 1846–1910.* Washington, D.C.: Smithsonian Institution Press, 1981.

————. "The World as Marketplace: Commodification of the Exotic at the World's Columbian Exposition." In *Exhibiting Cultures: The Poetics and Politics of Museum Display,* ed. Ivan Karp and Steven Lavine, 344–65. Washington, D.C.: Smithsonian Institution Press, 1991.

Hirsch, Susan, and Robert Goler. *A City Comes of Age: Chicago in the 1890s.* Chicago: Chicago Historical Society, 1990.

Holtermannn, Bernard Otto. *Gold and Silver: Photographs of Australian Gold Fields from the Holtermann Collection.* Ed. Keast Burke. Harmondsworth, Eng.: Penguin, 1973.

Horgan, Stephen. "Photo-Engraving Pioneers No. 6: William Kurtz Introduced Three-Color Halftones." *Photo-Engravers Bulletin* 15 (August 1926): 323–26.

Hrdlička, Aleš. *Physical Anthropology: Its Scope and Aims, Its History and Present Status in the United States.* Philadelphia: Wistar Institute of Anatomy and Biology, 1919.

Hull, Roger Piatt. "*Camera Work,* An American Quarterly." Ph.D. diss., Northwestern University, 1970.

Hyde, W. Lewis. "John William Draper, 1811–1882." *Applied Optics* 15 (July 1976): 1726–30.

Illinois. Board of World's Fair Commissioners. *Brief History of the Charitable Institutions of the State of Illinois.* Chicago: John Morris Co., 1893.

————. *The Illinois Building and Exhibits Therein at the World's Columbian Exposition, 1893.* Chicago: John Morris Co., 1893.

————. *Report of the World's Fair Commissioners at the World's Columbian Exposition.* Springfield: H. W. Rokker, 1895.

Index to Awards: World's Columbian Exposition; List of Exhibitors at the World's Columbian Exposition for Whom Diplomas Were Prepared by the Bureau of Engraving and Printing. Washington, D.C.: Bureau of Engraving and Printing, n.d.

Ingram, J. S. *The Centennial Exposition, Described and Illustrated.* Philadelphia: Hubbard Bros., 1876.

Internationale Ausstellung von Amateur Photographien in der Kunsthalle zu Hamburg, 1 Oktober bis 20 November 1893: Offizieller Katalog. Hamburg: Rudolf Mosse, 1893.

Italy: One Hundred Years of Photography. Text by Cesare Colombo and Susan Sontag. Florence: Aliniari, 1988.

Ives, Frederick. "The Lumière Lippmann Color Photographs: A Communication to the Photographic Society of Philadelphia, November 8, 1893." *Journal of the Photographic Society of Philadelphia* 1 (March 1894): 49–51.

J. Landy's Catalogue of Celebrities. Cincinnati: Landy's Gallery of Photographic Art, n.d.

Jacknis, Ira. "Franz Boas and Exhibits: On the Limitations of the Museum Method in Anthropology." In *Objects and Others: Essays on Museums and Material Culture,* ed. George W. Stocking, Jr., 75–92. Madison: University of Wisconsin Press, 1985.

————. "Franz Boas and Photography." *Studies in the Anthropology of Visual Communications* 10, no. 1 (1984): 2–60.

Jackson, William Henry. *Descriptive Catalogue of the Photographs of the United States Geological Survey of the Territories for the Years 1869–1875.* 1875. Reprint. Milwaukee: Q Press, 1978.

————. *Jackson's Famous Pictures of the World's Fair.* Descriptive text by Selim H. Peabody and Stanley Wood. Chicago: White City Art Co., 1895.

————. *Time Exposure: The Autobiography of William Henry Jackson.* New York: G. P. Putnam's Sons, 1940.

————. *The White City (As It Was): The Story of the World's Columbian Exposition.* Chicago: White City Art Company, 1894.

James, Peter. "Evolution of the Photographic Record and Survey Movement, c.1890–1910." *History of Photography* 12 (July/September 1988): 205–17.

Jenkins, Reese V. "George Eastman and the Coming of Industrial Research in America." In *Technology in America: A History of Individuals and Ideas,* ed. Carroll W. Pursell, Jr., 129–44. Cambridge, Mass.: MIT Press, 1981.

————. *Images and Enterprise: Technology and the American Photographic Industry, 1839–1925.* Baltimore: Johns Hopkins University Press, 1975.

Jenks, Tudor. *The Century World's Fair Book for Boys and Girls.* New York: Century Company, 1893.

Johnson, Rossiter, ed. *A History of the World's Columbian Exposition Held in Chicago in 1893 by Authority of the Board of Directors.* New York: D. Appleton & Co., 1897–98.

Johnson, William S. *Nineteenth-Century Photography: An Annotated Bibliography, 1839–1879.* Boston: G. K. Hall, 1990.

Johnston, Frances Benjamin. "The Evolution of a Great Exposition." *Demorest's Family Magazine* 28 (April 1892): 310–28.

————. *Mammoth Cave by Flashlight.* Washington, D.C.: Gibson Brothers, 1893.

———. *Women of Class and Station: An Exhibition Organized by the Art Museum and Galleries and the Center for Southern California Studies in the Visual Arts, California State University, Long Beach, February 12 through March 11, 1979.* Long Beach: The Center, 1979.

Jones, Bernard E., ed. *The Encyclopedia of Early Photography.* 1911. Reprint. New York: Arno Press, 1974.

Jussim, Estelle. *Visual Communication and the Graphic Arts: Photographic Technologies in the Nineteenth Century.* New York: R. R. Bowker Co., 1974.

Karp, Ivan, and Steven Lavine, eds. *Exhibiting Cultures: The Poetics and Politics of Museum Display.* Washington, D.C.: Smithsonian Institution Press, 1991.

Keller, Heinrich. "The Myth of Art Photography: An Iconographic Analysis." *History of Photography* 9 (January/March 1985): 1–38; 249–75.

Kirshenblatt-Gimblett, Barbara. "Objects of Ethnography," in *Exhibiting Cultures: The Poetics and Politics of Museum Display,* ed. Ivan Karp and Steven Lavine, 386–443. Washington, D.C.: Smithsonian Institution Press, 1991.

Knutson, Robert. "The White City: The World's Columbian Exposition of 1893." Ph.D. diss., Columbia University, 1956.

The Kodak Camera. Rochester, N.Y.: Eastman Company, 1890.

Levine, Lawrence W. *Highbrow/Lowbrow: The Emergence of Cultural Hierarchy in America.* Cambridge, Mass.: Harvard University Press, 1988.

Libby Prison War Museum Association. *Libby Prison War Museum: Catalogue and Program.* Chicago: Libby Prison War Museum Association, n.d.

Library of Congress. Reference Department. *Guide to the Special Collections of Prints and Photographs in the Library of Congress.* Comp. Paul Vanderbilt. Washington, D.C.: Government Printing Office, 1955.

Londé, Albert. *La photographie médicale: Application aux sciences médicales et physiologiques.* Paris: Gauthier-Villars, 1893.

Loy, Daniel Oscar. *Poems of the White City.* Chicago: Daniel Oscar Loy, 1893.

Lubove, Roy. *The Progressives and the Slums: Tenement House Reform in New York City, 1890–1917.* Pittsburgh: University of Pittsburgh, 1963.

McCabe, James D. *The Illustrated History of the Centennial Exhibition Held in Commemoration of the One Hundredth Anniversary of American Independence.* Philadelphia: National Pub. Co., 1876.

McCarthy, Kathleen D. *Noblesse Oblige: Charity and Cultural Philanthropy in Chicago, 1849–1929.* Chicago: University of Chicago Press, 1982.

MacKenzie, John M. *Propaganda and Empire: The Manipulation of British Public Opinion, 1880–1960.* Manchester: Manchester University Press, 1985.

Martin, J. F. *Martin's World's Fair Album: Atlas and Family Souvenir.* Chicago: C. Ropp & Sons, 1892.

Massachusetts. Board of Managers. World's Fair, 1893. *Report of the Massachusetts Board of the World's Fair Managers.* Boston, 1894.

Maudslay, Alfred P. *Archeology (Biologia centrali-americana).* 5 vols. London: R. H. Porter and Dulan and Co., 1899–1902.

Maxwell, William Quentin. *Lincoln's Fifth Wheel: The Political History of the United States Sanitary Commission.* New York: Longmans, Green, 1956.

Millard, A. J. *Edison and the Business of Innovation.* Baltimore: Johns Hopkins University Press, 1990.

Miner, H. Craig, "U.S. Government Building at the Centennial, 1874–1876." *Prologue* 4 (Winter 1972): 203–19.

Mitchell, Timothy. "The World as Exhibition." *Society for the Comparative Study of Society and History,* 31 (April 1989): 217–36.

Molella, Arthur. "The Museum That Might Have Been: The Smithsonian's National Museum of Engineering and Industry." *Technology and Culture* 32 (April 1991): 237–63.

Moore, Charles Bloomfield. "Women Experts in Photography." *Cosmopolitan* 14 (March 1893): 49–59.

Museum voor Volkenkunde (Rotterdam, The Netherlands). *Beelden van de Orient: Fotografie en Toerisme; Images of the Orient: Photography and Tourism, 1860–1900.* Amsterdam: Fragment, with the Museum voor Volkendunde, 1986.

Musser, Charles. *The Emergence of Cinema: The American Screen to 1907.* New York: Scribner, 1990.

Muybridge, Edweard. *Animal Locomotion: An Electrophotographic Investigation of Consecutive Phases of Animal Movements, 1872–1885.* Philadelphia: University of Pennsylvania, 1887.

———. *Descriptive Zoopraxography; or, The Science of Animal Locomotion Made Popular.* Philadelphia: University of Pennsylvania, 1893.

———. *Muybridge's Complete Human and Animal Locomotion: All 781 Pictures from the 1887 Animal Locomotion.* New York: Dover Press, 1979.

Nadeau, Luis. *Encyclopedia of Printing, Photographic and Photomechanical Processes: A Comprehensive Reference to*

Reproduction Technologies, Containing Valuable Information on Over 5,000 Processes. 2 vols. Fredericton, N.B., Canada: Louis Nadeau, 1989–90.

Naef, Weston, in collaboration with James N. Wood. *Era of Exploration: The Rise of Landscape Photography in the American West, 1860–1885.* Buffalo: Albright Knox Gallery, distributed by the New York Graphic Society, 1975.

National Archives and Records Administration. Still Pictures Branch. *Guide to the Holdings of the Still Pictures Branch of the National Archives.* Comp. Barbara Lewis Burger. Washington, D.C.: National Archives Trust Fund Board, 1990.

Naya, Carlo. Venice: The Naya Collection. Ed. Italo Zannier. Foreword by Alberto Moravia. Venice: O. Bohm, 1981.

Newbury, Spencer B. "Photographic Proofs and Apparatus." In *Universal Exposition, Paris,* 2:201–11. Washington, D.C.: Government Printing Office, 1891.

New York. Board of General Managers. *Report of the Board of General Managers of the Exhibit of the State of New York at the World's Columbian Exposition.* Albany, 1894.

Nir, Yeshayahu. *The Bible and the Image: The History of Photography in the Holy Land, 1839–1899.* Philadelphia: University of Pennsylvania Press, 1985.

Norton, F. H., ed. *Frank Leslie's Historic Register of the United States Centennial Exposition, 1876.* New York: Frank Leslie's Publishing House, 1877.

Notman, William. *Portrait of a Period: A Collection of Notman Photographs, 1856–1915.* ed. J. Russell Harper and Stanley Triggs. Montreal: McGill University Press, 1967.

O'Connor, Diane Vogt. *Guide to Photographic Collections at the Smithsonian Institution, National Museum of American History.* Vol. 1. Washington, D.C.: Smithsonian Institution Press, 1989.

Off for the World's Fair with a Trokonet. Rochester, N.Y.: Photo-Materials Co., 1893.

Oriental and Occidental, Northern and Southern Types of the Midway Plaisance. St. Louis: N. D. Thompson Publishing Co., 1894.

Orvell, Miles. *The Real Thing: Imitation and Authenticity in American Culture, 1880–1940.* Chapel Hill: University of North Carolina Press, 1989.

Palmquist, Peter E. *Catharine Weed Barnes Ward.* Arcata, Calif.: Peter E. Palmquist, 1992.

Palmquist, Peter E., ed. *Camera Fiends & Kodak Girls: 50 Selections By and About Women in Photography, 1840–1930.* New York: Midmarch Arts Press, 1989.

Pan-American Exposition. *Official Catalogue and Guidebook to the Pan-American Expostion.* Buffalo: C. Ahehart, 1901.

Panzer, Mary. "How the West Was Won: Reinventing the Myth of William Henry Jackson." *Afterimage* 16 (March 1989): 17–19.

———. *Philadelphia Naturalistic Photography, 1865–1906; Yale University Art Gallery, New Haven, Connecticut, 10 February–7 April 1982.* New Haven: The Gallery, 1982.

Pedzich, Joan. "John Howe Kent." *Image* 27 (March 1984): 1–10.

Perez, Nissan N. *Focus East: Early Photography in the Near East (1839–1885).* New York: Abrams in association with the Domino Press, Jerusalem, and the Israel Museum, 1989.

Peters, Lisa N. "Images of the Homeless in American Art, 1860–1910." In *On Being Homeless: Historical Perspectives,* ed. Rick Beard. 43–67. New York: Museum of the City of New York, 1987.

Peterson, Christian Anders. "A History of Exhibitions of Photography in America, 1887–1917." M.A. thesis, Syracuse University, 1976.

Phillips, David R. *The West: An American Experience.* Chicago: Henry Regnery Co., 1973.

Photographic Mosaics: An Annual Record of Photographic Progress. New York: Bernerman & Wilson, 1891–93.

Photographic Society of Philadelphia. *Sixth Annual Exhibition Under an Agreement Between the Photographic Society of Philadelphia, the Society of Amateur Photographers of New York and the Boston Camera Club.* Philadelphia: The Society, 1893.

The Photographic World's Fair and Midway Plaisance. Chicago: Monarch Book Co., 1894.

"Photographing Savages." *Popular Science Monthly* 42 (August 1893): 570.

Pierce, James Wilson. *Photographic History of the World's Fair and Sketch of the City of Chicago.* Baltimore: R. H. Woodward and Company, 1893.

Poignant, Roslyn. "Surveying the Field of View: The Making of the RAI Photographic Collection." In *Anthropology and Photography, 1860–1920,* ed. Elizabeth Edwards, 42–73. New Haven: Yale University Press in association with the Royal Institute of Anthropology, London, 1992.

Ponce de León, Néstor. *The Columbus Gallery: The Discoverer of the New World as Represented in Portraits, Monuments, Statues, Medals and Paintings.* New York: Néstor Ponce de Léon, 1893.

Potts, David. "Social Ethics at Harvard, 1881–1931: A Study in Academic Activism." In *Social Science at Harvard: From Inculcation to Open Mind*, ed. Paul Buck, 91–128. Cambridge, Mass.: Harvard University Press, 1965.

"Proceedings of Special Meeting, December 19, 1993." *Journal of the Society of Amateur Photographers*, n. s. 1 (February 1894): 9–10.

Ragan, Henry Harger. *Art Photographs of the World and the Columbian Exposition: An Album of Rare Photographs of the Wonders of the Universe.* Chicago: Star Publishing Co., 1893.

A Record of the Metropolitan Fair in Aid of the United States Sanitary Commission Held at New York in April 1864. New York: Hurd & Houghton, 1864.

Reilly, James. *Care and Identification of 19th Century Photographic Prints.* Rochester: Eastman Kodak Company, 1986.

Rhodes, Henry Taylor. *Alphonse Bertillon: Father of Scientific Detection.* New York: Abelard Schuman, 1956.

Root, Marcus Aurelius. "A Heliographic School: Its Implications." *American Journal of Photography and Allied Sciences* 3 (July 1860): 41–42.

Rosenblum, Barbara. "Photographers and Their Photographs: An Empirical Study in the Sociology of Aesthetics." Ph.D. diss., Northwestern University, 1973.

Rosenblum, Naomi. *A World History of Photography.* New York: Abbeville Press, 1984.

Rydell, Robert W. *All the World's a Fair: Visions of Empire at American International Expositions, 1876–1916.* Chicago: University of Chicago Press, 1984.

———. "The Culture of Imperial Abundance: World's Fairs and the Making of American Culture." In *Consuming Visions: Accumulation and Display of Goods in America, 1880–1920*, ed. Simon J. Bronner, 191–216. New York: Norton, 1989.

———. "The Literature of International Expositions." In *The Book of the Fairs: Materials About World's Fairs, 1834–1916, in the Smithsonian Institution Libraries*, 1–62. Chicago: American Library Association, 1992.

Sandweiss, Eric. "Around the World in a Day: International Participation in the World's Columbian Exposition." *Illinois Historical Journal* 84 (Spring 1991): 2–14.

Sandweiss, Martha, ed. *Photography in Nineteenth Century America.* New York: H. N. Abrams, 1991.

Schutt, Harold G. "World's Fair Tree: An Interview with Jesse Pattee." *Historical Bulletin of the Tulare County Historical Society*, no. 6 (October 1950): 1–2.

Schuyler, Montgomery. "Last Words about the World's Fair." *Architectural Record* 3 (January-March 1894): 291–301.

Sekula, Alan. "The Body and the Archive." *October* 39 (Winter 1986): 3–64.

Shakelford, Collin. *Souvenir Ride on the Ferris Wheel at the World's Fair, Chicago.* Chicago: American Engraving Co., 1893.

Shaw, Professor E. R. "The University Exhibit at the World's Fair." *University Quarterly*, 17, no. 1 (1893): 8–11.

Shepp, James W., and Daniel B. Shepp, comps. *Shepp's World's Fair Photographed: Being a Collection of Original Copyright Photographs Authorized and Permitted by the Management of the World's Columbian Exposition.* Chicago: Globe Bible Publishing Co., 1893.

Sinclair, Bruce. *Philadelphia's Philosopher Mechanics: A History of the Franklin Institute, 1824–1865.* Baltimore: Johns Hopkins University Press, 1974.

Sipley, Louis Walton. *A Half Century of Color.* New York: McMillan, 1957.

———. *Photography's Great Inventors.* Philadelphia: American Museum of Photography, 1965.

Smith, Harvey T. *Pictorial Album and History of the World's Fair and Midway.* Chicago: Foster Press, n.d.

Smithsonian Institution Libraries. *The Book of the Fairs: Materials About World's Fairs, 1834–1916, in the Smithsonian Institution Libraries.* Chicago: American Library Association, 1992.

Snider, Denton Jacques. *World's Fair Studies.* Chicago: Chicago Sigma Publishing Co., 1895.

Snyder, Carl. "Engineer Ferris and His Wheel." *Review of Reviews* 6 (September, 1893): 269–76.

Stanford University. Department of Art. *Eadweard Muybridge: The Stanford Years, 1872–1882.* Stanford, Calif.: Stanford University, 1972.

Stange, Maren. *Symbols of Ideal Life: Social Documentary Photography in America, 1890–1950.* Cambridge: Cambridge University Press, 1989.

Stevens, Mrs. Mark. *Six Months at the World's Fair: A Little Here and a Little There of the Great White City; The World's Fair.* Detroit: Detroit Free Press, 1895.

Stewart, Susan. *On Longing: Narratives of the Miniature, the Gigantic, the Souvenir and the Collection.* Baltimore: Johns Hopkins University Press, 1984.

Stillé, Charles J. *Memorial of the Great Central Fair for the U.S. Sanitary Commission, Held at Philadelphia, June 1864.* Philadelphia: U.S. Sanitary Commission, 1864.

Sunart Photo Company. *Sunart Catalogue and Manual.* Rochester, N.Y., 1893.

Taft, Robert. *Photography and the American Scene: A Social History, 1839–1889.* 1938. Reprint. New York: Dover Press, 1964.

Tagg, John. *The Burden of Representation: Essays on Photographies and Histories.* Amherst: University of Massachusetts Press, 1988.

———. *Grounds of Dispute: Art History, Cultural Politics and the Discursive Field.* Minneapolis: University of Minnesota Press, 1992.

Thomas Cook, Ltd. *The World's Fair at Chicago, 1893: Information for Travellers.* London: Cook, 1893.

Thompson, John. "Biographical Notes and Commentary on the Work of Henry Bosse." Unpublished report for the U.S. Army Corps of Engineers, Rock Island District, Illinois.

The "Time Saver": A Book Which Names and Locates 5,000 Things at the World's Fair the Visitors Should Not Fail to See. Chicago: W. E. Hamilton, 1893.

Todd, Frederick Dundas. *"Snapshots"; or, The World's Fair Through a Camera; From Recent Photographs by F. Dundas Todd, Assisted by W. H. Shuey and R. C. McLean.* Chicago: Union News Co., 1893.

Trachtenberg, Alan. *The Incorporation of America: Culture and Society in the Gilded Age.* New York: Hill and Wang, 1982.

Trennert, Robert A., Jr. "Selling Indian Education at World's Fairs and Expositions, 1893–1904." *American Indian Quarterly* 11 (Summer 1987): 203–20.

Triggs, Stanley. *William Notman: The Stamp of a Studio.* Toronto: Art Gallery of Ontario, 1985.

Trombino, Don, with research by John Pazmino. "Astronomers on the Hudson." *Skylines* 2, no. 3 (1978): 3–6.

Trombino, Don, with research by John Pazmino. "Henry Fitz: Locksmith, Photographer and Telescope Maker." *Skylines* 2, no. 2 (1978): 3–5.

Truman, Benjamin. *History of the World's Fair.* 1893. Reprint. New York: Arno Press, 1976.

Twyman, Robert W. *History of Marshall Field & Co., 1852–1906.* Philadelphia: University of Pennsylvania Press, 1954.

U.S. Centennial Commission. *International Exhibition, 1876: Official Catalogue.* Philadelphia: John R. Nagle & Co., 1876.

U.S. Commission to the Paris Exposition, 1889. *Reports of the United States Commissioners to the Universal Exposition of 1889 at Paris.* Vols. 1 and 2. Washington, D.C.: Government Printing Office, 1890–91.

U.S. Commission to the Vienna Exhibition, 1893. *Reports of the Commissioners of the United States to the International Exhibition Held at Vienna, 1873.* Vols. 1 and 2. Washington, D.C.: Government Printing Office, 1876.

U.S. Congress. *Report of the United States Commissioners to the Columbian Historical Exposition Madrid, 1892–1893.* 52d Cong., 3rd sess., 1894–95, H. Ex. Doc. 100.

U.S. Geological Survey. *Annual Report.* Washington, D.C.: Government Printing Office, 1891–99.

U.S. National Museum. *Annual Report of the United States National Museum.* Washington, D.C.: Government Printing Office, 1886–95.

Vaczek, Louis, and Gail Buckland. *Travelers in Ancient Lands: A Portrait of the Middle East, 1839–1919.* Boston: New York Graphic Society, 1981.

The Vanishing City: A Photographic Encyclopedia of the World's Columbian Exposition. Chicago: Lee & Laird, 1893.

van Rensselaer, M. "At the Fair." *Century Magazine* 46 (May 1893): 7–13.

Vidal, Léon. "Exposé de la situation morale de l'association et de l'oeuvre accompli dupuis la précédente assemblée." *Bulletin de la Association du Musée des Photographies Documentaires,* no. 2 (April 1896): 33–41.

Wade, Elizabeth Flint. "Amateur Photography Through Women's Eyes, No. 2." *Photo-American* 5 (June 1894): 235–36.

Walker, Francis Amasa. *The World's Fair, Philadelphia, 1876: A Critical Account.* New York: A. S. Barnes & Co., 1877.

Weaver, Mike, ed. *British Photography in the Nineteenth Century: The Fine Art Tradition.* Cambridge: Cambridge University Press, 1989.

A Week at the Fair: Illustrating the Exhibits and Wonders of the World's Columbian Exposition. Chicago: Rand, McNally and Co., 1893.

Welling, William. *Photography in America: The Formative Years, 1839–1900.* New York: Thomas Y. Crowell Co., 1978.

Wile, Frederic William. *A Century of Industrial Progress.* Garden City, N.Y.: Published for the American Institute of the City of New York by Doubleday, Doran & Co., 1928.

William H. Truettner, ed. *The West as America: Reinterpreting Images of the Frontier, 1820–1920.* Washington, D.C.: Smithsonian Institution Press, 1991.

Wilson, Edward L. *Wilson's Photographics.* 1881. Reprint. New York: Arno Press, 1973.

Wolff, Janet. "The Invisible Flâneuse." In *Feminine Sentences: Essays on Women and Culture,* 34–49. Cambridge: Polity Press, 1990.

Wood, R. Derek. "The Daguerreotype Portrait of Dorothy Draper." *Photographic Journal* 109 (December 1970): 478–82.

World's Columbian Exposition. *Catalogue of the Russian Section, World's Columbian Exposition, 1893, Chicago.* St. Petersburg: I. Libermann, 1893.

———. *Official Catalogue of Exhibits.* Pts. 1–14. Ed. Moses P. Handy. Chicago: W. B. Conkey, 1893.

———. *Official Catalogue of Exhibits on the Midway Plaisance.* Department M: Ethnology, Group 176. Ed. Moses P. Handy. Chicago: W. B. Conkey, 1893.

———. *The Official Directory of the World's Columbian Exposition.* Ed. Moses P. Handy. Chicago: W. B. Conkey, 1893.

———. *Official Views of the World's Columbian Exposition.* Chicago: Chicago Photogravure Co., 1893.

———. *Portfolio of Views.* Chicago: National Chemigraph Co., 1893.

———. *Report of the Committee on Awards of the World's Columbian Commission: Special Report on Special Subjects or Groups.* Washington, D.C.: Government Printing Office, 1901.

———. *Report of the President to the Board of Directors of the World's Columbian Exposition.* Chicago: Rand McNally, 1898.

World's Columbian Exposition. Council of Administration. *Minutes of the Meetings of the Council of Administration.* Chicago: Henson Brothers, 1893.

World's Columbian Exposition. Department of Liberal Arts. *The Bureau of Charities and Correction: What It Will Include and Instructions for Preparing Exhibits.* Department of Liberal Arts, Circular No. 6. Chicago: World's Columbian Exposition, Department of Liberal Arts, 1892.

World's Columbian Exposition. Department of Photography. *Portfolio of Views.* Chicago: National Chemigraph Co., 1893.

The World's Congress Auxiliary of the World's Columbian Exposition Congress of Photographers. Chicago, 1893.

The World's Fair at Chicago, 1893: Information for Travelers. London: Thomas Cook Co., 1893.

World's Parliament of Religions. *The World's Congress of Religions.* Chicago: International Publishing Co., 1894.

Wortham, John David. *The Genesis of British Egyptology, 1549–1906.* Norman: University of Oklahoma Press, 1971.

Wright, Helena. "The Division, the Smithsonian, and the Mission of Art: A Narrative History." In National Museum of American History, Division of Graphic Arts, G. A. 100: The Centenary of the Division of Graphic Arts, 21–35. Washington, D.C.: Smithsonian Institution, 1986.

———. *Imperishable Beauty: Pictures Printed in Collotype.* Washington, D.C.: Smithsonian Institution Press, 1988.

Ziolkowski, Eric J. "Heavenly Visions and Worldly Intentions: Chicago's Columbian Exposition and the World's Parliament of Religions." *Journal of American Culture* 13 (Winter 1990): 9–15.

INDEX

ABOUT THE AUTHOR

JULIE K. BROWN received her initial training from Boston College and earned an M.A. in Art History from the University of Rochester in 1966. She taught at the Rochester Institute of Technology and wrote weekly art reviews for the Gannett newspaper as well as worked on a grant in innovative art education for the Memorial Art Gallery of the University of Rochester.

In 1969 she moved to Australia where she lived for fifteen years. Here she taught in the Department of Fine Arts of the University of Queensland for five years. On completing a Ph.D. in the Department of History, she returned to the United States in 1985. She has taught at the University of Texas at San Antonio and in 1989–90 was the Fanny Knapp Post-Doctoral Fellow at the University of Rochester where she taught and did research for the present publication.

She has continued her researches on nineteenth and early twentieth century photographic exhibitions and most recently has been working on a grant on Exhibition Histories for a new database of the GEH Interactive Catalogue of the George Eastman House, International Museum of Photography and Film. She is currently researching and writing a history of photographic exhibitions as an independent scholar and lives in San Antonio, Texas.